CACTUS COUNTRY

CACTUS COUNTRY

A Boyhood Memoir

ZOË
BOSSIERE

ABRAMS PRESS, NEW YORK

Library of Congress Control Number: 2023950085

ISBN: 978-1-4197-7318-1
eISBN: 979-8-88707-257-9

Printed and bound in the United States
10 9 8 7 6 5 4 3 2 1

This memoir is a work of nonfiction. Names and identifying characteristics of some individuals have been changed.

ABRAMS The Art of Books
195 Broadway, New York, NY 10007
abramsbooks.com

To Dowker

"I toss the stone of my story into a vast crevice; measure the emptiness by its small sound."

—Carmen Maria Machado, *In the Dream House*

CONTENTS

AUTHOR'S NOTE

This work has been adapted from my life and is subject to the limitations of memory and perspective that make true stories so deeply human. In cases of conflicting accounts, I have often privileged my own version of events over other recollections. Some timelines have been purposefully collapsed or integrated in the interest of cohesive narrative storytelling. In many instances, names and identifying details have been altered to protect the identities of the real people I grew up with.

THE BEGINNING

THE BOY POSES FOR A photograph in an Airstream trailer, the scruffy family dog wrapped around his shoulders like a feather boa. His short blond hair is tousled, uncombed, his cheeks and the bridge of his nose marked red from a long afternoon spent playing, shouting, fighting with other boys under the harsh desert sunlight. Dust and sweat stain his wrinkled t-shirt, the pale skin on his neck and arms. He and the dog look directly into the camera's eye, their frozen gaze stretching like the night outside the trailer they stand in, forever waiting for the shutter to click.

Many people who've seen the photos from my childhood in Cactus Country, the trailer park I grew up in, have asked where they were taken, and whether the boy pictured is my brother. They are surprised when they learn the truth: I was that boy, that boy is me.

More than twenty years after this moment, he and I share the same wiry arms, the same lean face and long fingers. Our resting expressions are serious, our eyebrows thick and severe. But my hair is darker than his now, and long; I haven't cut it since leaving Tucson almost a decade ago. When friends ask if I'm considering a shorter style I shake my head and say that after a childhood of bowl cuts and bobs I've come to appreciate the versatility of longer hair, how it can be tucked discreetly away under a hat or run freely down my back like sheets of desert rain during a monsoon. How it encompasses both masculine and feminine possibilities.

What I often don't say is the way I feel about my gender and its expression has changed many times before. That it continues to change, even as I speak.

On the day this picture was taken in the Airstream, the boy I was had never heard the word *transgender*, didn't know to look it up in Dad's tattered dictionary, as he had with other words like *boy*, *man*, *male*, *sex*, and *change*. He didn't have the language then to talk about how it felt to be raised in a gender at odds with the way he saw himself. What it was like to pray to a god he didn't believe in that tomorrow he might wake up in a different body, one more like the bodies of the other boys he spent his days with in the desert, smashing beetles and chasing freight trains.

The story of the boy I was—of the person I am—is inextricably tied to the desert surrounding Cactus Country, and to the hard masculinity, stoicism, and camaraderie of the boys and men I knew in those years, who regarded me as one of their own.

But when people ask me about my childhood now, I rarely mention the desert, or the boys, or my gender. Instead, I tell the story of how, at ages two and three and until about four, years before my family moved to Tucson, I had an alarming tendency to slip away from wherever I was supposed to be.

My memories of these days are little more than shadows and light. There is only the brightness of a morning spent alone in the Smithsonian's vast courtyard. A flash of my preschool teacher careening from the reptile house at the zoo, her large body rushing toward my small one with all the imminence of an oncoming train.

According to my parents, nothing—not fear of getting hurt or kidnapped, not forces of nature or acts of god—could have kept me from wandering away. So, given my history as a flight risk, they probably shouldn't have been surprised the day I went missing at home.

When Mom tells this story, she describes a frantic search of our Virginia apartment. How she and Dad donned their winter coats and took to the streets, calling my name with increasingly hoarse voices. She recounts their panicked thoughts about the golf course behind the apartment, its deep sand traps and flowing creeks. Of the open road where cars sped around tight neighborhood corners without slowing for pedestrians.

Thirty minutes passed, then an hour before I was found safe on the playground at the center of the complex, naked, contentedly rooting in a mound of dirt. The relief my parents report feeling in this moment quickly gave way to frustration, the anger that comes after fear. Mom took me by the shoulders, looked me in the eyes, scolded me for leaving the apartment on my own. What was I thinking? Didn't I know better than to go and get myself lost?

If there is a defining moment of my childhood, it is probably this one: My tiny hands, still covered in dirt, waving indignantly in the air, insisting that my parents had told the story all wrong. That I hadn't been lost at all. That I was right *here*, where I intended to be.

Even so many decades later, after our move to Cactus Country and beyond it, my parents laugh when they highlight the incident as the earliest example of my contrary, wayward nature, what they have all my life called a "hardheaded" personality. The spark that would go on to stoke the blazing sense of independence they have come to know well. Or so they tell me.

I don't know how much of this memory is true. But we all grow up with anecdotes like these. Little stories that are supposed to explain how we became the people we are. Some, like mine, are passed down by our families. Others, we tell ourselves when we look back at pictures from our childhoods. We say things like, *I was such a tomboy—see how I wrestled with my brothers?* Or, *I knew I was gay, even then—look at my tiny feet in those heels!* We craft our origin stories, as much about who we were as who we want to be. *I have always been this way*, we say, which is another way of saying, *This is who I am*.

What I'm trying to tell you now is that somewhere in the space between the girl who ran away from home and the boy in the photograph is the beginning of a story that explains how and why I feel the way I do about my gender. It's the story I carried with me into the desert at eleven years old, the one that set me on the path toward a nascent boyhood with unwavering determination. The same story that, years later, compelled me to become a teacher and a writer, leading me out of the trailer park and into a life completely different than the one I had known.

The girl in the story is unhappy, except when she isn't. The boy wishes his body were different, except when he doesn't. The child searches for the place they belong, except when they feel content exactly where they are. There are many places like this I could start, but I'd be lying if I said how it begins is really all that important. Only that no matter how many ways I try to tell it straight, the story of my childhood always seems to wander.

But if I close my eyes and picture it, a memory, or something like one, begins to take shape. I see a lone, barefooted boy with short blond hair walking along the road in Cactus Country. The soles of his feet sting against the searing desert asphalt as he wipes away the sweat beading under his uneven bangs. Still, he presses on, looking for something despite feeling uncertain it could ever be found. Trusting that, no matter how far he strayed from the path home, he wouldn't find himself lost.

I. DESERT BOY

DAY ONE

MY BARE FEET CRUNCHED AGAINST hot gravel as I scanned the pavement, searching in vain for campsite 198. I'd never felt so thirsty in my life. Under the heat of the Arizona sun even my new short, bowl-style haircut wasn't enough to keep me cool. I licked my cracked lips, blood salty on my tongue. Cactus Country was so much bigger than I'd expected, its long roads leading me down endless campsite rows populated with RVs of every make and model—campers, coaches, pull trailers, park models, fifth-wheels, and motorhomes. Miles of untouched desert surrounded the park on all sides, interrupted only by the interstate and the distant train tracks.

I paused, squinting to make out a set of white numbers stenciled onto the asphalt. This was campsite 198, all right. Cady, the girl I'd played with earlier that afternoon—the one leading a sticky-faced toddler around—had asked me to meet her here after lunch. Paint peeled from her family's faded yellow camper like a bad sunburn. A shirtless boy about eleven, my age, sat at a picnic table in the shade of the camper's ripped awning, chewing on a pen cap as he glared at the electronic game in his hands.

"Your sister in there?" I asked, motioning to the trailer. The boy grunted, but didn't look up. I rapped my knuckles against the aluminum doorframe. A gaunt woman with long, graying hair answered, a lit cigarette hanging from her lips.

"Cady can't come out just now," she muttered, cigarette lilting as she spoke. Before I could open my mouth, she pulled the door shut again. Her raspy voice berated someone, maybe Cady, from inside the trailer. Thinking it best to wait, I took a seat beside the boy at the picnic table.

"What're you playing?" I asked, leaning over to get a closer look at the screen. The game looked like a hand-me-down, at least ten years old with a faded black and green display. The boy didn't answer, but scooted farther across the bench, away from me. I sighed, staring at the broken toys littering the ground at my bare feet, their bright plastic fragments embedded in the dirt and scattered among the rocks. Reaching under the picnic table, I grasped at an action figure's disembodied leg.

Without looking up from his game, the boy pulled a knife from his pocket. In one motion, he whipped it open, pointing its blade at my face.

"If you touch that," he said, "I'll cut you."

I froze, staring cross-eyed down the knife's sharp, gleaming tip. Before today, my vision of the Southwest had consisted of lonely cowboys on saddled horses, roving marauders in wooden stagecoaches, and bloody O.K. Corral–style shootouts against a vast landscape of sand. I knew the region had a violent history, but never expected another child to threaten me with a dollar-store pocketknife. Flicking my eyes from the blade to the boy's fierce, angry gaze, I realized three things: First, this boy thought I was another boy. Second, his threat was a test. And third, if I had any hope of surviving here, I needed to pass it.

The boy's blond hair was shaved close to the skin, prickly follicles shooting up the way cacti sprout from chapped earth. Out in the desert, a long cargo train rumbled over splintered tracks, its whistle echoing faintly against the trailers surrounding us in time with his ragged breath. A dog tied up in a neighbor's campsite howled back at the train. Another dog howled, and another, their calls sounding to my ears like a battle cry. The boy and I glared at each other through the broad sunlight, each of us trying hard not to blink.

"You're not gonna do anything," I sneered. I said it like a dare. The boy said nothing, but kept the blade pointed between my eyes, even as I pulled my lanky arm away from the toy. After a few long seconds, he lowered the knife, returning to the game he held in his other hand.

We sat at the picnic table in silence as I funneled dirt through my fingers onto my shorts just to have something to do with my hands. Though shaken, I tried to keep my face blank, my nerves hidden. To leave now, I knew, would be to fail the first real test of my boyhood. But the rules were still unclear to me. I wondered how long I would have to wait here, and when I would know if I'd passed. The boy's face twisted in sudden rage.

"Fuck this stupid game!" he spat down at the machine. The boy shot from the bench and slammed the trailer door behind him, leaving me alone at the picnic table. Slowly, I stood up and brushed the dirt off my shorts. I waited there a while, staring at the trailer. Maybe now, I thought, Cady would come out to play. But the door stayed shut. With a sigh, I began the long walk across the park back to my own campsite, where Mom and Dad sat in front of our Airstream, watching what would be the first of many breathtaking desert sunsets.

"Did you find your friend?" Mom asked, lifting her sunglasses. The shades left a white outline around her eyes. Even though we'd only been traveling through the Southwest for a couple of days on the road to Tucson, Mom's hair had already started fading to blond in the sun, her skin taking on a deep tan. Back in Virginia she'd worked long managerial shifts, hopping between mall retailers. No matter how tired Mom might have been when she came home to us at night, I'd never heard her complain about anything. I shook my head no.

"Well, it's only our first day in the park," she said. "You'll find your people."

We didn't have a third folding chair, so I settled between my parents on the ground, legs crossed under me. The hot gravel dug into my skin, its sting acting as a soothing balm to my disappointment. I ran what happened with the boy over again in my mind, trying to decide whether I'd passed his test. I had not shown my fear, and I had stood my ground. That was good. Still, I felt out of my element, unused to the ways of this strange, hostile place.

Compared to Reston, Virginia, where we had moved from, Tucson was another world. The laws of nature I knew didn't seem to apply here, where the sunlight was harsh and the threat of sunstroke imminent. All the local wildlife could bite, or sting, or both. Plants were sharp and stoic, not to be touched with bare hands. Kids threatened to stab each other with knives. Surviving here, I realized—as a boy, or otherwise—would be a lot more difficult than I thought.

After a few minutes of silence, Dad breathed a satisfied sigh. "Our own little slice of paradise," he said. He leaned back, shooting me a toothy smile as he ran a hand through his thick, unruly hair, shoulders broad under the loose orange tank top he wore. Dad might have worked with his hands for a living, but his great love was reading. Before the move, we'd each packed only a few of our things, and most of what Dad chose to keep were books. Some of his favorites had titles like *Be Here Now* and *Leaves of Grass* and *For the Time Being*, and he often read them out loud to us in the Airstream.

I glanced back at the trailer behind us, gleaming in the fading sunlight. Its silver, mirrorlike surface reflected the colorful hues of the clouds streaking overhead. *Our own little slice of paradise*. My family wasn't religious, but I'd always understood the word to mean a wonderland where all your most fervent wishes were granted—a place where what had once only been true in dreams sprang miraculously to life. I cupped a hand over my forehead and squinted up at my parents' faces, shining gold in the quickly fading light.

Though only eleven, I'd come to understand that Mom and Dad were a little unusual, as far as parents went. In an earlier era, before my birth, they'd worked a season as sea lion trainers in a Hungarian circus. They'd tried to make a go of living in Paris, France, though neither of them could speak the language. They'd had so many big dreams in their life together—of growing vegetables on a family farm in Oregon, of running a guided backpacking tour company in Eastern Europe, of traveling full-time around the United States in a modified school bus—but few of these ventures ever seemed to work out the way they planned. Now we were here in Tucson, at the start of a new dream.

I sat quietly on the ground as my parents sipped their wine, head in my hands. I wouldn't tell them about the knife, because part of being a boy meant not telling on other boys, even when you could get hurt, or killed. It meant keeping secrets from adults, and settling scores on your own. In the weeks and months and years that followed, I would come to know dozens of kids like the one I met on my first day in the park. Hard desert boys who roamed Cactus Country on bikes, armed with pocketknives, BB guns, and slingshots. Boys who shot birds out of the sky, slammed saguaro cacti with baseball bats, and beat each other's small bodies into the dusty earth. Among them, I would become the boy I was meant to be.

That next morning, I woke up early to buy a pocketknife at the Cactus Country park store. The green saguaro cactus painted on its handle faded quickly in my sweaty hands as I practiced flicking the knife open with a snap of my wrist and pointing it at an imaginary set of eyes, as the boy had done to me. I practiced until I could do this without looking, expecting another Western-style showdown when the boy and I saw each other next. This time, I would be ready to pass his test. But by that afternoon the boy's trailer was long gone, the only evidence he'd ever been in the park a few broken toys scattered in the dirt under a picnic table.

BOY SCOUT

IN THE SHADE OF THE Cactus Country bathhouse, I lay against the cool brick path with my hands in the air, watching blood seep from my split knuckles. Tucson's dry climate was hard on a body. By early afternoon, with the sun at its highest point in the sky, the playground's metal monkey bars could sear blisters onto my fingers. The black rubber of the cracked tire swing felt like sitting on a campfire, burning angry welts on the backs of my legs. I scratched at my ashen arms until they stung red and raw, aching in an almost pleasant way. Since the boy's family left, there had been no other children in the park to run or play or fight with. Nothing for me to do on long hot days like this but sweat it out in the shade until the sun went down.

I held a thin page of comics from a copy of the Arizona *Daily Star* over my head, the back of my skull grinding uncomfortably against the pavement as I read. After each strip, I glanced down from the paper and across the street, checking to see if Mom had come out of the Airstream to look for me yet. Our new home on wheels reminded me of an airplane, with interior storage compartments that folded up like overhead bins, cockpit-style bay windows at the front and back of its rounded ends, and an awning that stretched out from its side like a bird's wing. Our neighbors often stopped on their walks to admire the Airstream, and in the days since we arrived in the park I'd overheard Dad answering the same questions again and again.

"It's a 1978," he would say, "an Excella 500, a thirty-one-footer." These, I'd come to know, referenced the Airstream's year and model and length—all essential statistics in the world of recreational vehicles. The neighbors would nod, murmuring appreciatively. We were the only family in the park who lived in an Airstream. I could tell Dad enjoyed talking about the trailer by the way he'd stand with his hands on his hips, grinning widely as he gestured to this or that feature. Sometimes the neighbors would ask what had brought us to the Southwest, and Dad would always say, "Oh, to get away from it all."

In private, my parents had listed more specific reasons for the move, but I understood these only in abstract terms. Reston was too expensive. They were sick of suburbia. Of working too hard and too often for the privilege of living in a cramped apartment they didn't even own. Dad had bought the Airstream from an online auction site the year before on an adventurous whim, and it happened to be located in Arizona. By the summer, my parents had gone from dreaming of the vacations we would one day take in the trailer to serious talk of living in it full time. Just a few months later, we'd shed most of our belongings and undertaken the journey westward.

I folded up the comic strips and placed them under my head like a pillow. Mom still hadn't emerged from the Airstream. We were supposed to drive into town to buy a pair of shoes for the start of school the next day. I lifted my head to consider my bare feet. Cactus Country's campsites weren't paved, but covered in a thick layer of sharp white gravel. I loved the feeling of being barefoot, of the hot stones crunching under my callused toes. Tomorrow would be the first day in weeks I'd have to cover them.

I had never been the new kid at school before, least of all as a boy. In Virginia, I'd often fantasized about showing up to class with short hair, a daydream in which my friends and teachers would somehow understand that I'd actually been a boy all along. My new school in Tucson would be full of kids who'd never known me as a girl, and tomorrow would be my one chance to make the right impression. Thinking about it made my head feel hot, almost feverish, my stomach roiling the way it did when I played too long in the sun.

I felt a sudden, sharp prick on my earlobe and bolted up, swiping frantically. A red ant fell from my hair onto the pavement. I smashed its body with my palm, rubbing it hard into the brick. The Airstream's tall, spring-loaded door creaked open, Mom's tan, sandaled foot just visible underneath as she stepped out onto the gravel. She peeked around the door and waved me over, signaling the time had come for us to leave.

EARLY THE NEXT morning, Mom drove our battered minivan with the driver's seat pushed up as close to the pedals as it would go, her long sun-bleached hair clipped into a messy bun. Our destination was situated deep in the heart of Rita Ranch, a sprawling suburban neighborhood on the outskirts of Tucson, just a few miles north from Cactus Country. My insides swished uncomfortably with each turn in the road. I winced, steadying my backpack against my stomach.

"Just be yourself," Mom advised. "First days are always hard, but you'll win the other kids over in time. You've always known how to work a room." I nodded mechanically, too queasy to ask what room she meant. We pulled up to a colorful building towering like a beacon among waves of look-alike houses. The sign out front read: COTTONWOOD ELEMENTARY. Mom honked as I crossed into the schoolyard. Dozens of kids clustered around the playground, screaming as they chased each other over the blacktop, their excitement manifesting low in the pit of my stomach like dread. I turned around too late to watch Mom drive away.

A group of boys my age huddled on the basketball court, openly staring in my direction. I ran a hand through my hair and fixed my gaze on a weed growing between two slabs of sidewalk, trying to pretend I didn't notice or care. One of the boys, the shortest, broke from the group to approach me.

"Hey," he called. I looked up. The boy had soft brown eyes, his pudgy cheeks dusted with freckles. He hesitated, fiddling with the collar of his shirt.

"Um, so the guys over there, they—they wanna know if you're a boy or a girl." I glanced over his shoulder to the boys leering at us from across the playground. On its face, this might have been a fair question. Since my new haircut, Mom had often remarked that I was "too pretty" to be a boy, with my long eyelashes and slender, almost delicate features. Though all my life I'd seemed masculine for a girl, I hadn't yet perfected the more ineffable qualities of boyhood—the right way to move my body, or take up space in a room, or intonate my voice. Returning the boy's steady gaze, I knew his friends wouldn't be satisfied no matter what answer I gave. They'd already decided I wasn't one of them, daring me now to prove them wrong.

"What kind of stupid question is that?" I spat. "Go tell your homo friends to leave me alone." He shrugged, running back to relay my message as the morning bell rang out in the schoolyard. The boys from the basketball court called out to me as they passed, puckering their lips in mock affection, eliciting laughter from other kids waiting to enter their classrooms.

"Look at his backpack," the smaller boy shouted excitedly, pointing to the teal bag slung over my shoulder. I tightened my grip on its straps, eyes trained on the pavement.

"That's a girl's backpack!" the boys jeered. "He's a girl!"

My cheeks grew hot. I tried to ignore them, but to my dismay, the whole group lined up outside of the classroom I'd been assigned. I marched to the back of the line, hoping to make myself as inconspicuous as possible. But the rumors were already spreading. Eyes glanced not-so-furtively back at me, giggles erupting from huddled bodies.

He-she, I heard the voices whisper. *The new kid is a he-she.*

AS FAR BACK as I could remember, I'd played a secret game in the bathroom mirror of our Reston apartment. In my reflection, I saw the same kid I'd always been. Skinny arms, round face, green eyes, little brown dot on my left cheek. Straight dirty blond hair that came down just past my ears—the same hairstyle I'd had roughly since preschool.

In front of the mirror, I pulled my hair back into a loose bun, as I'd done countless times before. From this angle, I looked like a different person. One who lived the life I'd always wanted. I smiled at him, imagining the hair he held behind his head were gone. This version of me was much more handsome. He was tough and confident. He was happy. I liked the paradox of this game. How I didn't recognize the boy in the mirror, yet felt closer to him than I'd ever felt to the girl staring back at me when I let my bunched-up hair fall back down around my shoulders.

In the months after he bought the Airstream, Dad filled my imagination with fantastic visions about everything our move to Arizona would entail. Our new home in the Southwest would be the beginning of a real adventure where, he said, I would have the chance to reinvent myself into whoever I wanted to be. He promised me a dog, and brought home a small, wild-haired animal who would accompany us on the journey into our new lives. We named her Tucson after the place we were headed, and in the weeks leading up to the move, I spent a lot of time in front of the bathroom mirror, thinking hard about the person I wanted to become.

The day before we left Virginia, I asked for a new haircut over breakfast. Dad couldn't understand why I wanted any less hair than I already had.

"But your hair *is* short," he insisted, taking a sip of his tea.

"You said I could reinvent myself," I reminded him. "This is who I want to be."

Dad shrugged. A haircut was a small price to pay for an easier cross-country move. Later that afternoon, I sat in a pumped-up vinyl chair and asked the hairdresser to trim my hair short "like a boy's," demonstrating what I wanted with the mirror trick. She met my eyes, skepticism spreading across her slight face.

"You sure about this?" she asked. I nodded. She looked to Dad, who also nodded, and began the work of snipping my previous identity away. As strands of my hair fell onto the checkered tile, I closed my eyes, envisioning the boy who would get up from the chair. He'd brush some of the errant hair from his shoulders and go boldly into his new life, shedding the girl he used to be like an old skin, the way I'd once seen a lizard do. I couldn't wait to meet him.

"All done," the hairdresser said. My eyes shot up to the mirror. I turned my head to the left, then the right, frowning at my reflection. "Something wrong?" she asked. The transformation did not appear to be a success. I still looked like me, more or less, just a few inches shorter on the sides, a cool draft on the back of my neck. That was new.

"See?" Dad said back in the van. "You just don't look like a boy."

I crossed my arms in the passenger seat, trying hard not to betray my disappointment.

BACK AT SCHOOL, the whispering seemed to shadow me wherever I went—to the pencil sharpener, to the water fountain, out onto the playground. I wandered the schoolyard aimlessly, keenly aware of the many curious eyes following me around the blacktop. The boys from earlier that morning played a game of half-court basketball. One boy in a purple jersey dribbled the ball expertly between his legs. He was taller than most of the kids in our class, with frosted curls pressed up against the edges of his hairline from sweat. In my mind, he became "Curly." He must have noticed me watching the game, because the next time Curly had the ball, he threw it to me.

"Shoot, man!" he called. I caught the ball, my heart catching in my throat along with it. Before now, I'd only played basketball in gym class. But Curly had given me a second chance, a gift, and I was determined not to blow it. The other boys stopped playing to watch. I bounced the ball against the blacktop a couple times, took a shot from the free throw line, missed.

"Nice throw," they taunted. But Curly ran to catch up with the ball, tossed it to me again. He leaned over with his hands on his knees. My face burned, and it had nothing to do with the afternoon heat. I lined up the shot, took a breath, and threw the ball into the air with a little jump at the end, the way I imagined a real basketball player might. The ball bounced off the backboard, didn't even graze the rim. Curly shook his head.

"Man, why you wearing Shaqs if you can't shoot?" he said. I looked down at my shoes, stupidly, as though noticing them for the first time. White with red soles, SHAQ stitched onto the tongues, a silhouette of a man leaping into an impressive dunk shot on the sides. I'd picked them out at a discount store the day before with Mom. I chose the shoes because they fit me, and because I liked the story they told about the kind of boy I was. For a brief moment, Curly had looked at them and seen the potential for athleticism, agility, strength. But no shoe could hide the fact that I didn't know how to play basketball. No shoe would allow me to pass, to perform, to live up to other boys' expectations about who I should be. Curly and his friends laughed, returning to a game I was not invited to play. I retreated to the bench, staring down at my warped reflection in the metal clasps of my new shoes.

ON OUR LAST day in Virginia, Dad parked the van in front of what looked like a sporting goods store.

"Just need to run one more errand before we go," he said. A man with a blond handlebar mustache in a beige scouting uniform nodded as we stepped into the store, the rush of cool air conditioning like a fog over the damp humidity sticking to our skin.

Before us were aisles of patches adorned with bobcats, tigers, wolves, and bears. Neckerchiefs and merit badges. Baseball caps and socks to match. I leafed through a glossy handbook while Dad asked the man behind the counter about uniforms. He needed one the right size for a nine-year-old boy with the stature of a child about five, he said. The uniform was a goodbye present for Wade, a friend of mine from the neighborhood.

Wade was a quiet kid, and so small that people often mistook him for a kindergartener. His mother had recently separated from his father, an alcoholic prone to unpredictable rages. Wade didn't seem to care much for the great outdoors, but his mom had signed him up for Cub Scouts hoping he might benefit from the influence of what she called "some good men, for a change." Dad, who had a soft spot for boys with absent fathers, had offered to buy his scouting uniform.

The mustached man patiently answered Dad's questions about scout dens and packs and codes. He brought out a navy uniform with a matching blue belt, neckerchief, and Bear Cub cap, all the perfect size for Wade.

"Your son in the Scouts?" the man asked, nodding toward me. Dad turned to look, his eyebrows arched in surprise as I pulled the cap I'd been trying on from my head, hiding it behind my back. I'd been imagining how I would look as a scout. How I'd earn badges that Mom would iron onto my uniform, and ascend the ranks from Webelo to Eagle Scout. According to the Cub Scouts handbook I'd been perusing, that's what I'd be now, at eleven years old: a Webelo. Whatever that meant. Dad shook his head.

"No, not in the Scouts," he said.

"Well, that's a shame!" the man said, ringing up the uniform. "The Scouts is good for a boy his age. All my sons were scouts."

Dad nodded, appearing to mull it over.

"You like to go camping, son?" the man called out. I did like to go camping. I liked to climb trees and go exploring in the woods behind my apartment complex. The year before, my family had left Reston for the summer, living in a short school bus Dad had converted into a motorhome, complete with a working kitchen and foldout beds. We'd traveled around the continental United States in that bus, visiting every family friend and relative my parents could think of, touring every major national park, and sleeping in what felt like every Walmart parking lot in America. At the time, the trip had been more vacation than new way of life, but I liked to look back and reimagine the experience as a small taste of the sweet freedom Dad had promised would be ours every day in Arizona.

"I love camping," I said, inching closer to the counter, the Webelos cap still in my hands.

"He loves it!" the man echoed. "Come on, now. Buy the hat today, go home and think it over. This kid would make a great scout!" I beamed at him. The man had all the pitch of a practiced salesman. Dad sighed, half-smiling at me in a what-can-you-do kind of way. He tossed the cap onto the counter with Wade's uniform and promised the man he would. Think about it, that is.

AFTER MY FIRST day of school in Tucson, I sat down again on the brick pavement outside the Cactus Country bathhouse, this time on the other side of the building to catch the late afternoon shade. I'd shrugged when Mom and Dad came to pick me up from Cottonwood.

"Good," I'd said in response to all their questions. "Good. Everything was good."

I'd unceremoniously tossed my light blue backpack and Shaq shoes into the Airstream, eager to cast off the things that had betrayed me. Tomorrow I would carry my books in one of Dad's old packs and practice shooting baskets in the abandoned hoop at the back of the park. But for now, I watched the fire ants drag stray potato chips from under a nearby picnic table into a crack between the bricks and replayed every wrong thing I'd said and done at school that day.

The other boys in my class didn't see me as one of them. I was too weak, too sensitive, too feminine. Over the course of a single day I'd established a reputation that, I knew, would take the rest of the year to live down. It wasn't enough to look like a boy; I needed to learn how to act like one, too. I thought back to our last day in Virginia, when Dad and I set out from the Scout Shop.

"That man thought I was a boy," I'd said, grinning up from the van's passenger seat as I thumbed through Wade's Cub Scout handbook. The humidity seeped in through the open windows, warm air rushing in with such force I had to hold the rim of my new Webelos cap with one hand to keep it from flying away.

"He did," Dad said, then paused. "Probably because you were so interested in the hat." I rolled my eyes. The hat had nothing to do with it. Despite what I or my parents or anyone thought about my new haircut, the man in the Scout Shop proved to me that I had become the boy only I saw in the mirror. That now, other people could see him, too.

"Maybe, once we get to Tucson," I said, choosing my words carefully, "I could join the Boy Scouts for real." Dad shook his head, eyes still fixed on the road.

"There's no way that would work," he said. "You're not a boy."

"Please, Dad," I begged. "Can't we just *say* I'm a boy? No one would have to know." Dad flexed his grip on the steering wheel and sighed.

"I could never keep that story straight," he said, glancing over at me. "Besides, what's wrong with the Girl Scouts?"

I frowned, not sure how to explain that I didn't want to sell cookies, or wear that prim green vest-and-beret combo. How to say what I really longed for was the great outdoors, the camaraderie and adventure the Boy Scout handbook promised. I wanted to be a Boy Scout. But so much more than that, I wanted to be a boy. To slide with ease into the world people like Dad and the man at the Scout Shop and all the boys I knew seemed to inhabit without a second thought. But I couldn't begin to say any of this out loud. We sat in silence, dank wind from the van's open windows whistling between us.

Dad reached over, patted my leg, looked me in the eye.

Said, "I wish you could be one, too."

THE BEETLE KING

THE PALO VERDE TREE THE boys and I liked best forked into a V shape, its narrow green-barked trunk split two ways against the sky. On afternoons when the Arizona sun beat down too hot to wander the desert surrounding Cactus Country, we climbed into the palo verde one at a time, our bodies filling its branches like fruits. Our tree was shady, with long leaf-stems good for plucking and absentmindedly skinning with our fingers, dozens of tiny leaves fluttering to the ground until we held only a slender green straw.

"What should we do today?" Wesley asked. He yanked another stem from the branch, twirling it around his thumb. The straws were durable. Some of the Cactus Country girls wove them into lanyards and bracelets, but we boys preferred sticking them in our noses and one another's ears, or chewing them into a pulp and spitting them back out.

"Don't know yet," I said, shrugging. With a pocketknife I carved my initials—a jagged ZB—into the trunk. When I cut my hair back in Reston, I'd thought I might need to go by a new name to pass as a boy in Tucson. But it quickly became apparent I was the only Zoë most people I encountered had ever met. "Zowie, like David Bowie's son?" adults would ask. "Zooey, like that boy from the book, *Franny and Zooey*?" No one, least of all other kids, ever suggested my name didn't match my appearance. So I kept it.

On the branch below me, Arlo ripped down a fistful of leaves and pressed them against his upper lip like a green mustache. Some of the other boys giggled, plucking stems to make mustaches of their own. Monkey see, monkey do. From a distance, the seven of us could have been brothers. We wore shaggy home haircuts, our stained t-shirts full of holes. Our fair cheeks were always sunburned, the backs of our hands chapped red from the dry air.

But while my short hair and too-big shirts might have helped me blend in as one of the pack, I knew my body was different from the other boys'. My chest, which was beginning to grow round in the wrong places, had to be hidden no matter how hot or sweaty I became. Out in the desert I had to squat behind the cover of creosote bushes to pee. At home in the Airstream I was my parents' daughter, but up in the palo verde I felt like one of the boys. We sat in our tree for whole afternoons, each nestled into a different crook, talking, joking, and pulling pranks until dusk, when our moms called us in to our trailers.

During the winter in Cactus Country, campsites filled with seasonal residents locals called *snowbirds*, retirees from cold northern states venturing to the warmer Southwest and families chasing gainful employment across the country, often with their homeschooled children in tow. The parents worked as day laborers, independent contractors, schoolteachers, medical residents, tax consultants, and military personnel. One was even a prizefighter. To these families Tucson was merely a stopover, a bookmark in the longer story of their journey to somewhere else.

In the months since my parents had moved the Airstream into Cactus Country, I'd grown used to life as the only child in the park. But now, in a matter of weeks, our group of boys had swelled to three, then five, then seven, all of us between the ages of eight and thirteen. Though physically I had little trouble keeping up with the pack on the playground, I still had a lot to learn about becoming the boy I knew myself to be: How to shake off a sore arm or a stinging jaw after swapping playful punches. How to tell the kinds of crude jokes that made the other boys laugh. How to blend in, to pass as one of them. Up in the palo verde I watched my new friends closely, imitating their mannerisms. I wanted to speak their native tongue. To attune my instincts to theirs.

The most important rite of boyhood, I learned, was the dare. Not simply to dare other boys, but to *be* the most daring. We took running leaps over sprawling cacti, pedaled our bikes down the steepest corner of the concrete monsoon drain, climbed into the bed of the garbage truck stationed at the back of the park. When tensions with park staff were high, which was often, we retreated into the desert to build elaborate forts under gnarled ironwood branches and hunt jackrabbits with improvised slingshots. We ran alongside fast-moving trains, screaming and throwing rocks at their boxcars, chasing them like frightened animals out of our domain.

The games we played fluctuated with the size of our group as families moved into and out of the park. Few kids stayed more than a month at a time, and only two lived in Cactus Country throughout the entire winter season: Arlo and Wesley, who both knew I was a different kind of boy, but loved me like a brother just the same.

Arlo had a snaggletooth and brown eyes that lit up whenever he joked around. He was always pulling faces, crossing his eyes, tugging at his ears, hiking his shorts up to his belly button. I responded to his antics in kind. The two of us would set each other off, screaming with laughter until we gasped for air. Unlike his brother, Wes was tall and blond, with big ears and lean, angular features. Though two years older and a lot more laid-back than Arlo, he could be counted on to join us in whatever game we'd devised.

One day on the mile-long walk out to the train tracks, the three of us stumbled upon an abandoned pair of jeans, an empty beer bottle, a faded Altoids tin, and a penny, all seemingly arranged as a collection on the desert sand. We quickly made up a story about how the items had gotten there, picturing a drunk man who'd been frightened out of his pants by a rattlesnake coiled on the trail. The man had thrown the penny to create a diversion, then taken off running, bare-assed, through the desert. We doubled over laughing as Arlo reenacted this scene, flailing his arms as he ran.

"But what about the mints?" I asked once I'd caught my breath.

"He was probably on his way to meet a lady when he saw the snake," Wesley explained. "You gotta have fresh breath when you're smooching ladies!" He clasped his hands and leaned his cheek against them, puckering his lips. Arlo and I howled even harder than before, and soon Wes was laughing, too, all three of us melting a little in the heat and the pleasure of one another's company.

IN CONTRAST TO the warmth of Cactus Country's long afternoons, school felt like plunging headfirst into a twilight universe where kids called me *poor* and *stupid* and *trash* because I lived in a trailer, and *he-she* and *pussy* and *faggot* because my masculinity was more ambiguous than that of the other boys in my class. At school the desert—its stubby barrel cacti with needles curved like fishhooks, prickly pears whose spiny pads grew in confused bunches, agave plants with thick triangular leaves like green tongues—seemed impossibly far away.

Weekday mornings my family's battered minivan wound through Rita Ranch, cruising the immaculate suburban streets, passing row after unending row of faux-adobe homes. Dad adjusted the neckline of his orange tank top. Hot air from the open window swept through his thick brown hair as we drove.

"Why would anyone want to live in such ugly houses?" he said, gesturing his tanned arm toward them. "They're charmless. Absolutely devoid of personality."

I nodded from the passenger's seat, gripping my backpack against my chest as though bracing for impact. Dad and I had some version of this conversation whenever he took me to school. The Rita Ranch kids, my classmates, all lived in variations of the same earth-toned house with rounded clay roof tiles. According to Dad, kids who grew up in houses like these had no imagination, no vision, and no appreciation of life's rich possibilities. They didn't have the freedom to run wild the way the Cactus Country boys and I did. Dad said places like Rita Ranch stifled people's innate creativity.

"If anything, Zo," he said, raising one of his bushy eyebrows, "you should feel sorry for them." Dad flashed his crooked grin, reaching over to give my nose a sharp squeeze.

I wished we could talk about something else. We never spoke of my short, bowl-style haircut or the way I glowed when men called me *buddy* or *dude*, terms of endearment Dad used for other boys but never with me. We didn't talk about how I stared at the ground when he introduced me to friends and neighbors as his daughter, the bewilderment on their faces as they tried to reconcile this with the boy they saw standing in front of them. I didn't have the words then to tell Dad how I felt or who I really was. But I wished life at home and at school could feel as natural as being out in the desert with the Cactus Country boys.

Most mornings on the drive through Rita Ranch, I thought wistfully about what Wesley and Arlo might be up to. I'd spent enough time at their motorhome to know their homeschool days were shorter and more casual than my school days: an excursion to one of Tucson's historical sites or a couple of pages from a workbook. The brothers were a few grade levels behind me in their studies, but I never minded helping them count their loose change to buy popsicles at the Cactus Country store or reporting the park news aloud for them from the "What's Happening?" bulletin board.

Once, as we whittled sticks in front of his motorhome, Arlo asked what public school was like. He'd never been to one before. I talked him through a typical school day, downplaying all the parts about tests and homework to highlight the things I knew he would appreciate most: Pizza Fridays in the cafeteria, recess on the playground, the free cartons of chocolate milk.

"Would you ever want to go to a real school, you think?" I asked.

Arlo shook his head. He shaved a long slice from his branch, smoothing the wood with his thumb.

"Why not?" I asked.

He shrugged. "Sounds like a lot of work."

What Arlo said made sense. He had no grades, no bullies, and no real worries. A life without school sounded great. I knew Mom was too invested in my education to ever go for the idea, but the way Dad talked about the Rita Ranch kids gave me hope that he might be swayed. That night I begged him to let me stay home like Arlo and Wesley. I would do all my schoolwork in the Airstream! I would be more imaginative and visionary—more appreciative of life's rich possibilities! Dad's eyebrows rose and fell in amusement as I spoke.

"No way," he said finally, grinning even while he shook his head. "Not a snowball's chance in hell." No matter what I said, no matter how many of his own words I used in my argument, Dad wouldn't budge. I had to go to school.

"You'll thank us for it one day," he said, returning his attention to the book in his lap.

ONE CLEAR WINTER afternoon, the boys and I gathered in the palo verde tree. Arlo sat in the crux of the V, a desirable spot, but also the lowest to the ground. Wesley and I, as the oldest, occupied the highest branches in each of the tree's two trunks, while four other boys squeezed themselves into the lower ones. Seven sets of legs hung like fleshy branches, kicking idly in the air.

We'd just started talking about what game to play when Arlo let out a high-pitched shriek of terror, scrambling up until he sat on the same branch as I did. The tree shook with our laughter. We thought Arlo was goofing around, trying to spook us, but no telltale grin appeared on his face. I followed his gaze to the ground beneath us.

"What the heck is that?" I cried, pointing.

We stared, transfixed, as a beetle larger than any I'd ever seen emerged from a small hole at the base of the tree. Its shiny black body was easily the span of a child's open hand. Two thick antennae jutted sideways from its head. Large front pincers snapped open and shut. Six spindly legs gleamed in the sunlight. For a few seconds the beetle stood by the hole, twitching its antennae as though scanning the air for something. Then it turned and ambled slowly across the gravel toward the cactus garden. The boys and I exchanged glances from our perches in the tree. We had found our game.

A freckled boy in a black sports jersey leapt to the ground.

"You dare me?" he called up to us. We nodded, though we didn't yet know what we were daring him to do. Carefully the boy crept up behind the slow-moving beetle, reached out a sneakered foot, and lightly tapped the insect, knocking it over. Most desert creatures have some kind of defense apparatus: stingers, fangs, pincers, horns. We braced ourselves to run if the beetle launched an attack. But it was clearly not as threatening as it looked. The insect lay sprawled on its side, legs flailing in the air until finally regaining their balance. The beetle took a second to orient itself before continuing on its course across the gravel, albeit a little faster than before.

Now we were all curious. One by one, we climbed down.

"What should we do with it?" the youngest boy asked, brown eyes wide under the rim of his backward ball cap. As though answering this question, Wesley picked up a sizable rock from the base of the palo verde, one that fit nicely in his palm.

"Dare me?" he asked. Without waiting for a reply, he threw the rock at the beetle, which flew up on impact as though hit by a mortar shell. The insect landed helplessly on its back, pedaling its legs wildly. Arlo and a redheaded boy made a game of kicking the beetle back and forth between them until it grabbed hold of Arlo's shoelaces and clung. He screamed, trying to knock it loose. We laughed as the insect soared through the air, landing some six feet away. The beetle was fading, its antennae twitching weakly. Its body was mutilated, cracks visible in its armored shell, liquid seeping from its joints. Whoever came up with the coolest way to kill it, I knew, would be the winner.

"Wait here, guys," I said. "Keep it right there." I ran back to the Airstream, where Dad had gathered a pile of old cinder blocks and plywood with the intention of building a porch. I hauled up one of the blocks with two hands, holding it over my head as I staggered back to the playground. The boys hooted excitedly, hands over mouths.

"*Do it, do it, do it,*" they chanted, quietly at first, then louder, a rhythm of war beating in my ears. I stood over the helpless creature, its body darkened by my shadow. I raised the block as high as I could and, with all the force I could muster, drove it into the ground. The boys cheered, dancing around the cinder block in a flurry of ecstasy. I beat my chest and howled, radiating pride. The foe had been vanquished, and I felt like a king.

When I lifted the block again, the insect was unrecognizable, its body mangled, a white rice-pudding-like substance seeping from its abdomen—eggs, I realized, that would now never hatch. Its limbs twitched. Impossibly, it was still alive. Staring down at the beetle, I felt a sudden pang of guilt and worried, too late, that it was suffering. What I had done was cruel, maybe even evil. In that moment I wanted to save the beetle, to shield it somehow from the damage we had already caused. But the beetle was beyond saving. The other boys were still cheering me on, and if I stopped now, it would only show I wasn't one of them. This violence was the price of boyhood, of belonging. So I held regret in my throat like vomit as I hurled the cinder block back down onto the beetle. I stomped it with my bare foot, grinding the block into the insect's body in defiance of my better, more benevolent instincts. I swallowed my guilt until it was dull and toothless, overtaken by adrenaline.

"Look, there's another one!" a boy shouted.

ON A SUNDAY morning Dad asked for my help loading the van with window-washing supplies. A few months after our move to Cactus Country, he'd found steady work washing storefront windows around Tucson. Sometimes I came along to help him. I loved the long drives through town, scrubbing the insides of windows clean, writing out receipts for our clients, the satisfying soreness in my arms at the end of the day, and the pride I felt in helping earn money for our family. But most of all I relished doing manly work as part of what I saw as a father-son team.

We methodically packed blue rags and extendable metal poles into the van, filling jugs with water from our campsite spigot. With each step I grew more excited about the day ahead.

"So, what part of town are we hitting?" I asked.

"I'm taking Wes to finish up some jobs on the East Side," Dad said. Usually he took Wesley along only when I had school. Dad always bought him something in exchange for his help: lunch at a fast-food restaurant, a cheap toy, a new book. I saw these small tokens of appreciation as evidence that he thought Wesley was a better helper than I was. That maybe Dad would have preferred a real son over a daughter who just looked like one.

I tried to mask the disappointment on my face as I folded a pile of rags, smoothing the stack with my hand. "Why?" I asked, careful not to look Dad in the eye.

"It's good for a kid like Wesley to get out sometimes," he said. "He's the only teenage boy in the park, and he needs an older guy to look up to. You wouldn't understand."

This statement made my chest feel tight. I didn't like when Dad assumed I wouldn't understand something, especially if that something had to do with my gender.

We went into the Airstream for breakfast. "I still don't get why you're taking him instead of me," I grumbled, pushing scrambled eggs around my plate. "It's not fair."

Dad stuck his head out the open trailer door, glancing around to make sure no one would overhear us. He sat down and turned to me with the air of someone with a secret to impart.

"I'm helping him learn to read," Dad said, his voice hushed. He explained the gist of the operation: He would write a list of words and give them to Wesley to study in advance. Wes would spell them out loud while they washed windows. Then he'd practice writing the words in sentences as Dad drove them to the next job.

"Wesley can't know I told you any of this," he concluded. "He would be mortified."

"Why don't his parents teach him to read?" I asked.

Dad squinted down at the table and shook his head. "I don't know," he said quietly. "But try to understand: Wes needs this. He's thirteen years old and can't read a menu, for Christ's sake. Imagine for a second what that would be like. Think about how you would feel."

I tried, but any sympathy I might have had for Wesley was eclipsed by the sense that Dad cared more about the boy across the park than the one sitting right in front of him. Even with my short hair and skinned knees, my sun-beaten face and callused feet, I knew Dad didn't really think of me as a boy. I carried this knowledge inside of me, certain I must be a disappointment to him. Dad had always seemed proudest when he could see himself in me, and I tried to emulate him in my work ethic. If I washed the windows well, Dad would be proud of me. If he were proud of me, I could be proud of myself.

"Okay, but can't I just tag along?" I asked. We stood in front of the van's open back hatch now, mixing window-cleaning solution into spray bottles. "I could sit in the backseat. I won't bother you guys, I promise!"

Dad sighed, massaging his forehead between his thick thumb and pointer finger. "If I asked Wesley to spell a word with you in the car," he said, "he'd never trust me again. All the work we've been doing would be for nothing."

"But—"

"Don't be selfish," he said sharply, slamming the hatch shut.

I wanted to talk to Dad about the distance between the way he saw me—as a tough girl, a tomboy—and the way I wanted to be seen. To tell him the body I had didn't match what I knew in my heart to be true. To say I was his son.

But I knew better than to press his temper. Instead I smiled when Wesley showed up at the Airstream carrying a notebook. I told Dad to work hard, that I'd see him later. Waving as they drove away, I swallowed my hurt, which settled hard in the pit of my stomach until it digested into something like anger. That day Arlo and I spent the afternoon hunting palo verde beetles.

IN TIME THE boys and I learned how to summon the beetles on command, and thinking of new ways to kill them became one of our favorite pastimes. We poured water from a campsite spigot down the beetles' holes to flush them out, then ambushed them with the sharp edges of rocks, skewered them alive with sticks, burned their appendages with lighters.

We killed the beetles because we were angry. Because it was hot. Because we were bad. Because there was nothing else to do. Because we lived in trailers. Because the kids at school called us *trash*. Because our parents weren't around to stop us. Because we weren't enough for anyone. Because we didn't like the faces we saw when we looked in the mirror. Because we lacked control over our lives. Because we had the power to decide which beetles would live and which would die. Because killing the beetles made us feel strong, if only for a little while.

I didn't like to think about what we were doing. Through perfecting our techniques, we'd also learned the beetles were gentle giants. They had pincers and wings but didn't put them to use. No matter how we brutalized them, they never retaliated, never flew away. If I thought about that too hard, the now-familiar guilt would bubble back up inside me and threaten to spill over, to drown the stoic, masculine exterior I had cultivated as one of the Cactus Country boys.

Occasionally park staff would try to intervene. Maybe they sympathized with the beetles, or maybe they were just tired of seeing their body parts strewn over the sidewalk. After a stern reprimand the carnage might stop for a day or two, but we'd always come back to it. Each night I went home to the Airstream dusty, wounded, and utterly exhausted. I had thrown myself headlong into boyhood, and my body ached from the impact.

THAT SPRING THE once-dull desert cacti bloomed to life in bursts of vibrant color, their flowers almost too bright to look at. Mom shook me awake early one morning to watch a crown of orange-red bulbs unfolding one by one on a barrel cactus. Their petals opened at sunrise and closed again at dusk. The arrival of spring meant the snowbirds would soon be flying north. Every afternoon I counted more empty campsites than the day before. Our group of boys dwindled until we were just three. Before long it was time for Arlo and Wesley's family to travel home, too.

On the morning of their departure I hugged my friends goodbye. Their motorhome pulled away from its campsite and onto the road. Arlo sat in the bay window, waving. I waved back. As the motorhome picked up speed, I began to chase it. My bare feet smacked against the asphalt, stinging. I followed the motorhome through Cactus Country and out of the park until I couldn't keep up anymore. My lungs burned as I watched it travel to the end of the long road and turn left and out of my sight, maybe forever. This perennial loss was the nature of living year-round in Cactus Country. Every friendship, no matter how close, was temporary.

With the motorhome gone, I hung my head and began the long, slow walk back to the palo verde tree, now the only child left in the park to climb it. Sitting in the crux of its two trunks, I spread dirt around with my bare feet, sniffing back tears. I would not cry, though I wanted to. Boys did not cry, even when no one was around to see them do it.

A slow prickle crept across the bottom of my foot. I leapt up, pulling both knees to my chest. A palo verde beetle poked its head out from the hole my heel had been covering. Anger welled up in me, fierce and hot. I raised my foot, ready to strike, but stopped short. The beetle wasn't far enough outside its hole for me to get a clear shot. I watched with a furrowed brow, waiting as the insect climbed out slowly, one gangly leg at a time, its body gleaming in the morning sunlight. I'd never noticed how pretty the beetles' armor was—a rich, almost reddish brown. My anger was dissipating, the old guilt taking its place. This time I let it wash over me. It wasn't the beetle's fault it had scared me. It wasn't the beetle's fault I was angry or sad. I put my foot down again, a more benevolent king, a gentler kind of boy.

Hanging from the trunk of the palo verde tree, I swung my hand down in front of the beetle. The insect tested its weight against my skin with its front legs, then gingerly climbed onto my palm. I raised the beetle up and held it in my cupped hands. Its pincers looked even more menacing up close, but it didn't try to pinch my fingers. I knew it wouldn't. Considering the creature in my hand, I thought maybe we weren't so different. I couldn't imagine then what my future would hold, or how to reconcile the girl Dad saw in me with the boy I knew myself to be. But if I had to stay in Cactus Country while the other boys left, maybe that meant I belonged here, like this beetle did, in our desert kingdom.

The insect ambled slowly to the tips of my outstretched fingers, antennae waving through the air. In seconds the beetle opened its great wings, launching itself from my hands and into the bright expanse of the sky, startling me. I'd never seen a palo verde beetle take flight before. I watched it go, waiting to see where it would land.

HORSE GIRL

"DO YOU HAVE GIRL PARTS, or boy parts?" she whispered. I leaned over the spout, sipping a slow stream of water, thinking carefully about how to answer her. Though I didn't want to lie, I also didn't want to give this girl or anyone else at Cottonwood Elementary a visual description of what was going on in my underwear. Most of the time I allowed other kids to assume my gender, and didn't correct them no matter which set of pronouns they picked, figuring neither guess was exactly wrong. But direct questions were harder. I stepped away from the drinking fountain, Sage's blue eyes trained on me from behind her glasses.

"What do you think?" I said, wiping water from my lips.

"I don't *know*, that's why I'm asking," she said, taking her turn at the spout.

"Well, I'm not going to tell you," I said. She rolled her eyes as though to say *fine*, and sauntered back to the playground. Sage's habit of asking too-personal questions might have unnerved some kids, but I didn't really mind. She had a maniacal, cackling laugh that reminded me of a witch and liked chasing shy boys around the playground with her arms outstretched, trapping them into hugs as she whipped her long blond hair into their faces. I once saw her launch into the tallest boy in our class, the one who always called me *trailer trash*, sending his massive body hurtling to the blacktop. She leapt on top of him, snarling like a wild animal, clawing at his eyes as he bleated, "*I'm sorry! I'm sorry! I'm sorry!*"

No one knew what he'd said to her, but the entire class watched in awe as Sage flew off of him before our heavily pregnant teacher, Mrs. D, could reach them.

"We were just playing a game!" she shouted over her shoulder as she ran. The kid, still heaving on the ground, was too embarrassed to admit otherwise.

"Yeah," he muttered, wincing as he brushed dirt out of his hair. "Just a game."

I thought Sage was great. Better than great, actually. If the mystery of my gender kept her interested in talking to me, I was resolved to keep the secret as long as possible.

SATURDAY MORNINGS, I worked a four- or five-hour shift at the local horse corral. I had no special passion for horses, but Mom grew up riding them, and both of my parents considered this work an activity that would help me build Southwestern character, what Dad called "true grit." Soon after our arrival in Tucson, they made a deal with the owner of the corral, a leathery man who wore a ten-gallon hat, real snakeskin boots, and a graying handlebar mustache. In exchange for mucking out the horses' pens, the old cowboy promised to teach me to ride.

At first this prospect excited me, despite the grueling nature of the work. The old cowboy showed me how to shovel piles of dried horse shit into a wheelbarrow with a manure fork, and where to deposit it out behind the barn. Shoveling most pens required multiple trips. The pile would swell into a great stinking mound until men in pickup trucks came to haul it away. My round face ripened like an apple in the morning sunlight. The denim overalls I wore scorched my legs, the metal clasps singeing my bare arms. By noon I felt almost delirious from the heat, head throbbing as I staggered onto the barn porch for a drink.

I heard shouting and watched, wide-eyed, as a spooked stallion bucked one of the younger cowboys, Slim, from its back and kicked him in the head. Slim crumpled to the ground, clutching his face while the horse thrashed and neighed above him. The old cowboy rushed to calm the horse as his wife guided Slim to the safety of the barn. Slim recovered on the porch, holding a bag of frozen corn to his head with one hand and fishing some chewing tobacco from a can with the other. He sneered at me, a nasty bruise flowering around his left eye.

"Hey, who the hell's this kid?" he called.

Slim was lucky. The hoof had barely clipped him, and he would survive the kick with nothing worse than a battered ego. But the incident changed the way I saw the horse corral, my excitement replaced with a new wariness of the horses that kicked, the saddles that slipped, and most of all the cowboys who would try to sculpt me into something more reminiscent of a man.

AT SCHOOL, I embodied many kinds of otherness. Always last in line, I counted the ways I was different from my classmates on my fingers, mouthing each one silently. I—one—lived in a trailer park, was—two—new to the school, and—three—to Arizona. I was a boy with—four—a girl-body, who—five—sucked at sports and—six—smelled like horses. The list went on. Most kids avoided talking to me unless a teacher forced us to work together.

My least favorite boy in class had long, fidgeting fingers, a permanent scowl etched onto his face. He and I once sat together for a group project, blank posterboard laid out before us. The boy carved a hole into the desk with a pair of scissors as the girls in our group took turns looking up facts about the solar system in an encyclopedia. Whenever I opened my mouth to contribute, the boy paused his carving to mutter a stream of obscenities under his breath. He spoke quietly, head turned away from me to further disguise his taunts from the teacher.

"That's not funny," I said, pencil shaking in my grip. "Shut up."

"Fucking make me, pussy-ass faggot bitch," he whispered, still not looking at me. "The fuck are you gonna do about it?"

The girls pretended not to hear him, taking a sudden interest in their textbooks. Tears stung the dry corners of my mouth, but I knew better than to tell the teacher. Mrs. D was studiously oblivious to most bullying, and the few times she'd pulled the other boys aside only made their harassment worse. She'd just tell me to ignore him. Sticks and stones. I glared down into my lap at my open hands, hating the boy, but hating myself more for crying, for failing to counter his insults like a man.

ON A LATE Saturday afternoon, Slim and the old cowboy sat smoking on the barn porch. Usually one or both of them would be out on the trail with a group of riders this time of day, but business had been slow that morning and now it was near closing time. They rocked in chairs with their legs splayed out in worn bootcut denim and leather chaps, spurs adorning their heels. Both wore wide-brimmed ten-gallon hats, even in the shade.

Despite how I'd pictured Tucsonans before moving to the Southwest, I hardly saw anyone dressed like this outside of the horse corral. Through their old-fashioned ranchero way of life, men like Slim and the old cowboy held strong to the dregs of American Southwestern masculinity from the heyday of Tombstone and the Earp brothers and the O.K. Corral, an era that had passed long before their births. In modern times, cowboys had become desert tour guides, their horses standing saddled and ready at the fence for snowbirds to come through and pay for a horseback ride, which few ever did.

That afternoon, with the pens shoveled and the horses fed and watered, I had nothing to do but kill time on the porch until my parents showed up. I made a game of tapping at the old cowboy's leg, my thumb closed into a tight ball.

"Ain't no way to throw a punch," he said. "You'll break your thumb like 'at." He grabbed my hand and roughly fashioned it into a proper fist, thumb on the outside of my folded fingers.

"Hit me," he said. "Hard as you can, now." I jabbed at his open palm a few times and the old cowboy nodded approvingly, taking a long drag off his home-rolled cigarette.

"Soon you'll be fightin' like a man," he said, blowing smoke from his nose.

All the cowboys smoked or chewed, sometimes both at once. The old cowboy's youngest son practiced all the time. He'd hold the stem of a chocolate sucker to his lips with his thumb and pointer finger, spitting the brown juice onto the ground between licks. I couldn't understand why someone who spent all day in the desert heat would want to light a fire and breathe it in, but these men didn't seem to figure it that way. Studying my small clenched fists, I wanted to harness the power of their stoicism, to break it like I'd once seen the old cowboy do to a wild mustang.

IN THE SCHOOL cafeteria, I held my lunch tray as I scanned the long tables for Sage amid rows and rows of unapproachable faces. But I couldn't find her. Sighing, I took a seat instead across from a girl and a boy from our class. The girl wore dark clothes, heavy mascara, and a chain wallet. The boy had soft features and tended to make grand, effeminate gestures with his hands as he spoke. In the social hierarchy of our school, these two were far from popular, the kind of kids who knew how bullying felt. I'd never talked to them before, but this made them seem like good candidates for friendship. They exchanged glances as I sat down, erupting into a fit of giggles.

"No, *you* ask him," the girl whispered. Pretending not to hear her, I took a bite of the lasagna on my tray and frowned. The pasta was somehow both rubbery and dry. I spat the wad into my napkin.

"Um, not to be rude," the boy started, "but, like, what are you?"

"Oh my god, you can't just *ask* what someone is!" the girl said, smacking him playfully on the arm.

"What do you mean?" I said, playing dumb.

"Like," he began, running a large hand over his face as he stifled a grin, "like, are you a guy, or—?" He let the end of his question hang, the absent word containing all the slurs other kids had spat at me in the courtyard for months.

"What do you *think*?" I said, daring him to finish the sentence.

"A girl?" His tone made clear this wasn't a genuine guess, but a jab at my masculinity. I clenched my fists under the table, thumb over fingers like the old cowboy taught me. Though taller than me, I felt sure this boy wouldn't be able to hold his own in a fight.

"He looks like a guy to me," the girl chimed in. The boy rolled his eyes, turning his attention to his fingernails. I glared at him, taking another cautious bite of lasagna. The more I ate, the more passable it got. The trick was to chew quickly so that you got the tomato flavor and not the consistency. More whispering and giggling from the other side of the table.

"Hey, so, uh, are you a virgin?" the boy asked.

"What's that?" I snapped.

He smirked at me. "Just say yes or no."

"How can I tell you if I don't know what it is?" I looked to the girl, who smiled.

"Give us your best guess," she said, brushing a short black curl behind her ear. She seemed nice. Friendly, even. I considered how to answer the boy's question, deciding it might be better to say I wasn't something if I didn't know what that something was. That would be the safest bet.

"No," I said. The boy gasped, holding a fist to his open mouth. The girl stifled a laugh behind her hands. I felt an immediate, piercing shame for placing my trust in her.

"Oh my god," the boy said, loud enough for the entire cafeteria to hear. "You're *not* a virgin?"

"I don't—I don't even know what that *means*," I cried, desperately appealing to the kids at other tables. The whispering swelled like a wave. I tried to be stoic like the cowboys, to keep my face blank when kids pointed and laughed on the playground. But inside, my throat clenched tight with the same silencing powerlessness I felt at school almost every day.

In my shoes, a man like Slim would've probably challenged the boy to a fight out behind the barn. But school wasn't the horse corral. I didn't have the old cowboy here to back me up. Fighting with my fists might shut one kid up for a while, but the teasing wouldn't stop. I had dozens of tormenters, outnumbering me, and they had the school system on their side. Rita Ranch kids never got in any real trouble for the things they said or did. Teachers knew the truth about me, and where I came from. They could count the ways I was different.

I buried my face in my arms, wishing I could skip ahead to Saturday. At least nobody at the horse corral asked me stupid questions I didn't know the answers to.

"AROUND HERE WE put in a full day's hard work, hear?" the old cowboy said gruffly, spitting brown tobacco juice from behind his teeth onto the dusty earth. I nodded, gripping the straps of my overalls, staring down at the splintery porch where moments ago he'd caught me sitting idle in the shade, running my fingers over the rough edges of a crescent-shaped piece of hoof I'd found hanging over the clothesline.

"Some manure needs shovelin' yonder," he said, nodding toward a fresh pile steaming in the dirt. "See to it."

I grabbed my fork and wheelbarrow, bracing my body for a return to the heat. Though I tried to keep pace like the old cowboy asked, I didn't have the endurance. Shoveling became an equation. I learned to stretch the task to use as little energy as possible while gauging how much longer I could stand out in the sun before collapsing. Slim, for his part, had taken to dunking me in the water trough whenever he caught me slacking. Nothing was more disgusting than taking a bath in cold horse spit, even if it did offer some relief from the heat.

Despite the old cowboy's promise to my parents, after months of work I could count the number of riding lessons I'd had on one hand. Conditions had to be just right. The old cowboy only saddled me up on slow days with the shoveling all done, and only then if I reminded him and he didn't have anything better to do. Before heading back to the small pen where little kids took pony rides at birthday parties, we'd each pick our horses from those tied to the fence.

I always chose the oldest horse, Blackie, because his dark, peeled-grape eyes didn't dart around like the young stallions Slim had broken. I'd lean forward in my saddle and talk to him, tugging on the reins to coax him this way or that. I could see what people liked about keeping horses when I helped the old cowboy refill his water trough or haul a fresh hay bale into his pen. Blackie chewed sideways, his lips flying up his gums when I held out an apple or a sugar cube.

"Palm up," the old cowboy reminded me. "Else he'll take one of your fingers with it."

THE HUMILIATION OF the cafeteria incident was still fresh in my mind after the final bell that day at school. I sat on the curb in the parking lot, glaring at my closed fists, wishing I'd hit the boy when I had the chance. Regret roiled in my stomach as I imagined how good the ache of his cheekbones would have felt against my knuckles. The slow-motion surrender of his body to gravity as he fell backward onto the cold linoleum. The dark blood running freely from his busted nose onto his upper lip.

I felt a sharp pinch on the back of my neck and whipped around, ready to fight whichever boy dared taunt me this time. But it was only Sage. She smirked at me, flipping her long hair away from her eyes. I sighed a breath of frustration.

"What do you want?"

"I heard you're not a virgin," she said.

"Yeah, me too," I said, turning back toward the street.

"Is it true?" she demanded.

"How should I know?" I said. "No one will tell me what a virgin is." Sage glanced furtively around the parking lot before cupping a hand to my ear. I twisted my face in disgust.

"Ugh, that's gross! Why wouldn't they just *say* that?"

"Because they're stupid, obviously," she said, plopping down next to me on the curb.

"I should've punched that kid in the nose, huh?" I said. Sage grinned, her braces gleaming in the harsh afternoon sunlight.

"You definitely should have," she agreed. We swapped jokes and rumors about my latest bullies, and soon the day hadn't seemed so bad. I waved to Sage through the van's open window as Mom drove us homeward to Cactus Country, a smile spreading like a rash across my cheeks.

"Was that a friend of yours?" Mom asked. I nodded indifferently, stifling my smile behind the stoic face I'd wear to the horse corral the next morning.

BATHROOM BLUES

"ZOË, YOU HAVE TO," MOM said, her voice hushed. Our fight had escalated from the privacy of the Airstream onto our front porch, a low plywood and cinderblock platform. Fresh from the Cactus Country showers, she'd dressed for the morning heat in a sleeveless button-up shirt, capri shorts, and sensible sandals. Her long, sun-streaked hair, still drying, hung limply down her back.

She folded her arms against her chest, glancing around to see who might be in earshot of our spat. A lady with a dog strolled along the pavement adjacent to our campsite. Across the street, a couple sat drinking coffee at the picnic table in front of their motorhome. Conversations and television sets blared through open trailer windows. Mom never raised her voice in public. I knew she wouldn't want to make a scene in front of the neighbors.

"No, I don't," I said, calmly. "You can't make me do it."

"You have to brush your teeth," she repeated. "You have to take a shower."

"I won't."

Mom bit her lower lip, squinting at me as though I were a puzzle she didn't know how to solve. At twelve years old, I spent my days barefoot. Dirt crusted my toenails. Plaque caked my teeth. My greasy blond hair shone in the sunlight, and a fine layer of grit coated my sunburned face like a second skin.

"Why don't you want to take care of yourself?" she asked.

"Because it's a waste of time," I insisted. I didn't see the sense in washing up today when I'd be dirty again by tomorrow. But my protest wasn't just an aversion to cleanliness. In or out of the shower, I tried hard not to think about the ways my body was changing. I couldn't stand to look at its widening hips or its narrowing waist, the two puckered lumps like anthills on the once-smooth plain of my chest. As the cool water flitted across my skin, I often fantasized about cutting off the lumps in two clean slices, imagining how light I would feel playing outside with the warmth of the sun on my bare shoulders. Sometimes in the shower I beat my body like a wild animal, slamming fists into flesh as hard as I could until the lumps stung with frustrated bruises.

Over the past few months, Mom had tried to guide me through puberty in her own, quiet way. One morning I'd found a new bottle of acne wash left next to the Airstream's bathroom sink. Another day, she'd casually asked whether I needed any "support." I cocked my eyebrows until she pressed her hands under her breasts and pushed upward, miming what she meant. Mom breathed a long, audible sigh as I left the trailer without a word, its aluminum door slamming behind me.

Her latest effort had been to leave a battered copy of *The "What's Happening to My Body?" Book for Girls* on my pillow. I opened the book exactly once, turning to a random page with a diagram of a woman inserting a finger into her vagina and touching her cervix. The book encouraged readers to become acquainted with their bodies in this way. I didn't even want to admit I had a vagina, let alone go rooting around in it. Scandalized, I snuck the book from the Airstream under my shirt and tossed it into the park garbage truck.

Back on the Airstream porch, Mom moved her hands to her hips.

"Please," she said, her voice cracking. "Just be reasonable." I crossed my arms, shook my head. Mom clenched her jaw and rubbed her hands hard against her face. Her shoulders began to heave. Once, then twice. Electric shame surged from my heart to my fingertips. Everything in me wanted to reach out to touch her, but I resisted the impulse, looked away. I didn't mean to make Mom cry. But I also couldn't bear to face my body in the shower again. I stared at the plywood in guilty silence, waiting for her to compose herself.

Mom sniffed hard as she wiped her cheeks with the backs of her fingers. She caught my gaze, her eyes red and tired. Nodded, as if to ask, *So what do you say?*

I bit my lip and shook my head once, a defiant *No*. One I hoped would also, somehow, explain why I couldn't do what she begged me to do. That I was sorry for pushing her away, for refusing the help I didn't know how to receive. But after weeks locked in this power struggle, my message was lost in translation.

"You're *dirty*!" she shouted, angry tears stinging at her eyes. "You're going to get sick, and your teeth are going to rot out of your skull! Is that what you want? Is it?"

Mom's outburst hit me like a flipped switch. My guilt of seconds ago was gone, replaced with a fiery rage to match hers.

"Yes, it *is* what I want!" I shouted back. "If they fall out, I won't have to brush them!"

"Fine!" she screamed, waving her arms. "I don't care!" She wheeled around and into the Airstream, slamming the door with such force the trailer shook on its axles.

The blaring televisions of minutes ago had all gone silent. The picnic table couple looked up at me from their coffee mugs. Even the lady with the dog had stopped walking to listen, pretending to inspect his paws for cactus spurs. My face flushed, and it had nothing to do with the morning heat.

"I've tried everything," I heard Mom sob through the Airstream walls. "She's just so damn stubborn. I don't know how to get through to her."

"Let her learn, Susan," Dad counseled. "If her teeth rot, they rot. It's the most natural consequence in the world."

I felt bad for upsetting Mom, but I couldn't apologize. If I did, I'd have no choice but to give in and take a shower. In time, I'd learn from the Cactus Country boys how to douse my hair in the bathhouse sinks, to run my wet fingers behind my ears and neck. I'd wipe the dust from my face and arms with damp paper towels and head home to the Airstream, pretending to be clean. But for now, I would lay low, hanging out at the playground until our fight blew over. With Mom, it usually did by dinner time. She'd never been one to hold a grudge.

I STOOD IN the school courtyard, facing two closed doors—one marked GIRLS, the other, BOYS. Two choices, both somehow wrong. Opening either door could lead to trouble, depending on who might be around to see me walk through it.

Everyone at Cottonwood had heard the rumors about my gender, but nobody seemed sure what to believe. My classmates immediately recognized me as a boy, and used masculine pronouns—even the bullies who taunted me for being too effeminate. My teacher, Mrs. D, meanwhile, had initially seemed surprised when the boy who showed up to the first day of class didn't match the girl in her files. But after a quick call to my parents she corrected herself, from then on referring to me as "she" and "her."

When faced with tough questions on the playground, I could usually get away with convincing the kids in my class that they'd misheard "he" as "she," or that Mrs. D and the other teachers were confused. But maintaining this plausible deniability required constant vigilance to avoid any mention of my pronouns. I hid my face behind a book whenever Mrs. D walked by my desk. I never raised my hand in class, even when I felt sure I knew the answer. By evading the attention of my teachers, I was able, tenuously, to preserve my identity as a boy at school.

I sighed, craning my neck to survey the courtyard. The art teacher strode along the sidewalk, her heels clicking against the pavement. She waved to me. I bent over the fountain between the bathrooms, pretending to take a long drink until she'd passed.

Despite the dry desert climate, I usually avoided drinking water at school. Sometimes this helped me hold off on going to the bathroom until I got home. But other days, like today, I couldn't wait. I watched the teacher disappear into a classroom on the other side of the school. All clear. Eyes still fixed on the courtyard, I slipped behind one of the bathroom doors—and ran smack into a girl.

"What're you doing in here, you sicko?" she demanded, pushing me back outside. "This is the *girl's* room." The teacher reappeared from the far classroom, looking curiously in our direction.

"Oops, sorry," I said, feeling both pairs of eyes on the back of my head as I took a deep breath—though not too deep—and returned to class, bladder full and spirit deflated.

The news spread quickly on the playground.

"You went into the girl's room!" the boys chanted in high, singsongy voices. For the rest of the day, they called me "it," narrating my every move aloud as though I were an exotic animal in a nature show. They echoed animal "mating" calls at me from their desks, burying their faces in their arms and giggling whenever I looked up. For once, I didn't care what the other boys said. The pressure building in my abdomen overwhelmed any attention I might have given them. By the end of the day, I could hardly walk. Breathing was agony. Mom noticed my stiffness and silence on the drive back to Cactus Country.

"What's wrong with you?" she asked.

"I really, really, really have to pee," I whispered, arm held between my legs.

Mom pulled over at a gas station and I rushed inside. The relief, sitting on that grimy toilet on a Tuesday afternoon, was like none I'd ever known. I thanked God for single-stall gas station bathrooms.

"Why didn't you just use the bathroom at school?" Mom asked when I hopped back into the van, her blond eyebrows creased in concern.

"I didn't have to go then," I said. She eyed me suspiciously. I tried not to return her gaze, picking at a scab on my knee.

"It's not good for your bladder to hold it in," she said. "You'll get an infection. Promise me you'll go when you have to go from now on." I nodded and said that I would, knowing full well what Mom asked of me—to be kind to myself, to take care of my body—was impossible.

AT THE HEIGHT of the winter season, the Cactus Country boys and I raided the park laundry room for lost quarters, fishing under the machines with wire clothes hangers. We pooled the coins we found, burying them at the foot of our favorite palo verde tree until Sunday, when we dug them up to buy popsicles from the park's general store. Twin pops were cheapest—just 50 cents for two—and we bought as many as we could afford, splitting them down their centers and swapping them so we each got at least a couple licks of every flavor.

At the park store, we basked in the air conditioning, listening to Cactus Country's assistant manager tell us her childhood stories about climbing trees and picking fights with boys. Carol had short, spiky black hair, sharp eyebrows, and a gruff edge to her voice. Neighbors sometimes complained about Carol's blunt nature, but I liked her. She gave me things—old candy bars, unpopular ice cream flavors, leftover seasonal trinkets—that she never doled out to the other kids.

One Sunday, Carol rang up our popsicles distractedly, rushing through each transaction without the usual small talk. When I walked up to the counter with my sweaty handful of change, she met me with one of her characteristic side-eye glances.

"You and me need to talk, kiddo," Carol said. She looked over my head at the other boys. "The rest of you kids, scram."

My friends whooped on their way out the door, sure I must be in some kind of trouble. I tried to think what I'd done wrong. Did Carol know we'd been slaughtering the palo verde beetles again? Had she seen the barrel cactus we'd carved our initials into by the playground? Or maybe she'd heard it had been my idea to climb from the trees onto the roof of the public bathhouse?

"A man came in the office this morning saying a little girl went into the men's room and sat down in the stall next to his," Carol said. Her dark eyes locked onto mine. "You wouldn't know anything about that, would you?" My eyes widened in false surprise.

"It wasn't me," I said. She shot me a stern look, exhaled a deep breath from her nose.

"I know it's hard—" she began, then stopped. I stared at her, wondering what, exactly, she knew was hard. But Carol didn't elaborate. "I'm sorry, but you can't go into the men's room anymore."

"Okay," I said, "but I didn't—"

"I understand, but you can't, okay?" Carol said, her expression softening in a way I wasn't used to. "I wish you could, but you can't." She said this last part quietly. I looked down at my bare feet, ashamed.

"Now, I won't tell your parents anything about this," she said. I nodded. Carol reached under the counter and pulled out a handful of expired chocolate bars.

"Share these with your friends," she said, passing them to me. "And tell them you're my favorite." Carol winked. I smiled at her, gathering the candy in my hands. She'd given me a cover, and in that moment, I loved her for it.

"This is the best Sunday *ever*," one boy declared, his mouth full of cracked M&Ms. The others seemed to agree, licking the quickly melting chocolate from their fingers. Ripping into a too-hard Butterfinger bar, my thoughts turned to the man who reported me, one of hundreds of snowbirds I'd never met and never would. Why did he care who used the stall next to his? Didn't other boys sometimes sit to pee? I wished I could explain to this man—to everyone—how it felt when I averted my eyes in the women's room to avoid the startled faces and uneasy stares I often encountered there. How walking into the men's room made me feel wonderfully ordinary, like I was any other boy. Two choices, both somehow wrong. I scraped the chocolate from the bar's peanut butter center with my teeth, wondering why bathrooms had to be separate at all.

ONE MORNING LATER that spring, I woke to a sharp, throbbing pain in my abdomen. Mom and Dad slept on the foldout couch as I stumbled sleepily into the Airstream's tiny bathroom and sat on the toilet. The release made the ache feel better, at first. But when I wiped, the paper came up stained a deep and alarming red.

Immediately, I remembered the health warning going around school that week. A boy had contracted a rare disease that caused, among other things, blood in the urine. The principal sent a letter home to parents listing the symptoms, which kids pored over in the parking lot after school, imagining each stray sniffle, cough, and itch as evidence our bodies had succumbed to the virus.

I slipped back into bed, panic flooding me like a shiver in the cool morning air. The ache in my gut seemed to be getting worse. Maybe I'd grown a tumor. Maybe my organs were shutting down. Maybe this was the first sign of the plague. I tossed my blankets aside and quietly padded over to where my parents slept, gently nudging Mom awake.

"Mom," I whispered. "Mom, I think there's something wrong with me." She opened her eyes slowly, peering up at me through half-open slits like a lizard. I led her to my twin bed midway through the Airstream and explained my theory. Mom regarded me with a patient expression, seeming less worried than I'd hoped, but listening carefully until I finished. She licked her lips.

"You might be right," she said. "Or . . . " her voice trailed off. I waited for her to finish the thought, but she let it hang. I didn't understand. What else could it possibly be? Twelve-year-old boys didn't just spontaneously start bleeding. I nodded, urging her to go on. Mom's eyes brimmed with so much affection I couldn't bear to meet her gaze.

"What?" I said, suddenly embarrassed.

"Why don't you go in and check one more time?" she asked. She said it so tenderly, and that's when it hit me, the reality of what this might actually mean. Stiffly, I got up from bed and went into the bathroom again, closing the door slowly behind me. I sat down on the toilet. Yanked a sheet of paper from the roll. Wiped.

I didn't want to look, wishing with my whole being that, in fact, I did have the disease. That Mom would rush me to the hospital and I could go on antibiotics or through several rounds of painful treatments and stay home in the Airstream until I recovered enough to go back to school. Or that, any minute now, I would wake up to find this scenario a hazy, distant memory, like trying to remember a dream that took place in another lifetime.

But most of all, I wished that what was happening to me just wouldn't happen, ever. That my body would not betray me. I didn't believe in God, but I prayed to him. *Please, let me be a boy just a little longer. Please, let me be sick.* I had never wanted anything so much as I wanted this.

With a shaking hand, I held the darkening paper up against the morning desert light, and began, silently, to cry.

GROWING PAINS

"Aw, c'mon Zo," Dad said, shouting over the hot air blasting through the van's open window. "It's not so bad." He stole a quick glance at me, one eye still locked on the road.

So far, I'd been sullen and moody on the more than thirty-minute drive through sprawling Tucson, on our way to wash windows at the Check Into Cash payday loan chains. I didn't want to talk. I didn't want the radio on. Not even a break from working at the horse corral was enough to lift my spirits. My arms folded tightly against my chest, I faced the passenger seat window, looking at but not really seeing the storefronts and strip malls rushing by.

"Oh, really?" I retorted. "It's not so bad to bleed all over the place? You should try it sometime, then. You might like it."

Dad sighed through his nose, but let the sarcasm slide.

"I don't know what it's like. That's true. But I do know it doesn't change anything about who you are," he offered. He reached over and gave my knee a loving squeeze before shifting into third gear. I couldn't think of anything smart to say to that. Having a period didn't change anything about who I was. But it did make it harder to become the person I wanted to be.

"Try to cheer up, honey," he shouted, gesturing toward the cloudless blue sky. "See what a nice day it is?"

"All I see is darkness," I said bitterly.

In the days since my period started I'd settled into a kind of numb reality. One where I felt cranky no matter how much sleep I got, and my body ached worse than side stitches after a long run. Once I'd composed myself enough to let Mom into the Airstream's bathroom, she'd searched the tiny cabinet with a furrowed brow for a box of sanitary pads, pushing aside the stash of half-empty shaving cream cans and bottles of shampoo she'd collected from whatever last year's snowbirds had abandoned in the Cactus Country showers.

"Here," she said, blowing the dust from the box's cardboard lid. "You can use these for now. I don't need them anymore." She unwrapped one of the pads from its plastic packaging and showed me how to stick it to a fresh pair of underwear. How to fasten the wings around the middle so it stayed securely in place.

"Let me know if you need help," she said. "I'll be right outside."

I took the panties from her, closed the door. Pulled them over my legs and around my waist. The pad felt bulky, like wearing a diaper. With a sanitary pad strapped to my underwear, I didn't feel free to run and play. I couldn't go swimming, or climb trees. But worst of all, the pad ensured I wouldn't be able to stop thinking about my period. Not even for a second.

DAD HAD PLOTTED the day's stops out on a map, ten jobs across Tucson's east side. We pulled into the parking lot of the first Check Into Cash store on 22nd Street and set to work. He dumped a gallon of water from the cooler into a bucket as I poured in a cap of concentrated soap. I mixed them together with my hand while Dad buckled the squeegee belt around his waist.

He would wash the outside of each window with the scrubber and wipe them with the squeegee before the water dried in the sun—a process that on hot days took only seconds. I took care of the detail work, spritzing smudges with a spray bottle and wiping the windows clean from the inside. That done, I wrote out invoices and waited for the manager to fork over the six or eight dollars we got for each job before raiding the free sodas and candy bars they left out for payday loan customers. When I came along to help Dad wash windows, I could eat as much candy and drink as much soda as I liked. But today, even the promise of unlimited sugar couldn't cheer me. I walked past the snack table with the money, taking nothing.

Washing windows usually felt like a treat. For lunch Dad would spend a little of the money we earned on Taco Bell burritos. Later in the day, we might browse the used books and video games at Bookmans Entertainment Exchange on Speedway Boulevard. But my favorite thing, hands down, was the Check Into Cash tellers—typically men—who gushed about Dad and I working together as a father-son team.

"Training to take over the family business someday, eh?" they'd chuckle as I wiped soap from the interior windows in circles with my blue rag, the way Dad taught me. I always nodded along, flushing with pride. Never mind that window washing was a part-time gig and not anything close to a family business. Dad had no special interest in windows, and didn't make particularly good money washing them. Still, I liked being part of this fantasy of patriarchal legacy, the passing of a trade from father to son.

The manager of the second Check Into Cash store grinned at me from behind the counter as I came in. "Learning the ropes from your old man, son?" he asked. I nodded, but couldn't bring myself to return his smile. Dad and I weren't on the same team anymore, even if we looked the part. My eyes burned. After six days living at the mercy of its whims, I wanted to punish my body, to make it hurt. Turning my back to the manager, I scrubbed the windows in wide circles, harder and faster, until my muscles ached. Once the windows shone, I went back to the van and put our supplies away with exhausted arms, leaving Dad to deal with the invoice.

"I hate to see you so upset," he said. I shrugged. We drove to the next few Check Into Cash stores in silence, save for the gusts of hot air whipping through the van's open windows. At around our seventh stop, I grabbed my spray bottle and a fresh rag. But before I could head into the store, Dad waved me back to the open hatch.

"Want to try it?" he asked. I eyed the scrubber with some awe. Washing the outsides of the windows required upper-arm strength and finesse, as you could accidentally make streaks if you went too fast. Too many streaks, and you'd have to go over the window with soapy water all over again, wasting valuable time and expensive soap solution.

"Sure," I said, a grin spreading across my face. Dad adjusted the belt several notches down to its smallest size, but it still hung loosely from my frame, the holster knocking against my knee. I balanced it on one hip, staggering unnaturally from the van to the windows. Dad showed me how to fit the scrubber onto the end of the extendable pole. How to dunk it into the soapy water—first one end, then the other, with a little twirl to ensure minimal spillage.

On my toes, I held the scrubber up to the top of the tallest windowpane and pulled it down, creating a long, satisfying trail of soapy water. Using the squeegee proved harder. I had to quickly swap heads on the pole, and wipe the blade dry between pulls. Starting at the top left corner of the window, I dragged the squeegee down until it slipped. The blade went sideways, making a huge streak across the pane. I straightened the pole and tried going over it again. Residual soap dribbled down from the window's middle. I sighed, lowering the pole.

"I really suck at this," I said.

"No, that's good for a first try," Dad said. "We can clean up those spots, no problem."

He went over my work with a rag wrapped around the end of an extendable pole. Once he smoothed the streaks, the window didn't look bad. The job took twice as long as usual and spillage from the crooked holster drenched my legs, but a little ember of pride smoldered in my chest as I piled our window washing equipment back into the van.

We'd worked well into the afternoon now, our bodies sticky with layers of dried soap and sweat. Dad splashed a little water from the cooler onto his head and sighed.

"Let's take a break from this heat, huh?" he said. We drove to Bookmans to cool off in the air conditioning. Dad went to peruse the magazines while I loitered in front of the restrooms, waiting for a good time to furtively slip into the women's room and change my pad. After wandering the store's vast maze of bright orange bookshelves, I spotted two redheaded boys around my age standing close enough to a display case for their breath to cloud the glass. The taller one pointed to a game cartridge, his finger smudging the surface.

"No way, they have it! They *never* have this one," he said. "Quick, get the guy!" The shorter boy ran to find the clerk, a squat man in his twenties with shoulder-length greasy blond hair who followed him with a bored swagger, the epitome of cool, humoring the boys' excitement.

"Awesome," the clerk said dryly. "This must be, like, the best day of your whole lives."

I watched him unlock the case, the boys bouncing on their toes. In a few short years, these kids would grow tall and muscular. Red hair would sprout thick on their jawlines. Their voices would deepen to a baritone. Soon they would become young men, as the clerk once had.

The boys galloped to the register, holding up the backs of their loose pants as they ran. I took their spot in front of the case. My face reflected translucently in the glass, cheeks pink from sun exposure and hair stiff with sweat. I had become the boy I wanted to be. But boyhood was fleeting, transitory. When I tried to picture myself as an adult, the only face I could imagine was Dad's—his light green eyes and thick brown hair and prominent brow, features so unlike the ones staring back at me. I looked until Dad tapped me on the shoulder, signaling it was time to leave. Back in the van, he pulled a thick paperback from his bag.

"Got you something for helping out today," he said, flashing his toothy smile. Dad knew I loved to read, and that a good book was hard to find in Cactus Country. The recreation hall had a disorganized wall shelf filled with cheap romance paperbacks and mystery thrillers where young women ended up either ravished or murdered—sometimes both, and not necessarily in that order. I mostly read the stray books my parents brought into the Airstream. Other than Dad's David Sedaris essay collections, Annie Dillard books, and *The Far Side* comics, some of my favorites were *To Kill a Mockingbird*, *A Tree Grows in Brooklyn*, and *Coffee Will Make You Black*—any story about a kid reckoning with their place in an uncertain world.

I took the book from him, turning it over in my hands. On the cover, a young woman crouched over a stretch of highway, thumb extended, waiting for a passing car. I read the title aloud: "*Even Cowgirls Get the Blues* by Tom Robbins."

"I really loved this book when I was just a little older than you," Dad said. "I used to hitchhike around the country like she did, and I always thought she was really cool—definitely her own kind of girl, like you. Maybe you'll think so, too."

I studied the woman's stalwart expression, her eyes shadowed under the brim of a cowboy hat. Though I understood what Dad was getting at, and appreciated his attempt to make my bad day a better one, I didn't want to be my own kind of girl. None of the characters in my favorite books lived in trailers way out in the Sonoran Desert. No novel I'd ever read had anything to say about boys with periods, or girls who wanted to punish the bodies they'd been born into. I wanted to read a story like mine, because I wanted to know how that story would end.

"Thanks, Dad," I said, thumbing through the book's worn pages. He ruffled my hair.

"We'll get through this, motherfucker," he said, misquoting a line from a David Sedaris essay we both loved, the one that always made me laugh. "Just you wait and see."

I smiled. As Dad drove on to the next job, I opened the book and began to read, disappearing into the childhood of Sissy Hankshaw who, true to Dad's recollection, faced her looming adulthood with a courage I could not.

THE BULLY BOX

"I KNEW IT!" SAGE SAID, eyes beaming behind her glasses. "I *knew* you were a girl!"

We crouched together behind a creosote bush at the edge of the schoolyard. The day before the end of sixth grade, I'd pulled Sage aside to tell her the truth about my body in what I hoped would be a private place. I put a finger to my lips, frantically shushing her.

"Quiet, before the whole school hears!" I said.

"Why?" she asked. I opened my mouth to explain, but thought better of it. All year the mystery of my gender had been enough for us to form something like a friendship. But I wanted Sage to like me for who I was. I'd overheard a few things about middle school from the other kids. Incoming seventh graders would be split into three "teams" for their classes, and we had no way of knowing in advance which group we'd be sorted into. After today, Sage and I might not see each other again. Sage held out her wrist, handing me a pen.

"We should hang out this summer," she said. "What's your number?"

LIKE MOST RITA RANCH kids, Sage lived in a single-story home with a sparse, gravel-paved front yard. The first time I came over, we hung out in a small, dark room furnished with a Dell computer, a desk, a rolling chair, a stool, and a sizable hole in the door, made, Sage told me, by her father.

"Your dad punched a door?" I said. "Why would he do that?" I asked this, though I already knew the answer. Cactus Country was full of guys with tempers, and I'd seen with my own eyes how a man could go from frustrated to rageful in the time it took most people to finish a sentence.

"Because he's an idiot, that's why," Sage said. She explained her dad had been drinking one night. Sage locked him out of the room and, in response, he'd smashed his way through until his knuckles bled.

"He wanted me to get off the computer and go to bed or something," she said, rolling her eyes. I nodded as though I understood, could commiserate.

The computer, and more precisely, the internet, was Sage's all-consuming fascination. Dad had a laptop I borrowed to play web-browser games and care for virtual pets, but that summer Sage introduced me to a more grown-up version of the internet. To instant messaging, online personality quizzes, and fanfiction. I watched Sage fire off short messages, each one like a flash of lightning, to strangers she called her friends. We entered a private chat room with a guy, Wolfey59, who Sage said was her long-distance boyfriend. She translated the chatspeak for me—lol, irl, afk, bff, asl, rotfl—so I could follow their conversation.

"wolf i want u to meet my irl bff," she wrote.

"Write hi," she said to me. I pecked "hi" on the keyboard and pressed the return key.

"hi," Wolfey59 said.

"she has short hair n looks like a boy but is rly a girl," Sage wrote.

"lol kewl," said Wolfey59.

I frowned at the screen, not wanting Wolfey59 to know these details about me, even if I would never meet him in real life. As I opened my mouth to protest, Sage's dad abruptly burst into the room, broken door knocking hard against the wall. Sage scrambled to minimize the instant message window.

"You know the rules," he told her. "Keep this door *open*. I don't want you alone with no boys in here." He took his big hand off the doorknob to point at me, glaring.

"Oh my god, Dad!" she said. "That's a *girl*." His pointed finger went limp. He stood up a little straighter, smiling bashfully at me, the way a lot of adults did when they learned the truth about my body. Either tripping over themselves to seem apologetic, or otherwise reacting incredulously—as though my gender were an elaborate prank. In seconds, Sage's dad had gone from ready to rip my head from my skinny neck to murmuring a gentle string of apologies.

"Oh, is that so? Oh, I'm so sorry. Your short hair. I'm sorry. That's fine," he said, and was gone, the door shut softly behind him. I let out a long breath I wasn't aware of holding in. Sage rolled her eyes.

"Told you he was an idiot," she said, smirking at me. I felt embarrassed that both Wolfey59 and Sage's dad now knew my secret when hardly anyone else did, but I was willing to let it go in the face of what seemed like a convenient truth: Nobody was ever suspicious of two *girls* hanging out alone together.

Sage had boyfriends on the internet, sure, but they didn't seem like real people. They didn't get to sleep over at Sage's house, where we camped out in our sleeping bags, eating fistfuls of sugary cereal and watching Adult Swim late into the night. They didn't get to careen around never-ending Rita Ranch on a single bicycle, following its winding roads at random until we didn't care whether we ever found our way back.

"Why can't you ever come over on Saturdays?" she asked, clicking through an online personality quiz.

"Because I have to work," I said. I explained about my weekend job helping the old cowboy and Slim shovel, feed, and brush their horses. Sage wrinkled her nose.

"Horses? That's so gay," she said, eyes still on the screen. I nodded slowly, biting my lower lip. Yes, it was gay. Gay, meaning ridiculous. Ridiculous, like the idea that Sage and I could ever be more than friends, even as whatever was happening between us seemed to stretch beyond the bounds of friendship into some ill-defined place I didn't know how to name.

In the relative privacy of Sage's computer room, we would flirt, even hold hands. I'd return from long afternoons at her house to the Airstream in a haze of preadolescent infatuation, terrified of how I felt but wanting to keep feeling it forever. Alone in the trailer, I wrote about Sage in short, feverish bursts. Writing made the feelings seem real for a moment, my crush alive with possibility on the page. When I finished writing I'd tear the pages from my notebook, ripping them to shreds and disposing of the evidence so no one would ever see it.

Because in these secret, ephemeral pages I'd also write about how sometimes, late at night, our bodies illuminated by the staticky blue glow of the television screen, Sage's face would creep closer and closer to mine. Our eyes would lock, mine searching hers for something in them that told me whatever happened next would be okay. At the last second, I'd turn away and Sage would giggle into her pillow. No matter how many times we played this game, I always lost. I knew if I closed my eyes, if I leaned in, there would be no going back. Hers was the sweet face of oblivion, and I was too afraid to find out whether she would still be there, smiling at me, on the other side.

DESERT SKY MIDDLE SCHOOL'S massive student body—three grades each split into three teams, with classrooms spread across three courtyards—afforded me an anonymity I didn't have in elementary school. Every hour on the hour, hundreds of us streamed like ants across the courtyards from one classroom to another. No one at Desert Sky knew me as the weird, gender-ambiguous kid from out of state. Middle school was the great equalizer, a place where everyone fell somewhere on the spectrum of gangly, awkward, blemished, and stinky. Most kids were too busy dealing with their own pubescent hang-ups to pay much attention to mine.

The only thing I didn't like about middle school was Sage's budding interest in dating and romance. She spoke openly about her crushes on the other boys in our classes—who was hot, who was not—yet continued to flirt with me in secret. A few months into the school year, I found Sage in the courtyard holding hands with her first official not-online boyfriend.

He and I were about the same height, with the same round, boyish face. We both wore our bowl haircuts slightly long and draped loose, too-big clothes over our lanky bodies. In homeroom, I watched the school news broadcast in the dark, feeling listless as Sage sat next to me, covertly carving the letters of his name—A-L-E-X—into her forearm with a straightened paper clip. Staring at the TV, I didn't notice Sage put the clip down until she'd slipped a folded note under my fingers. I opened it slowly, careful to obscure it under the table from our teacher, Mrs. Goldwasser, who sat behind us at her desk. Mrs. G was notorious for reading notes she confiscated aloud to the class.

"Whats wrong," the note said. I could feel Sage's eyes on the side of my face.

"Nothing," I wrote. Sage scribbled a new line and passed it back.

"You can tell me," it said.

I shrugged and turned to the TV. Sage added something else to the note and pressed it, insistently, against my fingers.

"Please," it said. I sighed, trying to find the words for how I felt. I wrote and erased and rewrote my thoughts over and over until the page was smudged gray. Finally, I settled on: "How do you really feel about me?"

Mrs. Goldwasser's chair groaned as she stood up from her desk. Scrambling to hide the note in my lap, I waited for Mrs. G to return to her seat before tossing it to Sage. I tried not to look at her as she read it. In no time, I had a response.

"Youre my best friend & I love you," it said. I smiled, though I knew this was a dodge, telling me what I wanted to hear without saying anything at all. Emboldened, I pressed for more.

"But when you say love what does that mean?"

"It means I LOVE you!" Sage wrote, the word capitalized and underlined a few times for emphasis. She was going to make me ask the question I'd been trying to avoid. I gritted my teeth, pressed my pencil to the paper.

"But do you love me like a friend or—" Before I could finish the thought, Mrs. Goldwasser appeared over us, snatching up the note like a bird of prey and swooping back to her desk in the dark. Sage and I exchanged panicked glances as we heard the crinkling of paper unfolding behind us. Mrs. G looked up at us, then down at the note, then up at us and down at the note again. She did not read the note aloud.

At the sound of the first-period bell, Sage and I darted away from each other and toward our next classes at opposite ends of the courtyard. My stomach was in knots all through American History, Algebra I, and

Personal Finance. At lunch, I walked the perimeter of the soccer field alone, pacing to give the anxiety in my body somewhere to go. Liking Sage wasn't gay, exactly, because I was a boy. But I worried what would happen if anyone found out how we spent our weekends. Other kids would taunt us, maybe try to hurt us. We would certainly be separated into different classes. We might even be expelled. How I felt about Sage could only lead to trouble, I'd always known that. But I hadn't considered how my feelings might get her in trouble, too.

BY THE END of the school day it became easy to push the note to the back of my mind. In just under an hour I'd be home, in Cactus Country. But during final period, my English teacher got a phone call in the middle of our lesson. He held the receiver to his checkered button-down, telling me to pack my things and report to the vice principal's office. My heart dropped.

"Why?" I blurted. He pulled his glasses down and peered at me over them. The other kids snickered. My arms felt too heavy as I gathered my planner and notebook into my backpack. I told myself the call didn't have anything to do with the note. I'd nearly convinced myself there had been a family emergency when I saw Sage across the courtyard. She'd been called to the vice principal's office, too.

"Do you know why?" I asked, my voice deflating.

She looked at the ground, shrugged. "The teacher didn't say."

We walked toward the administrative office at the front of the school, the courtyards quieter than I'd ever seen them. In an hour, the bell would ring and these same yards would flood with kids thinking only of the weekend ahead. Sage stared at the ground as her feet moved over it, one after the other, like a solemn march to the gallows.

In our year of friendship, I'd never known Sage to be afraid of anything, her confidence and charisma unwavering. She could command the attention of a room and become friends with everyone in it. I admired these qualities, and it pained me now to see her in such obvious distress. A fiery determination grew in my chest, stronger with each step. Earlier in the day I had wanted to hide from these feelings, but I wouldn't anymore. I would tell the vice principal that the note was my fault. That my feelings were unrequited. But I was going to own them all the same, and in doing so, demonstrate to Sage what she meant to me. If they wanted to kick one of us out of school, I would shoulder that burden. And I would do it gladly.

The vice principal, an imposing man named Shannon Woolridge, seemed to be expecting us. He waved us into his office.

"I've received a disturbing report about the two of you," he began. Sage's knuckles were white, hands shaking in her lap. Woolridge put on a pair of wire-framed glasses with his big hands and pulled a badly crumpled sheet of notebook paper from his desk. He held it up and began to read aloud in his booming voice:

"On Friday after school, I was walking home when Zoë and Sage threw dirt clods at me. They laughed and said it was because I was fat. They are bullies. That is why I am reporting them to the bully box."

He glanced up at us over his glasses, as though attempting to gauge our reactions. I looked to Sage, but she had the same confused expression on her face that I probably did.

Desert Sky Middle School's anti-bullying campaign encouraged students to make anonymous complaints through a shoebox in every classroom called the "bully box." The goal was to empower kids to report on behavior that might have otherwise gone ignored. With the bully boxes, our teachers said, each of us had a direct line to the vice principal's ear. We would not have to suffer in silence. But, in a great irony none of the adults at Desert Sky seemed to anticipate, kids mostly used the bully box as a more sophisticated tool to bully one another.

When I asked who wrote the note, Woolridge either wouldn't or couldn't say, muttering something about confidentiality. We needed to account for our whereabouts on that day.

Suddenly, I remembered perfectly. Sage and I had gone to Cactus Country. We'd spent the afternoon watching cartoons on the couch in the Airstream, inching our bodies closer with each commercial break.

When we were close enough to lace our fingers together, she leaned over, gently resting her head against my shoulder. We sat like that for the rest of the show, my skin buzzing with warmth where it met hers. I remembered wishing the moment would transcend the afternoon and stretch on into eternity—for every day of the rest of my life to be, in some small way, like this one.

"That's impossible," I said, "because my mom picked us up that day." Sage remained silent, hiding behind her long hair.

"If I called your mother, would she tell me that?" Woolridge asked.

"Yes," I said.

"Really," he said. "Is that so." He said it like a statement. Like he'd made up his mind already. I leaned over and picked up the phone on his desk.

"Why don't you call her right now?" I said, handing him the receiver. He looked from me, over my unblinking face, to Sage. Woolridge leaned back in his chair and folded his arms across his broad chest. He scratched his beard, as though considering what to do with us.

"Okay," he said, finally. "Get back to class."

Our secret was safe for now. I thanked Mrs. Goldwasser silently, promising, in my gratitude, never to pass notes in her class again. With only twenty minutes left in the school day, we sat on a bench in the courtyard, speculating about who might have made the false report and plotting our revenge.

"You know what would be funny?" I said. "What if we found out who did it and then *actually* threw dirt at them!"

"Or we could report Mr. Woolridge to the bully box!" Sage suggested. We were getting punchy now, imagining the absurdity of our vice principal opening the bully box to find himself reported—of Woolridge taking the steps to discipline himself, to call his own parents, to expel himself from the school.

"Really," I said, imitating Woolridge scratching at his beard. "Is that so." Sage cackled into her hands, flashing a mouth full of braces. I wanted her to keep laughing.

"He looks like a turkey!" I said, pulling my cheeks together until my lips resembled a beak. This was a baseless accusation, but it didn't matter. Sage went with it, like I knew she would.

"*Mr. Turkey*," she gasped. At this, we both burst out laughing.

At first, we laughed at how bad the joke was, and then we laughed because we were laughing at such a bad joke, and then we laughed because we were still laughing and couldn't stop. We laughed as our muscles ached and there were tears in our eyes and it was hard to breathe. We laughed as the final bell rang and the other kids began to file out of their classrooms and into the courtyard. We laughed as they stared at us, whispering to each other, for once not caring what they would think.

JAVELINA SUNSET

What started as a rumor, sweeping from one end of Cactus Country to the other like a tumbleweed, had become fact: the pigs were back. From the playground, we boys surveyed the evidence, marking what we knew on a crude map of the park drawn in the dirt with a stick. The javelina herd had been spotted three nights in a row by various neighbors out walking their dogs. We'd seen their small, heart-shaped tracks imprinted in the dry riverbed. Their unmistakable scat, lumpy pellets strewn over the earth like busted rolls of quarters.

The javelina had come to drink from the shallow birdbaths and eat the seed that dropped from feeders along Cactus Country's barbed wire fence. The same fence meant to keep ranchers' cows from wandering into the park, to protect them from getting hit by massive, rumbling Class A motorhomes and trucks hauling long, triple-axle fifth-wheel trailers. But the javelina could duck under that fence, no problem. Much smaller than wild boars, their closest relative, up close the javelina had short, stocky bodies, with spiky black hair and tusks that gleamed white in the moonlight. I knew this because I'd seen the herd while out walking my neighbor Terry's dog, Max, the night before. Six grown pigs and a few babies, crossing the dry riverbed into the park.

Max had barked a big game, lunging at them like they were a harmless colony of jackrabbits. But the javelina didn't scatter. They stood their ground, glaring as though daring us to come closer. Max wanted those pigs bad. He practically choked himself to death tugging so hard against his lead. If he got free, I knew I'd never catch him. The javelina would've taken him down for sure. I told this story to the other boys at the playground, pausing for dramatic effect.

"So then what'd you do?" Arlo asked. He and his brother Wesley had come back for the winter season, and though we were older now, our friendship had picked up more or less where we'd left off two years before.

"I grabbed Max by the collar and pulled his ass back to the trailer," I told him. "Once the pigs were out of sight, he forgot all about 'em."

"Damn," another boy said. "It was close, huh?" I nodded.

The javelina were protective as all hell and had already gored a couple dogs this season. To get between a mother javelina and her babies was about the stupidest thing a body could do. But dogs didn't know that. Most people didn't, either. The park staff posted signs all over the public bathhouses and the recreation hall with warnings not to approach the javelina or leave food out where they could get to it. They took up the birdbaths and seed, but this only encouraged the javelina to come farther into the park in search of nourishment.

Sightings proliferated until the javelina were all anyone—adult or child—seemed to talk about. Neighbors crowded around picnic tables and swapped stories over morning cigarettes. Cactus Country staffers could be overheard discussing javelina diversion strategies over two-way radio as they scooted around the park in their golf carts.

Conversation among us kids always centered on who'd seen them the night before, and where. Though diminutive as far as pigs go, we played them up in our stories. With each retelling, the javelina grew taller and fatter. Their tusks became longer and sharper. Gradually, they acquired an unquenchable thirst for blood.

One of the younger boys, Aiden, swore on his mother that he'd seen a javelina standing on its hind legs, peering through his trailer window to where he slept on the couch.

"Son of a bitch stared right at me," he said. "His eyes were glowing red as the devil."

We gasped, cupping our open mouths with our hands. *Holy fucking shit*, we breathed, though we knew damn well Aiden was a liar. It didn't matter. Nothing much happened in the park, and his story had exactly the kind of excitement we craved.

Plenty of kids might have boasted they weren't scared of the javelina, but I knew only one person bold enough to mess with them. Crazy Larry was a slender retiree with short, wispy white hair, often stuffed under a ball cap. The first time we noticed him circling the outer perimeter of the park's fence with a pair of binoculars, we thought he might be bird-watching. But didn't he know all the seed was gone? The boys and I stopped our bikes to ask him.

"You ever heard of a luau?" Larry asked, peering through the binoculars.

"Huh?" I said.

"It's a kind of party they have in Hawaii. They put a pig on a spit and roast it over a fire," he said, miming a cranking motion. "If we caught a javelina, we could have a luau right here in the park. What do you boys think about that?" He looked at us expectantly. We exchanged glances, none of us quite sure what to say.

"Are you stupid?" Aiden blurted.

"That's very disrespectful, young man," Larry said. He returned his attention to the desert, waving us all away as though dismissing us from class.

"*Is* he stupid?" Aiden asked once we'd pedaled out of earshot.

"Maybe," I shrugged.

Every time I saw Crazy Larry after that, he had javelina on the brain. To anyone who would listen, he talked about digging a deep barbecue pit in the middle of his campsite and what kind of seasoning he would use. The roasting would take all day, he said, and he would need volunteers to rotate the pig so it got cooked all the way through. He showed me elaborate drawings in his notebook of the javelina traps he'd devised. Once I even saw him skinning a long ocotillo branch into a spit, as if to have it on hand at a moment's notice.

"What do you suppose javelina meat tastes like?" he asked me as I walked Max one afternoon.

I wrinkled my nose. "I don't know, gamey?" I said. Larry looked at me thoughtfully for a moment before making a note in his pocket-sized ledger.

"That's a beautiful dog," he added. Larry reached down and gave Max a scratch before heading on about his javelina business. Max looked up at me, tongue lolling from his open mouth. He *was* beautiful: a golden retriever with soft, sandy fur. Strong, too; it took all I could muster in my scrawny thirteen-year-old body to keep him steady on the leash when he saw another dog or—God forbid—a rabbit darting back into the creosote bushes along the edges of the park. Max was so fearless that I had to walk him alone, even if I had other dogs waiting, to make sure he didn't get away from me. But I didn't really mind. It was all part of being a good dog walker.

"C'mon, boy," I said, whistling.

We continued along the fence, Max stopping to carefully sniff each of its poles, while I thought about the person Larry used to be, long before the first javelina sightings. A year back, when the desert still seemed safe enough to wander, all the neighbors knew Larry as a social drinker who was pretty good with a harmonica. He and his wife hosted barbecue parties in front of their camper where the adults stayed up laughing and drinking late into the night while we kids hunted around the surrounding desert with flashlights. One boy would dress up in an old Halloween costume, wearing the mask from *Scream* as he chased the rest of us through the cacti.

But over the summer, Larry had gone hiking by himself in the Oregon wilderness and couldn't find his way back. He spent three days and nights lost in the outdoors without food or water before he found his way home again. Other than being dehydrated, he'd seemed okay at first. But Larry was never quite the same after that. The few times I heard somebody quietly ask his wife about him, her answer was always buried in a sigh. She still loved him, but the neighbors whispered that he'd become a handful and a burden. There would be no more barbecue parties.

As Max and I rounded the corner back to Terry's trailer, I wondered whether Larry missed the person he used to be. Maybe, I thought, all this javelina stuff with the luau was his way of trying to get things back to the way they were. Or maybe he was nuts. No real way to tell.

I climbed the wooden deck steps up to Max's trailer and knocked on the door to let Terry know we'd come back from our walk. Terry wore an oxygen tube for his emphysema, so he couldn't get up from his armchair and answer the door, let alone take Max outside.

"Hey, Terry," I said, unhooking Max from his leash. "You need me to come by tonight and take him out again?" He nodded.

"Lori's working late," he said. Terry's wife, Lori, was a professional nature photographer. She was the one who'd answered the ad I posted on the Cactus Country "What's Happening?" bulletin board that read: "Zoë's Dog Walking Service — Reliable. Professional. Good with dogs." Underneath I had drawn a picture of me with a smiling puppy, a speech bubble that read DOGS LOVE ME emanating from my mouth. This last part was only partly true, as my own family's dog, Tucson, was less than fond of me for reasons Dad explained probably had to do with pack hierarchies. But I enjoyed walking my neighbor's dogs, and the money I made doing it. I agreed to walk Max every weekday afternoon after school, and again in the evenings as needed. In return, Lori paid me $20 a week, usually leaving the cash with Terry.

"Money's on the table," he said, pointing to a couple of folded bills tucked under a vase. He pulled a fresh pack of cigarettes from the front pocket of his blue bathrobe and smacked it against the palm of his hand.

"That's bad for you, you know," I said. I knew Lori didn't like it when he smoked.

"Well, I've already come this far, right, kid?" Terry said, holding a lighter to the cigarette between his lips. "Can't stop now. Then I'd be a quitter." He grinned at me.

I liked Terry. He'd ask me about middle school and then regale me with stories from his own youth—the meals his mother used to make, his favorite class subjects, how he'd gotten in with the wrong crowd as a teenager.

"That's where I learned to smoke these," he said, considering the smoldering cigarette between his fingers. When he wasn't talking about the old days, Terry would catch me up on the latest episode of *Monk*, a show I'd never seen but that was his favorite.

I could tell Terry was lonely because of the way he'd talk and talk and talk. It occurred to me that, apart from Lori, I might be the only person he saw on a regular basis. He hadn't heard anything about the javelina herd, for instance. That night, I asked Mom if we could bring our dinner over to Terry's trailer on plates and eat with him. She said yes. I dashed across the park and breathlessly told him my idea. My mom made pesto chicken and rice! She could bring it over right now! We could even watch *Monk* while we ate! Terry smiled, but said no thanks. He was still in his blue bathrobe—the same one he always wore. I'd never noticed how stained and faded it was, or how stale his trailer smelled. I hadn't considered how my gesture might put him on the spot.

"Can I bring a plate just for you?" I asked, awkwardly. Terry shook his head. He wasn't hungry, he said. I told him I'd be back after dinner to take Max out one more time.

"Kid?" he said as I turned to go. "Thanks. I mean that."

AN HOUR LATER, I returned with Wesley to pick up Max. Almost fifteen now, Wes had grown tall and lanky in the years since I'd seen him last, a few new hairs sprouting on his upper lip. As the oldest kid in the park, he thought himself too mature to join the rest of us in our games and javelina lore. "They're just pigs," he'd scoffed when Arlo and I told him Aiden's story about the red-eyed beast stalking him through the window.

At twelve, a few months shy of my thirteen, Arlo wasn't allowed to leave his family's motorhome after dark. But Wesley went on a walk every night—the only person I knew other than Crazy Larry who was unafraid to go out alone during the javelina scare—and joined me whenever I had dog-walking duty.

I appreciated his company. Even in the moonlight, the desert was dark—a black mass of sharp shadow and relief. I'd heard kids at school tell stories based on local native and Mexican folklore about people getting pulled into the desert by mysterious creatures much bigger and scarier than javelina, never to be seen again. Anything could be hiding out there. Max sometimes paused to growl at unseen things in the darkness, which was enough to terrify me.

But none of it seemed to bother Wesley. We'd talk about video games and the girls he had crushes on back home in Maine. Other times we walked in silence, listening to the hum of cicadas, or the whistle of a faraway train. I admired the way Wes walked nonchalantly in the darkness, fists stuffed into the pocket of his hoodie. He didn't believe in monsters of any kind. And for an hour at a time, walking along the fence with him, I could be just as brave.

That is, until it came time to drop Wesley off and head home. Alone in the dark, I swore I felt a sinister presence in the desert. Following me. Watching me. Biding its time. Though I told myself I was imagining it, the feeling proved impossible to shake. Before bed, I made sure to draw the curtains of all the windows in the Airstream, keenly aware that its thin aluminum frame was the only barrier between me and whatever lurked in the darkness.

THE NEXT MORNING, Crazy Larry came to the playground with a javelina-related announcement. He'd written a new song to the tune of "Hello! Ma Baby" and wanted us to sing it with him. None of us were interested, but Larry insisted we should all learn the words.

"I'm not going anywhere until you kids sing!" he said.

"Leave us alone, Larry," I said. "You're being annoying."

"Yeah, go away, Larry!" the boys echoed from their perches above the monkey bars. But he wouldn't go, instead singing at the top of his voice: "Hello, my jav-eh! Hello, my li-na! Hello, my tas-ty pig . . ."

What began as a few kids trying to push him away from the playground quickly became an all-out brawl, with one of the bigger boys practically shoving Larry to the ground. As Larry stumbled, Arlo stole the notebook from his back pocket and tossed it to Aiden, who threw it back, monkey-in-the-middle style. Another kid snatched Larry's hat from his head.

"Stop that, boys!" Larry cried, his lean face pink and flustered. "Stop that right now!"

"Get out of here, you crazy old man!" Aiden shouted. He ran across the street to the cactus garden, sinking Larry's notebook into the pads of a sprawling prickly pear. We went on chanting at him to *go away* until one of the Cactus Country staffers came along in a golf cart and threatened to call all of our parents if we didn't leave Larry alone. He made Arlo return Larry's hat, shooting us a menacing look before scooting away in his cart. After that, most of the kids retreated to the playground.

Larry hunched over the prickly pear, trying unsuccessfully to whack his notebook loose with a stick. I sighed and crouched down in the dirt, sticking my arm slowly, carefully, into the space between the cactus pads to retrieve the notebook. Fine, hair-like needles sprinkled from the pads onto my bare arm as I pulled the book from its hiding place. I plucked some of the errant spines from its cover and handed it back to Larry, who took it silently, his expression unreadable, and left.

THE WINTER SEASON seemed to go quickly that year. Soon, the snowbirds traveled north for the summer and most of the boys in the park scattered back across the country to the states they called home. To me, though, Cactus Country felt most like home in the winters, when the park teemed with new neighbors and the possibility of reuniting with old friends. So that next season, when Lori returned to Cactus Country with a new trailer in tow, I looked forward to walking Max and visiting with Terry again. But they weren't with her.

The story going around the park went like this: They'd been staying at a KOA campground in Utah. Terry had dozed off with the TV on, a lit cigarette between his fingers. It fell onto his oxygen canister, setting off an explosion with the force and power of a pipe bomb. The trailer windows shattered, their glass blown out all over the street. The fire department arrived too late to save him or Max from the blast. Lori heard what happened from a neighbor over the phone, rushing home from the grocery store to find the trailer a smoking husk.

I sat on one of the swings in the playground, kicking dirt around with my bare feet, trying not to think about what had happened to Terry and

Max. Violent images flashed through my mind: blood spackling the walls of the trailer, skin and fur baked into the carpet, bodies engulfed in flames. I shook my head, as though I could get rid of the images if I disagreed with them hard enough. My eyes stung, but I smacked my cheeks raw to keep the tears away. I didn't want any of the other boys to come out and see me crying. I didn't want to have to explain myself to them.

I was considering going to hide in the desert when I saw Crazy Larry walking along the road in front of the playground. Even though I didn't call out to him, he noticed me and ambled over to talk about his latest javelina scheme. Larry had only been back in Cactus Country a week, but he'd had all summer up north to think about his plan. Nobody in the park had even seen a javelina yet this year.

"Do you really think you're going to catch one?" I spat through clenched teeth, rubbing tears into my face. "It's just so fucking stupid." Larry wasn't going to catch a javelina this year, or ever. Of course there would be no luau. Adults were supposed to know how the world worked. But Larry only knew how to tell stories, and they weren't even the ones anyone needed to hear.

Larry stared at me for a long second, his mouth hanging slightly open like he wanted to say something but was thinking hard about what.

"I don't know," he said, softly. "It's just something to do." I curled my toes into the dirt and looked up to the horizon, the anger of seconds ago departing on a breath. Larry didn't mean any harm. He took the swing beside mine and we sat together in silence for a long time, watching the broad sunset streak across the sky in hues of purple and red. The kind of sunset snowbirds would come out of their trailers in the evening to watch. They were supposed to be beautiful here like nowhere else in the world, but I'd never really appreciated them.

A sunset meant it would be getting dark soon. In a minute, I'd have to get up from the swing and go inside for dinner. I would wake up the next morning and go to school. When I got home, some of the boys I remembered from last year—Wesley, Arlo, Aiden—might be back, or they might not. The javelina would return this season, or they wouldn't.

I thought back to last winter, to Terry and Max's final night in the park. The season had been nearly over, then, the Tucson spring well underway with desert cacti in various stages of bud and bloom. No one had seen the javelina herd in months, and the big talk surrounding them had died down considerably. Most boys, including me, took Wesley's perspective and insisted they'd never been scared of those pigs anyway.

But that night, as Max and I headed back into his trailer from our walk, a stray javelina lunged at us from under the deck. Max bared his teeth, snarling and struggling against me to fight back. I hauled him up the stairs by his collar while the javelina retreated somewhere under the trailer. It must have gotten separated from the herd, I thought. The rest couldn't be far behind.

"What was all that noise?" Terry asked. With Max still barking, I hadn't bothered to knock before coming in. I told him about the javelina. We checked the dog all over for any broken skin, but he was okay. I poured Max his dinner and lingered for a long time with Terry, saying my goodbyes to both of them. But it was getting late, and I had school in the morning. My parents would be worried if I didn't come home soon.

I stood on Terry's deck, steeling myself for the run. From across the park, I could see the Airstream shining in the dim moonlight. I took a deep breath and vaulted myself over the side of the deck, hitting the ground hard. My bare feet stung from the impact, but I was too scared to care. I could almost hear the pigs galloping behind me, their hooves clicking against the pavement, the shrill squeal of their battle cries. Blood pounded in my ears as I gasped for breath in the warm night air. I dashed through the Airstream door, slamming it behind me. Mom looked up, alarmed, from where she sat watching TV on the foldout couch.

"What's wrong?" she asked, but I didn't answer. I ran to the back of our trailer, to the large bay window facing the way I'd come, looking out to see how narrowly I'd escaped the herd. But it was pitch-black. I couldn't see a thing.

PALMER'S KISS

"YOU'LL GO PLACES," MR. HAUER said as I leaned against the wall, first in line to enter his eighth-grade English classroom. He'd said it before, always apropos of nothing, accompanied by an encouraging smile, sometimes a wink. I shrugged and looked away, pretending his praise embarrassed me. It did, a little. But privately, I appreciated Mr. Hauer's confidence in me, even as I had my doubts. *What places?* I wanted to ask him. *Where?*

Most mornings, I arrived at Desert Sky Middle School with grit under my fingernails, a greasy sunburned face, and permanent bedhead. I didn't have fashionable clothes or good personal hygiene. But what I did have, according to Mr. Hauer, was what he called "a calming effect" on the other kids in class. I couldn't be sure what he meant by this. But Mr. Hauer often paired me with his most challenging students, such as the strange, troubled boy he assigned to the seat next to mine.

Wyatt had a head of curly hair unkempt enough to rival my own, and liked telling long, impossible stories. He was a black belt who could snap a grown man's neck with a single, well-aimed punch. An alien baby sent down to Earth to surveil and eventually murder his unsuspecting parents. A part-boy, part-wolf hybrid who transformed by the light of the midnight moon and romped around the desert with packs of coyotes. I had a hard time keeping track of Wyatt's complicated personal lore—a stream of tall tales always stretching to new heights.

The only consistent aspect of Wyatt's personality was his moodiness. Some days he was too quiet, communicating with muted facial expressions and shrugs. Other days he couldn't stop talking. In his excitement, he might scream in your ear or karate chop you in the back or put you in a surprise headlock. His unpredictable behavior was deeply fascinating to

Sage. She talked about Wyatt incessantly, and this is what frustrated me about him most of all.

"Did he say anything in your class today?" she demanded, meaning about her. We waited with our trays in the lunch line, me rolling my eyes. In the year since our run-in with the bully box, we'd spent more time together than ever. The only point of contention in our friendship now was Wyatt. Sage asked about him in the mornings before homeroom, in Cactus Country on weekday afternoons, at her house on weekend nights. *Did he say anything about me?*

Wyatt said lots of things, though rarely about anyone but his fictional selves. As Sage and I sat down to eat, I recounted Wyatt's latest story—something about developing multiple personalities, many of which had superhuman powers. Sage hung on every word.

"Wait, you don't actually believe this stuff, do you?" I asked. Sage just shrugged, smiling to herself. Despite her insistence, I tried to ignore Wyatt during Mr. Hauer's class. If I pretended he was just another kid and not the current object of Sage's affections, it was easier to focus on the readings. English was my favorite subject. I liked learning how to decode the secret messages Mr. Hauer said were hiding in every book—what meanings the author intended versus what meanings came later, once readers got their hands on it, interpreting and reinterpreting the words for, sometimes, hundreds of years. Today we read from a play, *Romeo and Juliet*.

"What are they talking about here?" Mr. Hauer asked. "Any guesses?"

The passage seemed impenetrable. I furrowed my brow, hunching over the textbook as though the answer might be hiding somewhere in the spaces between the letters in each word. I mouthed them over and over, willing them to mean something:

ROMEO

If I profane with my unworthiest hand
This holy shrine, the gentle fine is this:
My lips, two blushing pilgrims, ready stand
To smooth that rough touch with a tender kiss.

JULIET

Good pilgrim, you do wrong your hand too much,
Which mannerly devotion shows in this;
For saints have hands that pilgrims' hands do touch,
And palm to palm is holy palmers' kiss.

Mr. Hauer encouraged us to take it one line at a time.

"What does Juliet's 'palm to palm' look like?" he said. "Try it and see." We put our books down, held our hands out. Pressed them together as though in prayer.

"They're lips," I said, astounded. Right before my eyes this once-incomprehensible text had begun to take shape. Romeo wanted to kiss Juliet, but he couldn't be sure how she would react; Juliet wanted to kiss Romeo, too, but she didn't want to initiate the encounter. The characters on the page were no longer Shakespeare's, but two teenagers dancing around their mutual desire for each other, neither one bold enough to make the first move.

That year, Sage and I continued playing a perpetual game of chicken at our sleepovers. She still won, but I was getting more brazen now, gazing into her eyes as she drew closer, closer, and turning away milliseconds before her lips could meet mine. Sometimes, they brushed my cheek—a near miss—and we'd giggle silently, careful not to wake her parents. We'd fall asleep hand in hand, our faces inches apart, breathing each other's air.

Our game came to a sudden culmination that Halloween, in the darkness of a haunted house. There, surrounded by papier-mâché ghouls and fake blood splattering makeshift walls, I finally closed my eyes. I leaned in. It was soft, electric, holy—a ghost of a kiss, so ephemeral I could scarcely believe it had happened at all. Until this moment, the intimacies between Sage and I had always remained insinuated, unspoken. Now, there was no turning back, and with this realization came an exhilaration and terror greater than any haunted house I'd ever dared to enter. I held this new secret tight in my chest like a breath.

Later that week, Mr. Hauer asked the class to write a letter to our future selves, an assignment to be collected and then delivered back to us at the end of the year. Sage and I hadn't spoken about what happened in the haunted house, and in the days since, I'd been too full of anxiety to put the words to paper, worrying that—maybe—I'd imagined the whole thing. Now, in a furtive, near-illegible scrawl, I wrote every detail I could remember. Every joy, every fear, every hope for the future, all in one long stream of consciousness. When I reached the end of the page, I hastily stuffed my confession into an envelope and licked it closed, writing my name on the outside. I handed the letter in to Mr. Hauer. With the secret out of my hands, I had no choice but to let it go.

GYM PERIOD MADE passing as a boy at Desert Sky untenable, at least in front of the girls in the locker room. I tried to maintain appearances, lingering in the hall outside as long as I could get away with and sneaking in once most of the girls had already left for the soccer field. Though I never used my assigned locker, instead carrying my gym clothes in my backpack to change in the bathroom stalls, the rumors spread faster than I could contain them. In time, the truth of my body became something of an open secret among the other kids at school.

One morning in science class, as I was absorbed in a worksheet on the inner workings of cells, I felt a sharp spring of pain on my shoulder. The boy sitting behind me had snapped the exposed strap of my white sports bra—a garment that passed to most as an undershirt.

"Hey, is that your *bra*?" he whispered, then laughed. In that moment, I felt a unique sense of humiliation I'd only experienced once before, when another boy kicked me square in the crotch during a scrap on the school playground. I'd always thought a blow between the legs couldn't hurt people with vaginas. But the pain shot from the point of impact down to my feet, throbbing with such intensity I curled up on the blacktop and held myself, breathing fast to keep from crying out. There was blood in my underwear, but I couldn't go to the nurse. I didn't want her to tell me

I shouldn't have been fighting with boys in the first place. That it was my fault.

As I stared down at the worksheet, a strange shame washed over me. I'd lived as a boy for the last two years, through female puberty, and until now my masculine gender expression had protected me from unwelcome male attention. But some of the other boys at school had begun to notice I was different, sometimes with mortifying consequences.

Worst of all on this front was Levi, a kid from my science fiction elective. At first, I'd looked forward to talking to him about *War of the Worlds* and *Invasion of the Body Snatchers* between classes. We played the same video games and often swapped cheat codes and final boss strategies. But when Levi learned which locker room I used he suddenly, inexplicably, wanted to be more than friends. One day before class, he loudly announced his intention to take me to a movie.

"I'm not gay," I said quickly, glancing nervously around the courtyard.

"But it wouldn't *really* be gay," Levi insisted. I shook my head. But Levi couldn't—or wouldn't—take a hint. He invited me to come over to his house almost every day, no matter how many times I said no. He followed me around in the mornings before class and, more than once, serenaded me in the breakfast line, oblivious to the kids who pointed at us, giggling with secondhand embarrassment. He'd sing as I covered my ears with shaking hands, fleeing the cafeteria to hide behind an agave plant in the courtyard until the bell rang.

Every morning I woke up hoping that Levi would be sick and have to stay home. This wish backfired spectacularly one day when he showed up late to class, the absolute picture of death. His acne glowed an unnatural rouge against the sickly pale canvas of his face, a yellowish mucus leaking from his nose onto his upper lip.

"I didn't want to be away from you," he said. I described Levi's face to Sage later that afternoon at lunch, partly to vent my disgust and partly to make her laugh.

"He looked like he was about to pass out," I said. "Like this!" I pulled my cheeks down with both hands, revealing the reds of my eyelids. Sage choked on her milk.

"Maybe you *should* go out with him," she said once she recovered, drying the table with a napkin. "I mean, he obviously likes you." My heart sank deep into my stomach as I stared at the french fries on my tray, trying to decode what this statement might mean, as though Sage's words were written in one of Mr. Hauer's books. I wondered if this suggestion was a test of my feelings for her, and how she would react if I actually agreed to go out with Levi. Maybe the idea would make her jealous. Maybe Sage wanted to see whether I would show romantic interest in boys, like she did. Or maybe this was her way of further distancing herself from me.

I thought about these interpretations for a long time, but didn't come any closer to a real answer. A couple months had gone by since Halloween. Though we never talked about the kiss, Sage and I weren't seeing each other as much on the weekends anymore. Whenever we did, she invited her new friends over—some of the prettier, better-groomed, and more popular girls in our grade, who didn't care for my company. I'd overheard a rumor in the locker room that Sage and Wyatt might be hanging out together after school, though I couldn't muster the courage to ask her if this was true. For now, our sleepovers had come to an end, Sage moving ahead into a world of adolescent girlhood where I was unable to follow her.

"*Levi?*" I said, finally. "You can't be serious." She shrugged.

"Just a thought," Sage said, reaching over to steal one of my fries.

OUR FINAL ASSIGNMENT in Mr. Hauer's class was to write a short story set in another country. I wrote about an American boy named Elliott, who lived in Thailand and looked a little bit like me. He liked to play pranks on American tourists—similar, in my mind, to the snowbirds in Cactus Country. Usually he got away with his tricks, but one day a tourist became furious with him after tripping face-first into a hole filled with whipped cream. The man grabbed Elliott before he could get away and locked him in the back of an unmarked van. Luckily for everyone involved, Elliott woke up, relieved to find the encounter had only been a dream.

This wasn't a particularly nuanced story, but Mr. Hauer encouraged me, writing in the feedback he scrawled into the margins that it was one of the best he'd read in the class. I read the story to Mom and Dad that night after dinner in the Airstream, and they thought it was good, too.

"We might have a writer in the family," Dad said, and I glowed with pride.

After this, I started writing short stories in my notebooks. I wrote about young boys who were thrust into adventure and rose to the challenge, exploring faraway, hostile landscapes and saving their homes from the nebulous evils threatening to destroy them. The boys in my stories were unflinchingly brave, spoke precious few words, and preferred to work alone. They never failed at anything they attempted. In the end, they always vanquished the beast, saved the townsfolk, won the girl's heart. Though I wrote often, I was a brutal self-critic. I'd reread my stories days or even hours after writing them and feel ashamed, like I had caught myself in a lie. The heroes I wrote were too perfect, their stories nothing like my own. I'd rip them out of my notebooks, throw them away, start again.

DURING MY FINAL week at Desert Sky, the eighth-grade student body and their families gathered in the gym for an awards ceremony. I sat with Mom and Dad in the bleachers, waiting as the vice principal called kids down to the podium. Mr. Woolridge called my name from a clipboard, a small trophy in his hand for me, one of the few kids who was graduating from Desert Sky without ever serving a detention. Mom and Dad clapped as I bounded down the steps to accept the trophy. Sage stood up to cheer for me, and I grinned at her on the way back to my seat.

Levi received a perfect-attendance award, and I rolled my eyes as he held it up, remembering the day he'd come to school looking like a walking corpse. Next, Wyatt's name rang out through the PA system as he stumbled down the stairs to accept an award for excellence in science. When he came back from the podium with his certificate, Sage ran down the steps to meet him. She grabbed his face, clutching the errant hairs of his newly budding beard, and kissed him full on the lips. The crowd whooped and cheered like a daytime television show audience. I couldn't breathe, my heart beating hard like a stone hurled against the inside of my chest. So the locker room rumors had been true.

No sooner had Wyatt and Sage sat down together than my name was called once again, this time for an excellence in writing award. I tried to smile as I came down the bleacher steps to accept the certificate from Mr. Hauer and shake his hand. A tight, burning sensation rose in my throat and settled there, lingering even as I posed for pictures. I held up my awards for Dad's camera, trying not to glimpse Sage and Wyatt holding hands through the crowd. Once we got back home to Cactus Country, I could go out into the desert and be alone with my feelings. I just needed to hold it together until then. But as soon as my parents and I got to the van, I threw the awards onto the seat beside me, collapsing into my folded arms. Mom and Dad traded alarmed expressions. I couldn't keep the secret anymore. Catching a shaky breath, I told them the truth about Sage and me.

"I thought something like that might be going on," Dad said. Mom reached back from the front seat to put a consoling hand on my knee.

"The first cut is always the deepest, lovey," she said.

"I don't know," I croaked, still sniffing back tears. "I don't want to talk about it anymore."

During that drive back to Cactus Country and for weeks afterward, I went over the facts obsessively. But no matter how many times I tried to interpret them, to make sense of why Sage would choose to be with Wyatt instead of me, even though she and I were better friends, even though we had kissed first, they didn't seem to add up. Or, maybe, I didn't want them to. Because much more than the pain of watching her go out with another boy was the realization that, while Sage might've liked flirting with me in secret, she would never kiss me with the abandon she had kissed him, in front of everyone. That, to her, I wasn't a real boy and never would be. I tried hard not to dwell on the promise of what we might have had if only my body were different.

ON THE LAST day of school, as promised, Mr. Hauer returned our letters. I waited until after class to open mine. Alone on a bench in the courtyard, I ripped open the envelope, scanning the first few lines. I found my words embarrassing in their earnestness, the me of only a few months ago hopelessly naive. I couldn't bring myself to finish it, not wanting to remember how I'd felt that night in the haunted house. Slowly, I shredded the letter into a small pile of confetti-sized pieces and let the wind blow them all around the yard. In just a few short months, Sage and I would be freshmen at different high schools. I wanted, for the second time in my life, a chance to reinvent myself, to start again. Summer couldn't come soon enough.

WHITE FACE, BLACK EYES

CACTUS COUNTRY WAS NEARLY EMPTY, save for a few year-rounders' trailers sparsely dotting the landscape. With school out for the season there was nothing much to do but languish in the afternoon heat, which on some days could climb as high as 110. Too hot even for the swimming pool. As the only two kids left in the park, Aiden and I spent our summer vacation chasing the shade, looking for any reason to hang out wherever the air conditioning was.

Aiden reminded me of a Norman Rockwell painting I'd once seen, with his big ears and freckles and devil-may-care grin. He was ten, and a little short for his age, with a tiny bald spot right at the top of his head where the ringworm had been. Lots of Cactus Country boys had caught it earlier that year from the dogs, who got it from rolling around in the dirt. Like most, I had the rings pretty bad up and down my arms, but Aiden got it worst out of everyone. Six months later and the hair still hadn't grown back. Kids used to pick on him for it, calling him an "old man," provoking him until Aiden ran crying to his trailer. But the kids had all moved away now, and no one in the park cared about Aiden's bald spot anymore.

Though I was only a few years older than Aiden, his mom paid me to keep him out of trouble while she worked. Sometimes she left for a few days and Aiden spent the night in the Airstream with my family, sleeping on a makeshift bed of couch cushions. Other days, she had friends over—different ones every time—and locked Aiden out of the trailer while they did whatever it was she liked to do on her days off, which I'd heard some of the neighbors speculate around the picnic tables might be methamphetamine.

Aiden didn't seem to mind the babysitting arrangement so much. I always took him to the Cactus Country store and got us ice cream sandwiches with some of the money his mom gave me. We'd buy them one round at a time, eating them on a bench right outside the store before they melted in the summer heat. On days like that we mostly did whatever Aiden wanted to do, usually hunting around the desert for jackrabbits with his .22 caliber rifle or catching lizards with our bare hands. Aiden was a terrible shot, but I'd never seen a lizard get away from him. He dove after them with the abandon of a baseball star sliding into home plate.

One afternoon as I sat on the foldout couch in the Airstream playing a video game, Aiden came rushing through the open door, his face covered in blood.

"Jesus, Aiden!" I said. "What happened?"

"Look!" he said breathlessly, holding up the fat yellow lizard squirming in his grip—a horny toad—with both hands for me to see. Horny toads blend in with the desert sand, making them hard to spot. One of their natural defenses is to squirt predators with acidic blood from their eyelids.

"Doesn't that hurt?" I asked, pointing to the red on Aiden's brow.

"Yeah, stings a little," he said. "But here, feel of her." I ran my fingers over her sharp armored body and rubbed the soft flesh of her underbelly. Aiden charged me with holding on to her while he washed his face. I expected the lizard to attempt an escape, but she seemed calmer now, maybe in shock.

"What do they eat?" I asked when Aiden came back.

"Probably ants," he said. We lugged a heavy ten-gallon fish tank out from under Aiden's trailer and washed the dust from its interior with a hose. I sifted handfuls of coarse desert sand through an old kitchen sieve to line its bottom. Aiden furnished the tank with some leftover hollow logs and a shallow water dish shaped like a rock from his last lizard. We used sticks to lure black ants from a nearby hill and knocked them into the habitat, but the horny toad wouldn't go for them. Some of them crawled over her mouth, but she didn't move, not even to blink. She just stood there, stiller than stone.

"Isn't she beautiful?" Aiden kept saying. "Don't you think she's beautiful?"

DAVE HAD SHOWN up in the park one day that same summer, soon after the last snowbirds had gone for the season. He was twenty-seven, with blond hair shaved close to his scalp, wire-framed glasses, and a faint goatee. He introduced himself to us as David Davis—"the third," he said. "But just call me Dave." I'd thought only kings went by titles like *the third*. His formality suggested pride in a familial legacy that the dusty camper trailer behind him seemed at odds with.

"Zoë Bossiere," I said dryly, extending a hand. "The first." Dave laughed.

"That's funny," he said, still giggling as he shook my hand. "That's real funny."

In the hotter months, Cactus Country was less a vacation campground and more a land of lost and wandering souls. Like most everyone else who moved to the park during that time, Dave didn't know how long he would stay, or where he would go next. He smoked roll-your-own cigarettes in his trailer, which was just big enough for a twin bed and a mini fridge he kept stocked with that week's cheapest beer. Dave also had an air conditioner, and for this reason Aiden and I came over daily. That, and to play with Dave's cat, Buster.

Buster used to live with Aiden, but earlier that month Aiden's mom had declared she didn't have the money to pay for cat food and litter anymore. They'd had Buster since he was a kitten. Aiden hadn't cried when he told me, but I could tell he was upset from the way he'd squinted at the ground, kicking at the dirt. Dave must have been able to tell, too, because he offered to keep Buster for him. He said Aiden could come over to see the cat any time he wanted.

Dave's trailer was littered with newspaper, dry cat food, loose beer tabs, stray bits of tobacco, and torn girlie magazines. He had a vast collection of knives he let us play with, including a Wolverine-like claw he kept hanging over his bed, and five well-worn copies of the same book in various colors stacked neatly together on a shelf. I picked up the nicest of the set, a blue cover with golden letters and a sword emblazoned on the front. It smelled musty and old.

"Be careful with that," Dave said, raising a lighter to the cigarette between his lips, "it's one of the special editions." I opened the book to its title page and studied the stylized typeface.

"*Mean Camp-f*," I whispered aloud to myself, sounding out the words. Since Dave had more than one copy, I thought it might be a religious text—something ancient and holy. I was used to seeing Bibles and prayer books out on picnic tables, but I'd never heard of this book.

"Why do you have so many?" I asked, flipping through it to look for pictures. Dave shrugged from his spot on the bed, blew a puff of smoke from the cigarette.

"I don't know," he said. "I just think he's got some interesting ideas, that's all." I couldn't be sure who Dave was talking about, but I nodded anyway. That was more or less what I'd heard people say about Jesus, too.

Later that afternoon, in the Airstream, I asked Dad about Dave over tuna fish sandwiches and warming cans of soda. Dad had been working odd jobs that summer along with his usual window washing. Sometimes he'd hire Dave to come along and help out for the day while I stayed in Cactus Country with Aiden. He'd even found Dave steady work at a plant nursery as a landscape apprentice. Dad didn't seem to like Dave all that much, but helping people like him—those who wandered into the park with nothing—was one of his mysterious ways.

"Why do you think he has all those books?" I asked. Dad exhaled a long, frustrated breath through his nostrils.

"Because he's a fucking idiot," he said.

"What do you mean?" I asked.

"Dave's a skinhead," he continued, taking a bite of his sandwich. I raised my eyebrows.

"A what?"

"A Nazi," he said thickly. I'd heard of the Nazis in school, how they'd collected Jewish people and forced them into labor camps. Gassed them with poison in group showers. I'd seen black-and-white photographs of the piles of emaciated bodies that soldiers found in the aftermath. But I'd thought the Nazis were all dead. The bad guys who lost a long-ago war. An enemy to be destroyed in video games with names like *Call of Duty*.

"Is Dave bad?" I asked.

"I don't know," Dad sighed, shaking his head. "He's just an idiot, that's all."

SOMETIMES, AIDEN'S MOM would let him go into the desert with Dave to practice his shooting. They'd head out in the morning with Aiden's gun and a jug of water, coming back an hour or two later covered in sweat, red-faced and rabbitless. I never wanted to go along on their hunts.

"Lots of ways to catch something without a gun," I teased.

"Ain't nothing wrong with guns," Dave said. "I had a rifle just like that when I was his age. My dad taught me to shoot." I shrugged, guessing Dave probably liked to see himself as a kind of father figure, since Aiden didn't have one. And even if he was an idiot, like Dad said, Dave seemed nice enough a lot of the time. He'd tell us dramatic stories about growing up in rural Virginia. How he'd fought his way into manhood, breaking knuckles against skulls and making some decent money selling weed. He showed off his faded green tattoos, most of which he'd gotten in prison, with pride: skeletons and eagles and crosses and symbols I couldn't begin to recognize.

At times, Dave seemed ecstatically, almost impossibly happy. He talked about his new chance at life here with us in the Sonoran Desert. His little trailer offered him everything he needed. He had good neighbors to drink with, a job he was beginning to love. Everything was perfect. But other times, Dave sank into a despair so deep he seemed beyond reason. Aiden and I would come to his trailer to find it locked, the air conditioner running, Dave's car parked out front. We'd knock and knock, but nobody would answer. Neither mood seemed to last more than a day or two, though, and soon we'd be back in Dave's trailer with Buster, listening to him tell his stories again.

One morning, Aiden pounded at his own trailer door, yanking at its metal latch in vain. His mother had locked it before leaving for work. Aiden's .22 rifle was inside, visible through the window but out of reach. He wanted to hunt rabbits with Dave, and they couldn't go without the gun. Aiden screamed, kicking the door so hard he left a deep dent where his foot had been. Dave and I stood watching from the road. When Aiden got worked up, it was near impossible to intervene. I'd learned to stand back and wait for the anger to run its course.

"I was a lot like that at his age," Dave said wistfully, taking a drag from his cigarette.

"What, acting stupid?" I asked.

"No, I mean it," Dave said. "It's hard to be a boy, you know?"

I nodded, though I didn't quite understand what Dave was getting at. Even on the hardest days, being a boy always felt easier, more natural to me than being a girl ever had. I associated boyhood with cool-headed stoicism, rugged self-reliance, the freedom to live on my own terms the same way Dave seemed to in the stories of his youth. But maybe there was something darker and more dangerous about the kind of boy he'd been, about the kind of man he was, than I knew.

In the three years I'd lived in the park, I'd encountered a lot of boys like the one with the knife I met my first day in Cactus Country. Boys who made games of knocking baby birds out of their nests and kicking the pads off of prickly pears in the cactus gardens. Boys whose rage was hot and pulsing, like the palms of our hands when we dared each other to hold them to the asphalt. Boys who spat insults like fire, who led with their fists, who always drew first blood. But Aiden wasn't like those boys. He was always gentle with animals, and I'd never seen him get into a fight with anyone. Watching Aiden take one last swing at the door, I wondered what else Dave thought he saw in him that I couldn't.

ON A HOT July afternoon, Aiden and I came by Dave's trailer to cool off in the air conditioning and play with Buster. The camper door was shut, but Dave's car was parked outside, so we knocked until he finally answered, a scowl on his lean face.

"The cat?" Dave huffed. "Yeah, fine, whatever. Come see the fucking cat."

"What's wrong?" I asked. Dave took off his glasses and pinched the bridge of his nose.

"Just got my paycheck. After the rent, cell phone, gas for my car, food for *this* one," he said, pointing to Buster, "I ain't got nothing left for shit." He opened the mini fridge, saw that it was empty, and slammed it shut again. Aiden and I stood in the doorway, sharing a glance. This was a problem neither of us knew what to do with.

"Yeah, that sucks," I agreed. Aiden reached for Buster, who rubbed his head against the back of Aiden's hand. Dave sighed and sat down on the bed, accidentally catching Buster's tail. The cat hissed in protest, taking a swipe at his leg.

"Damn it!" Dave shouted. "Fucking cat!" He grabbed Buster by the scruff of his neck and hurled him from the bed. Buster cried out as he hit the floor, scrambling to right himself.

"Hey!" Aiden yelled. "Don't you fucking touch him like that!"

Dave's face scrunched red with rage. He shoved us both out and slammed the door, the camper shaking from the force. Aiden and I heard another squeal, longer this time. I imagined Dave kicking Buster, or throwing something at him, or stabbing him with one of his knives. We pounded our fists against the door, kicked it with our bare feet until our toes ached. Aiden was in tears, howling so loud I couldn't hear Buster over him.

"Just give us the cat, Dave!" I called.

"I'll kill him if you don't leave me the fuck alone," Dave said. "I swear I will!"

"You—you *pussy*!" Aiden screamed, his voice cracking. "Come out here right now, you fucking *faggot*-assed chicken*shit*!" He grabbed handfuls of gravel from the ground and pelted them against Dave's front door, continuing his tirade through clenched teeth.

"You *asshole*, you *fucker*, you goddamn son of a *bitch*—"

Aiden's voice was getting hoarse. His face darkened to a deep red, freckles fading into the color. He looked older, somehow, his expression so much like the one I'd just seen on Dave. Aiden took a breath and summoned the worst word he could think of.

The slur tore nonsensically from his throat, bouncing from the side of Dave's trailer back at us, the echo of his high voice sounding it again and again. The word seemed to ring through the park, and in its wake came a second of the loudest silence I'd ever heard. I didn't know whether Aiden was out of breath, or just as shocked by what he'd said as I was—as maybe all three of us were—but for that second, the desert went quiet, and all I could hear was the sound of blood beating in my ears with the same ferocity as the sun beating down on our backs.

"What the *fuck* did you call me, boy?" Dave shouted. We heard a smash, as though Dave had thrown something made of glass against the door. Aiden opened his mouth, ready to start shouting again. But before he could, I grabbed him by the arm and pulled. I dragged him as he wailed, away from Dave's trailer and into the shade outside the public bathhouse. Aiden gasped for breath, hiccupping from his rage and the heat. I twisted one of the spigots in an empty campsite until the water ran cold and splashed Aiden's face in it.

"He don't get to—to *fucking* touch my cat like that," he huffed as I wiped his forehead with the sleeve of my shirt. "If I had my .22 right now I'd go back and kill his ass dead."

"I know you would," I said quietly. Aiden kicked at the ground. I put my hand on his sweaty shoulder.

"Maybe my dad can talk sense to Dave," I said.

We found Dad in the Airstream and breathlessly filled him in. He nodded without comment or surprise, following us across the park to

Dave's trailer. But by the time we got there, Dave's green car was gone, his trailer still locked. The A/C unit was quiet. I pressed my ear to the door as Aiden called Buster's name. We heard a soft mew. It was the middle of a hot summer day, the temperature easily more than a hundred degrees. The kind of heat where mirages shimmer in the distance and the asphalt appears to melt. Without air, the cat wouldn't last long.

"We have to get Buster out," Aiden pleaded. Dad fetched a metal bar and pried the door open. Aiden gingerly scooped the cat from the bed, held him close against his body in a tight hug. Dave's trailer looked even more ransacked than usual. Clothes lay all over the floor. The fridge hung open. His books and knives were gone. Dad shook his head.

"I don't think Dave's coming back," he said.

THAT FALL, THE neighbors in Cactus Country gathered every evening around the picnic tables to drink beer and shoot the shit. I stood in front of the table, showing off a tarantula I'd caught crossing the road into the park from the surrounding desert. The late summer's monsoon rains would draw them from their holes and into the waiting hands of children. But it was rare to find a tarantula so late in the year. I alternated my hands as his spindly legs crept across my open palms, gaining no ground. The adults gaped over their bottlenecks at the spectacle.

"Won't it bite?" a man asked. He was a paramedic who worked the night shift three days a week. His boys were a couple years younger than me and away for the season, visiting their mom someplace a few states over. The man's new girlfriend, an RN, sat beside him, watching the tarantula with disgusted fascination. I shook my head at his question, playfully asking the woman if she wanted to hold it. She shrieked, laughing into her hands as I brought the spider closer. The adults around us laughed, too. The sun hung low in the sky, casting a red glow over our sunbeaten faces. The burn was an inevitability, no matter how much sunscreen we wore.

Once the novelty of the spider had worn off, the adults started talking about Dave again. No one had seen him since his arrest, but that didn't stop anyone from speculating what he might have done to get the warrant.

"I bet it was something to do with drugs," said one man. "Growin' 'em, sellin' 'em. He seemed like the type." Several men nodded in agreement.

"I heard he was mixed up with the Klan," another said.

"You think you know a guy . . ." said a third, allowing his sentence to trail off into his bottle. Silence, the solemn shaking of heads. After another round of beers, some of the guys started telling raunchy jokes.

"What's the difference between a man's job and his wife?" one asked.

"I don't know, what?"

"After five years, the job still sucks!" The men around the table laughed. One even slapped his knee. The women rolled their eyes, the wife of the man who'd made the joke giving him a playful shove.

"Okay, I've got one," the RN giggled, taking another sip from her bottle. She burped, holding the back of her hand up to her mouth.

"Why do Black guys have such big dicks?" No one had time to guess before she blurted out the answer, an epithet about the coarseness of Black hair.

A few of the adults chuckled. The paramedic laughed heartily, stood up to get himself another beer from the cooler. "Good one," he said. I furrowed my brow.

"I don't get it," I said. All faces turned to me, still standing at the head of the table. I held the tarantula in my cupped hands, one gently over the other like a warm desert burrow. The spider had retracted his legs, huddled into himself. A second or two of awkward silence as the RN looked at me sheepishly, wispy blond strands framing her thin face. I was no stranger to cussing or the gross-out humor favored by middle-school boys. Some of the names we called each other out in the desert might have made this woman blush. Even so, though I couldn't say why or how, her joke made me uncomfortable, as if I'd walked in on something I shouldn't have.

"You'll get it when you're older," the paramedic assured me, but I wasn't so sure I wanted to. Recently, radio shock jock Don Imus had been in the news for the racist and sexist remarks he'd made about the Black women on the Rutgers basketball team. His brother, Fred Imus, happened to live year-round in Cactus Country, and was good friends with Dad. After the story broke, I'd heard Fred say the same thing about Don as Dad had once said about Dave, complete with the same sigh, that same look of resignation—as though nothing could be done.

He's just a fucking idiot.

I hadn't thought much of it at the time, but standing at the picnic table, this same phrase ran through my head, and it became easy to write off the adults as drunk, the woman's joke as merely stupid. But as I headed away from the group, I wondered what it meant to be an idiot in the way Fred and Dad seemed to think. How often in Cactus Country, the things our neighbors might dismiss as idiocy, like Dave and his books, seemed benign to everyone until suddenly they didn't. In the aftermath, the neighbors would piece together a story around the picnic tables from all the signs they'd missed, following them like animal tracks in the desert—the small imprints of a coyote's paws or the sideways drag of a snake's long body over sand. The steaming scat and the brittle shed skins and the bones from its last meal.

I'd gone tracking with the other boys lots of times. In the desert, the signs animals left behind were often imperfect, confusing. An unskilled tracker could easily mistake old tracks for new ones, following the signs for hours only for the trail to go cold and have to turn back. We boys never tracked down so much as a desert mouse out there, but I always wondered: even if we knew exactly what to look for, even if we followed the signs perfectly, even if we weren't afraid of what we might encounter, what were we supposed to do with the animal once we'd found it?

The tarantula was brown and hairy, his leg span roughly the perimeter of my open palm. He was beautiful. I thought about taking him home to my terrarium, as Aiden and I had done with the horny toad he'd caught that summer. As I'd done with previous tarantulas. I'd keep them a few months, but they didn't last long under my care, no matter how many crickets I fed them. He wasn't mine to keep. I walked to the edge of the desert where I'd caught him, opened my palm, and watched the spider slowly amble away.

A FEW WEEKS after he left Cactus Country, Dave's trailer was considered abandoned. The park seized it and later put it up for sale. Buster went to live with a couple Dad found on Craigslist and Aiden moved to Texas. That fall, I saw police cars pressed up against the desert's edge, raining red and blue light on Dave's green car, stalled in the dirt with hazards blinking, a trail of severed cactus arms and shorn creosote bushes in its wake. Afterward, I stood at the picnic table and listened to the neighbors tell and retell the story of how Dave had tried to escape. How he'd flung himself from the car in a desperate bid for freedom, sprinting through the sand with the cops hot on his trail, guns drawn. How two of them had tackled Dave to the ground, cholla needles digging into his face as they pressed it into the earth. How they'd hauled him up, cuffed him, and taken him away.

We would never know why Dave had chosen to return to Cactus Country. How the police found him, or what reason they'd been searching for him in the first place. Dave's car sat in the desert for days until a tow truck came to haul it away. The desert foliage grew in and around the place Dave's car had been, masking the harm he'd caused, and in time it became impossible for anyone to say where exactly it all happened, only that it did.

DESERT DOG

On the day Dave was arrested in Cactus Country, Dad sat waiting for us on the Airstream porch when Mom pulled into our campsite.

"So you probably saw that Dave came back this morning," he began. "But he didn't come back alone." He looked up at the cloudless sky as though thinking carefully about what he'd say next. "Now, you can meet her," he said, "but I want to be clear right up front that under no circumstances can we keep her." I stared at him, my eyebrows arched like a question as Dad slowly pushed open the Airstream's tall silver door.

Huddled on the floor of our trailer was a small, white puppy. She couldn't have been older than a few months, with huge front paws and a pair of ears that seemed too big for her head. The puppy whined as I gently scooped her into my arms. But as I pressed her to my chest, I felt her body relax into mine. She panted in the Arizona heat, a long, spotted tongue hanging from the side of her mouth.

"We can't keep her," Dad repeated, his arms folded across his chest as if to underscore this point. He listed a few reasons why—that the Airstream was too small for a second dog, that she would grow into a violent breed, that he didn't want anything to do with Dave's bullshit anymore, and so on—but I wasn't really listening. The tag on the collar around her neck read CHYNA. Cactus Country's park manager had found her panting and overheated in the backseat of Dave's car. He brought Chyna to us because he knew Dad and Dave were friendly—or had been, once.

"I couldn't fucking believe it," Dad huffed. "First the cat, and now a dog." We'd rehomed Buster despite Aiden's and my impassioned arguments to keep him. From Dad's perspective, Chyna had become one more problem to solve in the wake of Dave's disappearance, his frustration renewed every time she peed on the floor, or scratched at the bathroom door, or chewed on one of our shoes. Our scruffy terrier, Tucson, didn't seem to appreciate a new dog encroaching on her space, either. She growled at Chyna, baring her teeth whenever the puppy approached her water bowl.

I tried to keep Chyna out of the Airstream, figuring the less often Dad saw her, the fewer opportunities he'd have to think about giving her away. Maybe with enough time, he'd forget about rehoming her all together. Our time with Chyna stretched into a week, my hope of keeping her growing stronger by the day.

THAT SATURDAY, WE ate lunch as a family at the Airstream's foldout table. Dad and I slurped bowls of instant ramen while Mom chewed a slice of burnt toast with peanut butter slathered on one side. Tucson stared up at Mom from under the table, her tail thumping loudly against the wood floor.

"No beg!" Dad said. Tucson slunk toward the far end of the trailer and hopped onto my bed, still peering at the table. Chyna scratched at my leg, whining until I pulled her onto my lap.

"That reminds me," Dad said, twirling his fork around a noodle. "We need to have a serious talk about this dog. Today. Don't let me forget." The time had come to make my case. I took a breath, running through the short script I'd rehearsed in my head.

"I've been thinking, Dad," I started. "What if I kept Chyna? I'd take care of her myself and pay for her food with my own money. She'd be my responsibility. I mean, isn't there some way—"

"In hell, maybe," Dad said brightly, spooning broth into his mouth. I sighed into my soup bowl. Thwarted, at least for now. But the desert surrounding Cactus Country, I figured, was a little like hell—hot and full of devil-adjacent creatures like snakes and spiders and lizards. I took in another mouthful of noodles, planning a new way to approach the subject later on.

"Besides," Dad said. "The ad's already up." I dropped my spoon into the bowl, broth splashing onto the table.

"You wrote an ad? When?" I demanded.

"We took pictures of her yesterday while you were at school." I glared at Mom.

"What?" she said, her voice thick with peanut butter.

"She's my dog!" I cried. "You guys can't just give her away!" I slammed my hand down on the table, causing the dishes to jump. Dad's bowl leapt over the side, most of the soup spilling onto his shorts. I opened my mouth to apologize, but the words came too late.

"Goddamn it, this has gone on long enough!" Dad shouted, thick finger pointed at me. "We already went through this with the cat and we are not keeping the fucking dog! Do you hear me? You need to drop it, or else!"

I said nothing. When Dad was pissed off—which, these days, was more and more often—I never felt sure what would happen, whether this time he might lash out at me the way I'd heard the other Cactus Country boys talk about their parents doing. Spankings, or *whuppings*, as we called them, were common in the park, and often preceded by family arguments—like this one—that passersby could easily overhear through thin trailer walls. We all knew it when another boy was getting his. But afterward, when he came out to the playground rubbing his behind, we pretended not to have heard shit. Though I'd never been whupped, myself, in moments like these I didn't dare test Dad's resolve.

"I do *not* want to hear you talk about keeping that dog again," he said, his eyes huge. I held Chyna a little tighter, worried he might try to rip her from my arms. But Dad just threw his spoon down on the table and left, slamming the Airstream door behind him.

"Fuck you too, then," I muttered under my breath. Mom ignored this, taking a long sip from her coffee mug. Arguments in our trailer had become more common over the last few months. Dad had always had a temper, but I'd never seen him so close to the edge.

That fall, as I entered high school, some of our regular window washing gigs dried up. Several of the old Check Into Cash stores had permanently closed, while other businesses opted not to renew their contracts.

Dad complained about paying more in gas to drive farther into town for fewer jobs. And coming home to the park after a hard day's work offered little comfort. Life in Cactus Country, once *our own little slice of paradise*, had lately felt more like purgatory. Our neighbors liked to talk shit, and since Dave's dramatic return, Dad was catching all kinds of heat about how close the two had been. He'd taken to sitting alone in the Airstream with his books rather than around the picnic tables, his frustration hanging in the air like the stench of sweat on a hot day.

"How could you do this to me?" I asked, turning to Mom.

"Don't blame me," she said. "You knew we couldn't keep her."

Chyna burrowed sleepily in my lap. I held one of her soft paws in my fingers, smoothing the fur with my thumb. She needed me, and I wouldn't abandon her like Dave had.

When Mom left to take Tucson for her afternoon walk, I filled a container with dry dog food from the pantry. I collected a gallon jug of water, a half loaf of bread, a leash, a bowl, a pillow, a blanket, and a small tent. After scouting out a camping spot not too far from Cactus Country's barbed wire fence, I pitched the tent behind the cover of wispy creosote bushes and gnarled ironwood trees. Though I'd need to venture back into the park to siphon water from campsite spigots and grab more food from the Airstream, there was no way I would go back to stay. I didn't care how angry Dad got. He couldn't make me come home without Chyna.

NAMED FOR THE surrounding mountain ranges, Empire High School was new, built just a year earlier on a patch of desert that stretched farther than I could see. The land had been bulldozed and a winding road had been paved, linking the eastern edge of Tucson to Vail, a neighboring town. Compared to the mostly suburban Rita Ranch kids I'd gone to middle school with, several of the Vail kids at Empire came from wealthy families, their lavish homes custom built on pristine acres of desert flora with glistening private pools and fleets of luxury cars. Their parents didn't wash windows or worry about shit-talking neighbors. Empire's student body was full of jerks competing with one another to pick on you for the secondhand clothes you wore, or the supposedly "gay" way you walked, or the trailer you referred to as "my house," or, often, for nothing at all. If not for my friend Drew, who also lived in Cactus Country, I might have felt entirely alone at Empire.

At fifteen to my fourteen, Drew was a big kid with a soft, round face, forever sweeping his long brown hair away from his eyes. Drew's family—his mom, stepdad, and two younger sisters—had moved into the park with little more than their small camper a few months after a devastating house fire. They'd lost everything in that fire, but I never heard Drew complain about that or anything else. Unlike a lot of the other Cactus Country boys I'd known, he was thoughtful and quiet. The kind of kid who'd split his last candy bar with you or help you retrieve a lost basketball from the meanest snowbird's campsite. The kind to let his sisters—any little kids, really—hang roughly from his neck, their sharp nails digging into his skin like cholla, and swing them by their lanky arms as they squealed with delight, never letting them go until their feet met the ground.

Most afternoons, Drew and I ditched the younger kids for a few hours to play trading card games in the shade of the Cactus Country bathhouse, laying our cards against the cool brick pavement. There, we played best of three, then seven, then thirteen, talking about the latest high school gossip—which teacher was dating who, which girls might be pregnant, which kids got high in the parking lot. I'd never gone to school with a friend from the park before, and it felt good to commiserate with someone who knew firsthand how much Empire High sucked.

"QUITE THE SETUP you've got here," Dad said, his deep voice disembodied through the tent's canvas. Chyna and I had only been living out in the desert for a couple of hours before he found our camp. I was still mad but knew it wouldn't do any good to ignore him.

"What do you want?" I said, unzipping the door. He crouched down to look me in the eye.

"Why don't you come home," he said. "This is silly. You don't want to live out here." Though he didn't say it, I could tell from his calm, slow demeanor that he felt sorry for yelling earlier. Maybe he'd changed his mind about Chyna, too.

"Can I keep her?" I asked.

"No."

"Then I'm staying." I folded my arms, resolute. Dad sighed.

"We already have a dog," he said. "We live in a trailer. There's just no room for her. You know that." I didn't respond. There had to be some way to make it all work. Other people lived in trailers smaller than ours with more than one animal. The family dog, Tucson, had always preferred Mom over anyone else. I wanted a pet of my own to care for, a pure bead of life and goodness in an otherwise relentlessly cruel landscape. I wanted to grow something, to raise something to thrive out here in the desert, just to prove to myself that it could be done.

"Besides, there's a family from Vail coming to get her tomorrow," Dad said. "They have a little girl who's excited to take Chyna home. You don't want to disappoint her, do you?"

I didn't want to start another fight, so I kept the fact that I didn't give a shit whether some rich guy's daughter was disappointed or not to myself. Instead I shrugged, brushing the stray sand around the canvas tent floor with my hand.

"I'll give you some time to think about it," Dad said. He stood up. From this vantage point, I could only see his hairy legs and sneakers. "I know you'll do the right thing," his voice called.

I listened until I couldn't hear the crunch of his footfalls against the dirt anymore. Silently, I slipped out of the tent and watched through the creosote bushes as Dad ducked under the barbed wire and crossed the dry riverbed back into the park. The second he vanished behind a wall of white trailers, I began packing up the tent and all of our supplies. We would move to another spot deeper in the desert. Dad wouldn't be able to give Chyna away if he couldn't find us.

LATER THAT AFTERNOON, I lay on the dusty tent floor, Chyna panting beside me. We'd been staked out at our new location for a little more than two hours. I poured some water into my cupped hand and rubbed it onto Chyna's fur to keep her cool. She licked the water from her pink nose, then resumed panting. I listened to the doves cooing in the ironwood trees outside and thought over the logistics of our new life in the desert.

Though I wanted to, I couldn't stay here with Chyna all the time. I had school on Monday, and dog walking duties on weekday afternoons. Maybe, I thought, I could ask someone in the park to watch Chyna for me. A neighbor who would be sympathetic to my cause. Drew's family seemed like good candidates. He and his little sisters loved Chyna, and his mom didn't seem to mind having her around their trailer whenever I came over. I ditched the tent and wandered over to Drew's campsite with Chyna on a leash. Voices echoed from his open door long before I got close enough to make out what they said.

"Do you think I'm *stupid,* Andrew?" a woman shouted. I peered through the doorway to see Drew's mom with a hand held above her head, her short, straw-colored hair as wild as the look in her eyes. Drew raised his arm too late to protect himself as she swung her palm across his face. A sickening smack resounded through the air, echoing from the walls of surrounding trailers. "Don't you *ever* disrespect me like that again!"

Drew rubbed the spot where she'd just struck him. His sisters hid behind a pair of couch cushions. My mouth hung open. Drew's mom froze suddenly, cocking her head toward me. The rage in her eyes gave way to a softer, almost bashful expression. She smiled.

"Excuse me," she said sweetly. There was a hint of embarrassed laughter in her voice, as though I'd caught her with a finger up her nose rather than with her hand in the air. She reached out to grab the door handle and pulled it gently shut. I made eye contact with Drew in the split second before the door closed, his expression one I'd seen on his face at school before—not of anger or embarrassment, the way I might have felt in his place, but defeat.

"And don't leave the *fucking* door open!" I heard another slap, this time accompanied by a sharp cry of pain. The trailer shook as someone, likely Drew's mom, stomped from one end to the other. I'd heard her berating him lots of times as I walked by their campsite—the whole park had—but seeing it with my own eyes ignited my sense of indignation. How dare she smile at me, then beat her son behind a closed door as though I couldn't hear her. As though I hadn't just seen exactly what she was doing. While I might have feared the possibility of being struck when Dad raised his voice, I realized then, with certainty, that he'd never hit me the way Drew's mom did him. Slowly, I walked Chyna back in the direction of our tent, biding my time until later, when I could count on Drew to meet me at the playground for our usual card game.

THAT EVENING, DREW came outside with a couple of decks, one cheek visibly pinker than the rest of his face. He tried to cover it with his hair, and I pretended not to notice. We tied Chyna's leash to a nearby bench so she could nap in the shade without interrupting our game. I shuffled Drew's deck and he shuffled mine, methodically flipping the cards over one another in a smooth way I admired but didn't know how to replicate. Drew trained his eyes on the pavement.

"Sorry you had to see that," he said. "I mean, that stuff with my mom earlier."

"Does she hit you a lot?" I asked, handing his deck back. Drew shrugged, sniffed, wiped his nose on his sleeve. We drew our hands silently, setting our first cards into play.

"Why do you let her do that to you?" I asked. It was an unfair question, and one I regretted a little as soon as it left my mouth. But Drew was a big kid. Probably big enough, I figured, to defend himself if he wanted to.

"I could never hit a woman," he said, as though reading my mind. "I don't care what she does to me." We fell into another long silence. Drew's eyes flicked over each card in play. I wanted to diffuse this tension, to try and make him smile. This was usually easy to do.

"Your mom's kind of a bitch, huh?" I said, grinning.

"Yeah, basically," Drew said quietly. He beamed up at me from behind the cards splayed in his hands, cheek shining red in the harsh afternoon light.

DREW AND I shared a gym period at Empire High with a scrawny, mean-spirited boy named Jesse, who seemed to aspire to be like the bullies who taunted him in the locker room. He took every opportunity to humiliate us in front of the other guys in class. One morning during our warm-up stretches I watched Jesse pick at a scab on his outstretched leg. The scab was gray and thick, like a patch of elephant skin over his kneecap. He peeled it slowly until blood ran down his knee onto the gym floor.

"Shit," he muttered, quickly wiping it with his hand. The coach blew his whistle and we all stood up to go outside for laps. The more athletic guys ran ahead, Coach right along with them. Drew and I were always among the last kids to reach the track. We liked to jog at a pace slow enough to talk about the card games we would play after school.

"Hey, Drew," Jesse called. I saw it coming in slow motion, like the phases of the moon. Jesse's arm swinging, palm open, onto Drew's cheek. A wet slap I could feel in my bones. Drew hanging his head. Touching a hand to his face, examining the blood on his fingertips. Jesse laughing, wiping the rest of it on his black shorts, racing ahead to catch up with the others.

"Are you okay?" I heard myself ask. Drew didn't answer me, but stood staring at the ground like he wished he could shrink into the dirt under our shoes. As though that's where he belonged after what Jesse had done to him. Watching him, I was gripped with fury. An anger focused and centered, yet all-consuming, like standing in the middle of a fire. I didn't care what happened to me next. All I knew was I wanted Jesse dead.

"Jesse!" I shouted. His name echoed against Empire's brick exterior. A few kids walking to the track turned in alarm. Jesse wheeled around, his smirk gone. I'd never stood up to him before. He paused, then started walking back toward us, slowly, carefully.

"Oh, what," he said, mocking me, "is he your boyfriend or something?" A bold taunt, but I could tell Jesse was afraid from the way his voice shook. Only a couple inches more and he'd be within swinging distance. I balled my fists, knowing I'd only have one shot to land a good one, maybe knock out a couple of teeth. I glared at him.

"You're nothing but a little bitch," I spat. By now, several kids in our class had stopped running, watching from the track to see what would happen next.

"What did you call me, faggot?" Jesse asked. He inched closer. Closer. Then—

"Hey!" Coach said sharply. "What's this about?" He stepped between us, and I lowered my fists. I told him how Jesse had picked the scab from his knee. About his bloody hand, and the slap. Coach looked at me as though I were speaking another language. As though these words, together, couldn't mean what I was saying. He looked from me, to Jesse, to Drew, who looked at the ground, a smear of red still visible on his cheek.

"My god," Coach muttered.

"You," he said, pointing to Drew. "To the nurse." At this dismissal, Drew lumbered slowly back toward the gym. Coach turned to Jesse, his eyes bulging from their sockets, a vein pulsing on his temple. "What in the *hell* is wrong with you, son? Never in all my years of teaching have I seen something so depraved and disgusting as what you just did!"

Coach laid into him in front of the entire class. Jesse's eyes were wider than I'd ever seen them as spit flew from Coach's red, angry mouth and onto his face. One girl turned to another and said, loudly, "What a fucking freak." Jesse looked ready to curl up and die right there on the pavement, the way a bug might. I grinned, glancing back to see whether Drew was watching, but he continued to trudge toward the locker room. He didn't come back out to class that day, but I managed to catch up with him at lunch. Drew sat alone, hunched over his untouched tray.

"That was really fucked up, what Jesse did," I offered. Drew didn't respond, staring at something invisible on the table. I tried to start the conversation a different way.

"I've never seen Coach lose it like that," I said. Drew shrugged.

"Jesse looks like his mom fucked a hyena," I said. But Drew didn't laugh. Didn't even crack a smile. I'd stood up for us, but it didn't seem to make a difference. No matter what happened to Jesse now, Drew still had to get hit, still had to stand with someone else's blood running down his cheek as other kids looked on. No joke could change that.

"I really don't want to talk about it," he said.

So we didn't.

BACK IN CACTUS COUNTRY, playing cards in the shade of the public bathhouse, Drew grinned, shaking his head as I filled him in about the situation with Dad and Chyna.

"So you're, like, living out in the desert now?" he said. "That's awesome." I nodded, looking over the cards in my hand, but I wasn't really thinking about the game. A glorious idea had come to me. I put my cards down.

"Hey, why don't you run away, too?" I asked. "There's room in my tent if you wanted to bunk with us. We could be like hoboes or something, maybe even hop a train and skip town!" Drew looked at me with an expression I didn't recognize, had never seen on his face before. He squinted through the harsh sunlight, his mouth screwed up to one side.

"I can't just leave," he said. "If I were gone, who would take care of my sisters?"

"Your mom would," I said. It seemed obvious to me, but Drew just shook his head. He pulled a card from the deck. Studied his hand. Made his move slowly, deliberately.

"Your turn," he said. I began to understand then what Drew had known all along. When his mom got angry, someone had to take the hit. Drew was her punching bag so his sisters didn't have to be. Fighting back would only make life harder for them. Drew's self-sacrifice was not a sign of boyish weakness, as I'd thought, but of a man's quiet strength. His way of loving his sisters, of looking out for them, when, maybe, no one else would.

We played cards until it grew too dark to see them anymore. I wanted him to stay, to play one more game, but Drew had to get home. He wished me luck, his body receding into the night. Chyna shivered as a burst of cold wind rushed over us. I pressed her small body against mine, rubbing her back until she stopped. From where I stood, I could see Mom through the Airstream's window, watching TV on the foldout couch. She looked warm.

I was still angry but now saw the naivete of my resistance. Though I had promised to take care of Chyna, to never abandon her the way Dave had, I knew my love wasn't enough. I could dodge Dad for a few more days, maybe a week at most. But returning to the tent now would only delay the painful inevitability I'd soon have to face. Unless I gave her up willingly, it was Chyna who would weather the consequences—the sweltering heat of the days and the freezing desert nights. With the puppy asleep in my arms, I trudged toward the Airstream, ready to bury my anger so she could have a chance to grow, to thrive in a real house with a family whose love would give her more than I, a desert boy, ever could.

ANDROGYNY & ECSTASY

"I MET A GUY LAST night," Angel said, blowing a cloud of smoke from his lips onto the cigarette between his fingers. Angel was a big bear of a man with long, dark hair, a matching goatee framing his mouth. He held up the tip, watching it smolder. I'd seen Angel sitting outside his family's fifth-wheel trailer from the Airstream porch and come over to join him. Now we huddled around his picnic table in the brisk morning air, talking about what had transpired in the ten or so hours since we'd last seen each other.

"You met someone here?" I asked. It seemed impossible that Angel would find another gay man in Cactus Country, especially one confident enough to be out among our conservative neighbors. There was Buckley, who I knew Angel found handsome, but he was straight and dumber than a palo verde beetle. I'd bum cigarettes from him sometimes down by the park's concrete monsoon drain. Angel wouldn't share his packs with me. He said he didn't want me picking up the habit, but really cigarettes were expensive and the Cactus Country store didn't sell them. They required a miles-long drive into Rita Ranch and were therefore a precious commodity.

"Of course I didn't meet him here!" Angel scoffed. "I met him online. He drove up from the city." Online, meaning Craigslist. The city, meaning Tucson. One of Angel's young nieces opened the door of their trailer and leaned out to ask where the breakfast cereal was.

"Ask your mother, child," he said. "I'm not on babysitting duty until she goes to work."

At twenty years old, Angel had come to Cactus Country from a mid-size Midwestern city to live with his older sister, a registered nurse who needed after-school care for her two daughters while her husband was stationed in Iraq. Angel watched to make sure the door to the fifth-wheel had firmly shut before recounting in a hushed whisper how he'd met his hookup for sex at the empty group camping sites. The trailer he shared with his sister and her family was a no-go for casual encounters. He didn't have a car of his own, no way to get into town without catching a ride from somebody. So the guys he met online had to come here.

"On the *picnic tables*?" I said. "C'mon, Angel, people eat on those!" Angel rolled his eyes, took another drag from his cigarette.

"No, not *on* the tables, honey," he sighed. "And that's all I'm going to say. A good girl doesn't kiss and tell." He took one last suck from the cigarette and let the smoke bleed luxuriously from his teeth and lips. My mouth watered. Angel made smoking look delicious.

"Do you think anyone saw you?" I asked.

"Pffft, oh please," Angel said, waving his hand dismissively. "Ain't none of these old snowbird biddies out past nine thirty." The queer sage of Cactus Country, Angel was out, proud, and seemed to fourteen-year-old me to be profoundly wise. Any time I came to him with a problem, he would listen carefully before posing an elegant solution with his characteristic wit and charm. He swiped the stub of his cigarette on the ground to ash it.

"Now then," he said, his voice and demeanor taking on an air of playful formality. "What is it you wanted to talk about, young one? Please, step into my office." He gestured grandly at the other side of the picnic table and I smiled as I sat down opposite him. When Angel wasn't babysitting, he took online psychology courses for college credit. He practiced the techniques he studied on me, his friend and first patient. I took a breath.

"Well, it's—" I started. "Do you think I might be gay?"

Angel snorted. "Of *course* you are," he said. "The first time I saw you, I thought you were a little gay boy, remember?"

I always bristled at this description, feeling too old to go romping around the desert, playing made-up games with little boys. As a soon-to-be high school sophomore, I wore baggy, ripped jeans and long-sleeved skateboarding logo shirts. I'd grown out my bowl cut a little, the way lots of guys styled their hair, and still presented to most as an average teenage boy. But I knew I wouldn't be able to look this way much longer. The bones in my once-round face had become sharper and more angular. My hips had widened, and my voice would never drop low like the voices of other boys my age. I was quickly growing into not-a-man, the anger I'd once felt about my changing body maturing into an emotion closer to grief. That morning, I had come to Angel after a sleepless night, haunted by my inability to envision who or what I would become.

"Okay," I said, finally. "But wouldn't you thinking I *was* a little gay boy actually make me straight? A girl who looks like a boy who likes boys? Or something?"

"But you don't like boys," Angel said.

"I guess that's true," I said. Though it wasn't, exactly. Since Sage, I'd had a few fleeting crushes on people at my high school. There was the theater kid who belted out choruses from Broadway musicals in the lunch line; the goth girl whose entire personality seemed to be modeled on the anime adaptation of *Van Helsing*; the tall, quiet boy who walked with one hand in his pocket and the other on the messenger bag slung casually over his shoulder. But these attractions seemed to come and go almost at random, with no discernable pattern. I hadn't spent enough time with any of my crushes, in or outside of school, to tell whether I actually liked them or not.

"Listen," Angel said. "I've known a lot of fags in my life. You, honey, are queer. No doubt in my mind." I nodded along to his assessment of me. Angel owned several rainbow pride flags and flew them, much to the chagrin of our neighbors, every chance he got. He unironically rocked out to "OK2BGay," a newly released queer anthem by Tomboy, blasting it on repeat from his trailer's outdoor speakers. He told anyone who would listen about his experiences performing in drag and marching in Pride parades. Angel seemed so sure of himself, so comfortable in his identity as a gay man. I admired that about him, and trusted his judgment. But I still had questions about myself that I was starting to suspect even Angel couldn't answer. At night, while my parents slept, I burrowed under the covers with my school laptop to browse the internet through Cactus Country's newly installed Wi-Fi service.

Earlier that week I'd joined a popular site called Gaia Online, which allowed users to create an anime avatar for posting in chat rooms and on discussion forums. My character was buff and masculine, dressed in nothing but a pair of boxer shorts, a limp cigarette hanging from his mouth. I chose a tongue-in-cheek username, nodding to what Angel always said about me: "i_like_gays." On Gaia, I quickly befriended a group of teens around my age and regularly stayed up chatting with them until the early hours of the morning. One boy, Rox, whose avatar was decked out in a black punk rock tank and platform boots, seemed especially interested in my username.

"so u no how ur gay?" Rox asked.

"ya," I wrote.

"me 2," he confessed. "but no one nos . . . except u lol"

My hands hesitated over the keyboard. Rox was coming out to me, being open in a way he'd never been with anyone, while I hid behind my ridiculous naked avatar. I pressed my fingers into the keys, stumbling toward an explanation about how I both was and was not what I seemed. But the more I tried to explain myself, the more confused everything became. I'd been born a girl, I told him, but had always felt more like a boy. I crushed on girls, and sometimes, maybe, other boys, too— "but it doesnt rly matter who i like," I concluded. "its all kinda gay no matter what"

"um what," Rox said. "tht makes no sense"

"ya it does, cuz im a guy," I said, "but like also a girl in a way"

". . . ok," he said. "so wich is it? u cnt b both"

I didn't have an answer for him, but I wanted one for myself. After Rox logged off for the night, I read article after article about human sexuality and gender identity, following American queer history from the Stonewall riots to the contemporary fight for the legalization of gay marriage and other basic LGBTQ+ rights. There seemed to be so many ways a person could find themself in that ever-expanding acronym, its "+" containing multitudes. When I ran out of search terms, I trolled the Gaia forums for hours, seeking anything that might help me define the tension between the body I had and the person I wanted to become. I stayed up all night looking.

"YOU'RE *GOING*," DAD said, his voice a dangerous baritone.

A few hours had passed since my conference with Angel. I sat on the foldout couch in the Airstream, arms crossed over my chest. Dad and I had been circling a fight all week. It might have started with the confrontation in the park laundry room, where I'd ranted about the cheap powdered detergent that left streaks on all my clothes. Or maybe it began when I'd complained about helping him wash windows after school, a once-coveted job that now felt to teenage me more like a chore. Or it could have been the argument that had materialized out of Dad's perception that I was sullen and ungrateful, that I stayed up too late and spent too much time on the internet.

I'd managed each time, with difficulty, to stop the disagreement from escalating. Dropping the issue, I'd offer a quick, meaningless apology that would calm things down for a while. But with each new conflict, my resolve weakened. The tension between Dad and I had grown thicker than blood. Sensing an imminent showdown, Mom backed him up, her voice sharp.

"Zoë, you made a commitment," she reminded me.

"But I hate the horse corral," I said. "I've always hated it." I'd never developed an interest in the horses and couldn't understand why Mom and Dad were so united on this particular front when they, as parents, were so lax about so much else. They acted as though working at the horse corral was something I would thank them for later, once I'd established a successful career as a jockey or a circus performer. But these days, I barely had the energy to get out of bed in the morning, let alone shovel for hours in the heat. I couldn't stand the thought of spending one more Saturday in the company of the old cowboy and Slim and their godforsaken horses.

"You can't make me work there anymore," I said. "I'm not going." Dad put his hands on his hips, shook his head like he was disappointed.

"You know, I'm just gonna say it. You've been a real bitch lately," he said. "I'm sorry, but you have." I'd never heard Dad call any man a *bitch*, a word he reserved for only the most difficult women. That he thought of me in these terms stung like stepping barefoot on a cactus needle. His words pierced me, and I exploded, a high-pitched anger screaming from my mouth.

"*You're* the bitch!" I seethed, pointing a furious finger at him. "I fucking hate the horse corral, and this trailer, and Cactus Country!" My fists were balled, my face red with breathless rage.

"But most of all," I said, "I hate *you*!" Dad stared at me for a second with his mouth slightly open, looking like I'd smacked him. When he found his voice again, my punishment was swift.

"Get out of here!" Dad shouted. He kicked open the Airstream's aluminum door, crashing it into the side of the trailer. "Get the *fuck* out!" He grabbed my arm, pulled me to the door, and shoved me so hard I nearly lost my balance on our plywood porch. I caught myself, stood up to face him.

"Fuck you!" I shouted. Dad shot me one last menacing glare before slamming the door shut. I turned and walked to the edge of Cactus Country, to a stretch of desert bordering the long road to I-10. I wished, with a pang, that I'd left the park with Chyna when I'd had the chance. We could have hopped one of the slow trains and made our way up the West Coast. On the rails, we wouldn't have to answer to Dad, or the cowboys, or anyone. The two of us would have flown past all of them in an open boxcar, just a modern-day hobo and his road dog, onward to freedom.

I stared out into the vast expanse of creosote bushes and ocotillo stalks, wanting to disappear into them, the way I'd seen the flightless quail and roadrunners do. I wanted to run like they did, not just into the desert, but away from the park altogether. Away from Tucson, and my family, and my body. But I was stuck here, with anger pulsing through me and nowhere to put it.

Sinking onto a stack of abandoned cinderblocks, I ran my hands over the white gravel at my feet. I found a sharp rock and rubbed it impulsively against my left arm, slowly at first, then fast, as though trying to start a fire. At first it felt good, like scratching a nagging itch. Then, as the friction broke the skin, it was hot, searing. I winnowed it down, layer by layer until a small gash appeared. I dropped the rock and examined the wound—red, raw, and stinging, like my anger had been. But those feelings were gone now, transferred to this new mark on my arm.

In a daze, I walked back to the Airstream and calmly apologized to Dad for saying I hated him. He grunted, put a hairy arm around my shoulders and gave me a quick squeeze, the tension between us receding for the moment. He agreed that I wouldn't have to work at the horse corral anymore if I didn't want to.

"It's healthy to get all the anger out in the open," Dad said, his tone betraying a strange pride. "That's how families talk to each other sometimes." I nodded, eager to reconcile, to put our latest confrontation behind us. But I couldn't help feeling that what Dad and I had done wasn't actually talking at all.

IN THE PERENNIAL way of Cactus Country, Drew and his family had moved out of the park a few months before, into a house that replaced the one they'd lost in the fire. Within weeks, the campsite they left behind was occupied by a family with two new boys, Jake and Louis. Louis was eleven and stocky, with a buzz cut and a ready, mischievous grin. His thirteen-year-old brother, Jake, had light brown hair and a shy smile. Jake, like me, had been assigned female at birth but wore boy's clothes and sported a short bowl cut. When I first knew him, a decade before he came out as a trans man, Jake still used his birth name and feminine pronouns. Though we never talked about the ways we differed from other boys, he and I recognized something common in the other and became fast friends.

Together, the brothers and I were notorious Cactus Country pranksters, always looking for new ways to amuse ourselves with the park's limited amenities. We skimmed the romance novels that comprised the recreation hall library, reading aloud, with disgusted fascination, as "his throbbing member" met "the creamy crux of her curls." We played bad music in the Airstream, turning the volume up louder and louder with each song until it bled out into the streets, dancing as the trailer shook on its wheels. We made prank calls to local businesses on the public phones, breathing hard into the receiver before hanging up in a fit of giggles. We acted out elaborate comedy skits based on Angel's bootleg copies of *The Big Gay Sketch Show* on the long, runway-esque series of picnic tables in the group camping sites, bowing deeply for an imaginary audience.

The only other teenager in Cactus Country was Buckley, a nineteen-year-old who lived with his grandparents. Buckley wore holey wifebeaters and loose-fitting jeans. Tall, muscular, and idle, without a job or school to occupy his time, he spent most days in the park exercise room, bulking up at the weight bench. In the evenings, he and I would meet on top of a sloped concrete basin at the back of the park where monsoon flood water collected to drain. Behind us, miles of open desert stretched to the railroad tracks. Where we sat afforded us a good view of the park, and relative privacy. There weren't many trailers on this end of Cactus Country, and we'd be able to see anyone coming from a distance. Buckley lit up a cigarette.

"Can I hit that?" I asked. He handed it to me. I took a few puffs, inhaling slowly each time, still not used to the burn. I tapped some ash onto the concrete, passed the cigarette back to him.

"So you got any boyfriends or anything?" Buckley asked. I let the smoke out of my mouth in a slow stream, pursing my lower lip the way I'd seen Angel do. I still had short hair, still wore boy's clothes, still carried myself like a boy—still *was* a boy in every visual sense of the word. But none of that seemed to matter to Buckley. Hearing the neighbors talk about me using feminine pronouns was enough to compel him to hit on me every chance he got. His attempts at flirtation frustrated me. I didn't like how he assumed I'd be interested in him, or that I had even one boyfriend, let alone a group of them.

"Boyfriends?" I said, "Yeah, I got boyfriends. I got more than I know what to fucking do with. I got boyfriends falling out of my ears. What the fuck do you think?"

Buckley squinted at me, taking a long drag from the cigarette. I'd expected him to brush it off, maybe laugh. But he didn't.

When someone perceived me as a girl, which was more and more often these days, the rules of boyhood I'd internalized when I came to Cactus Country suddenly didn't seem to apply anymore. Behaviors that had been encouraged in me as a boy—stoicism, cynicism, machismo—instead made me seem cold, negative, difficult. Buckley stared at me in silence, and I was suddenly conscious of being way out here alone with him in the quickly fading light. I folded my arms against my chest, shielding myself against my growing unease.

"Just asking, damn," he said, finally. "You don't gotta be a bitch about it." Buckley dropped the butt onto the concrete. We watched it roll down the slope, orange sparks crumbling away from its still-smoldering tip.

THAT NIGHT ON the internet, I discovered a new word: *androgynous*. The post was written by a trans person named Tay who used neopronouns—tay/tays—and identified as neither male nor female. Tay described feeling intense gender dysphoria when tay looked at tayself in the mirror or took a shower, detailing tays struggles with depression and self-harm. I'd never read anything, by anyone, that I felt so encapsulated the totality of my lived, embodied experience. I consumed every one of Tay's posts, and the hundreds of responses from users questioning whether someone could both identify as transgender and exist outside of the gender binary. I valiantly responded to the skeptics and the trolls on Tay's behalf, defending tay—defending us—against a world that didn't understand. Too excited to sleep long after I'd logged off for the night, I couldn't wait to tell Angel everything I'd learned.

In the morning, I met Angel outside his trailer and breathlessly filled him in about Tay, about how I'd finally found a word for the way I felt in my body.

"But if you're trans, that would make you a boy," he said, taking a sip of his coffee. "That's how that works."

I shook my head.

"I don't feel like I'm either gender, though," I said. "I just feel like I'm—like I'm *me*, you know?" Angel pulled out a new cigarette, stuck the butt into his mouth. Held a lighter to his lips.

"I think you're just confused," he said. We sat in silence for a few minutes as Angel smoked. The high of last night's discovery was fading, a weary fatigue settling in its place. If he was right, and androgynous wasn't a gender someone could be, then what did that make me? A new question popped into my head.

"Angel, do you think I'm a bitch?"

"Who's calling you a bitch?" he asked. I shrugged, not wanting to get into what Dad and Buckley had said. Angel studied me, flicked his cigarette against the rim of his empty coffee cup. "Well whoever's saying that, honey, definitely take it as a compliment," he said, laughing to himself a little. "A bad bitch is a very good thing to be."

THAT AFTERNOON, BUCKLEY came swaggering onto the playground, full of his usual boredom and bluster. Louis and I sat on the swings while Jake leaned against a pole, all of us ignoring Buckley as he climbed onto the play structure. He stood on top of the monkey bars, stepping from one end to the other with his arms out as though walking on a tightrope.

We thought it might be funny to try and shake Buckley off his perch. Louis and I began to swing as high as we could, slamming down hard onto our seats. But we weren't strong enough, and Buckley gloated, climbing to sit on top of the long metal bar the swings hung from, the highest point of the play structure. He pulled up his sleeves and flexed his biceps, shaking the bar under him with his arms to try and jerk us from the swings.

"You kids ain't shit!" he called. But Buckley's showing off soon got the better of him. He lost his balance, tumbling backward onto the hard earth with a heavy thud that we felt under our feet. Buckley's enormous body lay sprawled on the ground, motionless.

"Is he dead?" Louis asked. Jake and I shrugged with open mouths, both of us momentarily lost for words. Louis picked up a stick and pressed it gently into Buckley's cheek. No reaction.

"Can you tell if he's breathing?" Jake asked me. I approached Buckley slowly, reluctantly. Crouching over him, I hovered my hand over his nose to feel whether any air was coming out. Buckley's eyes fluttered open. He gasped as though waking from the dead.

"Christ!" I said, leaping backward. Buckley sat up and clutched his head with both hands, wincing. When he finally opened his eyes, his left pupil appeared much larger than the right.

"You, uh, you okay?" I asked, but Buckley didn't answer. He stood up, unsteady on his feet, before staggering toward us with arms hanging in front of him like Frankenstein's monster.

"Zombie!" Louis shouted. The three of us took off toward the storm drain at the back of the park, laughing. But to our surprise Buckley followed us, first walking, then jogging, then sprinting along the road. He was gaining on us, and quickly. We couldn't be sure what, in his confused state, he would do once he caught up to us, but there wasn't time to stop and speculate. The brothers and I made for the desert. I pulled the barbed wire fence open with my foot as Louis and Jake darted through, hoping the drain's concrete slope might slow him down. But Buckley flew up the drain in two huge steps, then took a running leap over the fence, clearing it easily.

Louis, Jake, and I raced haphazardly through the desert, scraping our legs against cactus needles as we went, hot air tearing at our faces. We led Buckley through a forest of jumping cholla. We hid behind tall ocotillo spears and doubled back, trying to lose him. We ran silently, save for an occasional "Shit!" or "Come on!" or "Go, go, go!" Our feet crunched against the sand as we glanced back to see Buckley still tailing us. He tracked us doggedly over barrel cacti, under low-hanging ironwood branches, deeper and deeper into the desert. We ran for more than a mile, all the way out to the railroad tracks, dodging prickly pears and creosote bushes, before slowing to catch our breath. Jake wordlessly pointed to Buckley's figure in the distance, distorted and shimmering in the heat, staggering toward us like a drunk. The three of us turned and continued to run, this time back toward Cactus Country.

Never in my life had I been chased by anyone, let alone an adult, with the determination with which Buckley pursued us. Not ever so fast, or for so long. I forgot all about my body, my anger, my heartbreak. All there was in the world was one foot in front of the next, this cactus to swerve around, that rock to clear, a quick glance over the shoulder to check whether we'd lost him.

This would be, I somehow knew, the last real chase of my childhood, and I didn't want it to end. Whatever happened next, whether our bodies collapsed in the sand from dehydration and heat stroke, whether Buckley finally caught up to us and wrung our necks or slit our throats or committed some horror we were or were not capable of imagining, none of it would have mattered. I would have been happy to die out in the desert that day if it meant I could run with Louis and Jake and Buckley forever, fueled by the terror and ecstasy of this absurd moment, transcending space and time until all four of us disappeared in a spectacular burst of light, like the explosion of a dying star.

THE BOYS AND I doubled over when we reached the park's barbed wire fence, back the way we'd come. We coughed and sputtered, our hairlines and t-shirts soaked through with sweat. I could feel my heart beating painfully in my skull. My dry tongue ached with thirst. Angel sat at the picnic table in front of his family's trailer, helping one of his nieces with a homework sheet. He looked us up and down, his face scrunched in concern.

"What is *happening*, children?" he asked. But before we could answer, Buckley burst out from the desert behind us, his eyes rolling to the back of his head. Too exhausted to scream anymore, we pointed at him, gesticulating wildly. Buckley did look truly monstrous, his massive biceps red and shiny from the sun and his sweat, resembling a pair of cooked lobster claws. He buried his head in his hands and fell to his knees. Then he threw up into his lap, curled into a ball on the gravel, and went to sleep. Angel stared, his mouth open.

"He fell on his head earlier," I managed to say, as though that explained things. Angel called for his sister, the nurse. She stirred Buckley awake and led him to the shade of their trailer's awning, flashing a light into each of his eyes in turn.

"Well, he definitely has a concussion," she announced. "Probably heat exhaustion, too."

Buckley mumbled something unintelligible. His grandparents weren't home, so Angel's sister drove him to an urgent-care center. Buckley would return hours later with a bandage around his forehead, remembering nothing about either the fall or the chase. I recounted the whole story to him that evening on the storm drain over a cigarette. He shook his head in disbelief, picking dead skin from a severe sunburn that had already started to peel.

"That sounds crazy," he muttered.

"What were you following us for?" I asked. "Don't you remember anything?" Buckley paused, inhaling the cigarette slowly, as though deep in thought.

"I really don't," he said finally, allowing a cloud of smoke to billow from his mouth, enveloping us both. "I just remember feeling like I was running for my life, you know?"

I looked over my shoulder and out into the desert of my boyhood, recalling the thrill and terror of the chase, for once understanding exactly what he meant.

II. CITY SLICKER

BIRD ON FIRE

"WAIT, THIS IS FOR THAT school I was telling you about," Dad said. "Listen." He turned up the volume on the van's radio so I could catch the tail end of the ad: . . . *City High School, a community of learners located in the heart of downtown Tucson. Enrollments open now!* He drummed his fingers against the steering wheel, waiting for my response.

"Yeah, sounds cool, I guess," I said. Dad rolled his eyes.

"You *guess*?" he asked. Convinced that Empire High School was the source of my growing teenage malaise, and our frequent fights, Dad wanted me to transfer to a different school for my sophomore year, one in the city.

"It's the damn suburbs, Zo," he said, soaping up the long windows with a scrubber. "They're crushing your spirit." I didn't respond, scratching at the elastic bandage wrapped around my chest. The bandage flattened my physique, making my body appear less feminine, but its itchiness and constriction felt like slow murder in the heat. Dad flicked some bubbles from his scrubber onto the top of my head. I glared at him.

"See?" he said. "You've forgotten how to have fun!"

Dad might've had a point, I thought, brushing the bubbles from my hair. Lately I'd been restless, feeling I had no place to be alone. Mom and Dad were always in and around the Airstream. Our neighbors walked along the roads day and night with dogs on leashes, drinking wine from margarita goblets with green saguaro-cactus-shaped stems. The latest generation of Cactus Country boys populated the playground, their shrill cries carrying across the park on the wind. Even the vast desert surrounding us, once an expansive wonderland of possibility, felt smaller than it used to. I knew all of its well-worn trails and ironwood tree hollows. Most days I sat in the high branches of my favorite palo verde with headphones in my ears, wondering what life outside of the park might be like.

I dragged the squeegee down over the glass where Dad had just scrubbed. After practicing for hundreds of hours on thousands of windows I could wipe the glass clean without a thought, my mind occupied with the idea of a new high school. I figured that City High—hell, anywhere—had to be better than Empire. As I shifted away from the conventional masculinity of my boyhood and toward a more androgynous appearance, I'd been getting into some trouble at school. Most recently, for fighting with a boy who'd called me a transvestite and "Ellen Degenerate" in the courtyard at lunch. I couldn't wait to get home to Cactus Country every afternoon. Bored was a lot better than bullied.

"So what do you say?" Dad asked as we loaded the window washing supplies into the back of the van, money in hand and on to the next job. "Can't hurt to look, right?"

HOUSED IN A once-bustling department store building in Tucson's historic downtown, City High was a progressive charter school where teachers went by their first names. The small student body comprised an eclectic group of lovable misfits. Some kids had been homeschooled for most of their lives, while others had dropped out or been expelled from Tucson's more traditional high schools. But everyone, no matter their background, seemed to have enrolled seeking a place of refuge. The school was big on community spirit. All the teachers knew your name, even those whose classes you'd never taken and never would. On Fridays, teachers and students came together for a whole-school meeting where student punk bands played improvised sets and local speakers from Tucson's downtown area gave talks about various community initiatives. I spent a day shadowing a sophomore named Andrés Cano, and by the afternoon I was sold on City High.

Most mornings that summer, I begged Dad to drop me off at the bus stop so I could traverse the sidewalks around my new school, exploring downtown while the desert sunlight was low and sharp, the shadows still cool. The city reminded me of what might happen if someone dropped a giant cinderblock on the desert, a slab with cold government buildings and tall office towers, a few tunnels dipping under raised railroad tracks where cargo trains ambled slowly along, their whistles echoing against the edifices. Most landscaping downtown was gravel-paved, like the campsites in Cactus Country. Warm plazas decorated with colorful Mexican tiles surrounded pleasant patios shaded by mesquite trees, public gardens artfully arranged with cacti and creosote.

Downtown had Sonoran hot dog carts and pigeons that swarmed the uneaten buns. An unlikely patch of real grass on the rolling hill outside the metropolitan library, and a large, violently red, abstract sculpture that resembled a playground but was too high off the ground for anyone—let alone a child—to climb. Unhoused people panhandled at the bus station and huddled to sleep with their dogs in the doorways of condemned buildings. Police roamed deserted streets with a handgun in one holster and a battered baton in the other. Scattered shops and restaurants nestled between the abandoned structures, but nothing opened before lunchtime and everything closed on the weekends, when downtown Tucson was dead to the world. That's when I liked the city best.

The commute entailed a twenty-minute drive from Cactus Country to Tucson's easternmost public Sun Tran bus stop, then another hour on the bus to the Ronstadt Transit Center. I relished the adult freedom of taking public transport, the time spent alone. On the ride, I flipped through the well-worn copy of Kate Bornstein's *My Gender Workbook* I'd picked up from a queer bookstore until its spine came unbound. In my workbook, I experimented with new pronouns, writing different combinations in the margins. I liked the sound of ze/zem/zeyr or they/them in place of he/him or she/her, but I had trouble convincing anyone to actually try them. My parents would use my pronouns if I corrected them in the moment, but always defaulted back to she/her. Angel simply rolled his eyes, insisting I was going through something he called "queer puberty" and would come out on the other side either a trans man or a lesbian.

"I had a similar phase, you know," he said. "When I was a little baby gay I'd try on my sister's clothes and wish I'd been born a girl instead."

"What about now?" I asked. "Do you ever wish you could be a woman?" Angel made a face.

"And *waste* God's gift to men?" he said, gesturing to himself from head to toe, his voice rising in faux indignancy. "Can you *imagine*, honey?" We both laughed. Angel might not have understood how or why I felt the way I did, but he was still my friend, my one connection to queer youth culture in Cactus Country.

Over the summer, I'd read what little I could find online about androgyny and genderqueerness, relaying most of what I learned to Angel, despite his skepticism. Using a tutorial I'd found on a trans female-to-male blog, I had begun binding my chest with a spare Ace bandage from the Airstream's first aid kit. I loved how binding made me look, but sometimes wearing an extra layer of tight polyester made me feel faint under the hot Arizona sun. The wraps needed to be adjusted throughout the day or they would begin to slip from my sweat. I didn't want to take them off, even to sleep. But wearing the bandages too long made my skin red, leaving itchy welts where the seams had been. Angel encouraged me to ditch the elastic and order a real binder.

"Forty bucks is a lot cheaper than a cracked rib," he'd said.

I chose one from a website called T-Kingdom based on a recommendation from Tay's post on Gaia Online. The day it arrived, I eagerly wrapped the binder around my chest, fastening it to itself as tightly as I could. I slipped on a shirt and checked out my profile in the Airstream's bathroom mirror, smiling wide at the person I saw. My chest appeared flatter than it had when binding with an Ace bandage. With my feminine face and masculine body, a fitted shirt and baggy jeans, I could pass as a pretty boy, one of those teen heartthrobs in a band. Even Angel seemed impressed, whistling when I showed him my new physique.

"We gotta find you a little girlfriend or something," he said. I pretended to roll my eyes as he grinned at me over his psychology textbook.

That Saturday, Angel took the Sun Tran with me downtown to a space for queer teens and young adults called Eon. One of his hookups had told him about it. I hoped to find someone there who understood my gender, maybe even felt like I did. To show Angel there were more of us. Eon's three mismatched couches were arranged in a C shape around a coffee table covered in queer stickers. The space had computers with internet access and a small library. A fridge with sandwich-making materials. Free condoms and sex education pamphlets. Pop-up HIV and STI testing facilities. Eon was a safe haven for queer youth, especially those who—whether in crisis, or unhoused, or still closeted to their families—needed a place to feel seen and understood, a place to make friends with other folks in Tucson like them. Though never explicitly stated on its posters and flyers, Eon's mission was to keep queer kids alive.

Angel and I sat on one of the couches for a group support meeting. As the youngest in the circle, I waited nervously as everyone shared their name and pronouns. No one had ever asked for my pronouns before. When it was my turn, I introduced myself as androgynous.

"My preferred pronouns are ze/zem/zeyr," I said, "but I also go by they/them."

I was the only person in the group to use nonbinary pronouns. After the meeting, two older girls called me over to their side of the couch. Angel shot me a smirk before heading outside to light a cigarette. The first girl reminded me of a mermaid, with her long dyed-orange hair and green sequined shirt.

"What are your pronouns again?" she asked, her voice soft and sweet. I repeated them.

"I thought 'they' was, like, plural though," the second girl said. She wore intricate, glittery eye makeup, her lashes almost as long as her nails.

"It doesn't have to be," I said, shrugging. I ran into this argument about the singular "they" a lot, and always had trouble understanding the reluctance to bend grammar rules in the spirit of inclusivity. People already used "they" and "them" in singular terms all the time, whether they realized it or not.

Later, when I excused myself to use the bathroom, I overheard the girls talking about me in hushed tones.

"But what does 'androgynous' even mean?" the first asked, a giggle in her soft voice.

"I know, is that supposed to be a trans thing?" the second said.

"Doesn't *sound* like a trans thing," the first scoffed. "What, is she bi-curious, too?" They laughed. Embarrassment flooded my cheeks, its heat burning my eyes. I'd heard Angel talk disparagingly about bisexuals, often in that same tone, usually accompanied by an eye roll.

"Bisexuals are a myth," he'd said. In his mind, bisexual men were actually gay with one foot still in the closet, and bisexual women only got with other girls to titillate straight men. Bisexuals were the fence-sitters of sexuality, holding back the fight for equality with their self-centered hedonistic desire to have it all. Is that what these girls thought about my gender?

I met Angel outside, where he was puffing on the end of a cigarette.

"Can we go home when you're done?" I asked, arms folded against my chest, elbows pressing into my binder.

"Already?" Angel said. "We just got here. You don't like it?"

"No, I don't know," I said. "It's fine, I just . . . I don't think I belong here." I told him what the girls had said, but Angel just shrugged as if to say, *See what I mean?* We rode the bus home to Cactus Country in silence. After this summer, Angel's family would be moving out of the park. I'd hoped to find a new community at Eon, but I wasn't queer in the right ways for the kids who hung out there. Online, Tay's original post now spanned hundreds of pages, and every night Gaia users logged on to ask tay the same questions, making the same arguments about the gender binary without bothering to read any of the answers tay or I or anyone had already written. Nothing, it seemed, would convince them of what they didn't want to believe. Everyone I encountered seemed to treat my gender like a debate.

Everyone, that is, until I met Avery.

Avery went to an alternative school downtown, not far from City High. She had dyed-blue hair that was cut mid-length on one side and shaved close to her scalp on the other, a stainless steel ring pierced through her nose. Avery wore oversized hoodies and sat in the back row of my bus, taking furtive sips of tequila from a plastic water bottle. I liked sitting next to her because she always livened up an otherwise dull ride, cracking morbid jokes about everyone onboard, including herself. Together, we whispered about increasingly absurd ways to kill ourselves on the bus until we were both in tears with laughter. Other times we listened to music on Avery's iPod, one set of earbuds split between us as we took turns sharing our favorite albums.

"Man, I wish there were girls like you at my school," she said. "Everyone I know sucks."

"Well, I'm not—" I started. "I'm not actually a girl." Avery cocked her head, one eyebrow raised as I explained what androgyny meant.

"Okay, so you're not a girl," Avery said, "but you're also not a boy?" I shook my head, mentally preparing to field the inevitable follow up questions. The are-you-sures and how-do-you-knows I'd become accustomed to answering whenever anyone asked about my gender.

"Neither one," I said. Avery nodded knowingly.

"Like that song by Garbage," she said. "That's pretty cool." I smiled as she searched her music library for "Androgyny." Of all the conversations I'd had over the past few months about my gender, this was the first time anyone had accepted my answer without pushing back. We exchanged phone numbers, and before long I was spending my weekends across town in the dilapidated double-wide mobile home Avery shared with her mom. There, Avery taught me the finer points of shoplifting.

"Always pay for one small thing," she said. "That way they don't get suspicious." We stole from the Circle K one street over: glass bottles of iced coffee, double packs of bubble gum, king-sized candy bars, tall cans of energy drinks. Anything we could stuff into the waistbands of our jeans or the front pockets of our loose hoodies. We smuggled our loot back to Avery's bedroom, feasting on the spoils as we passed a joint back and forth.

Weed was always available in abundance at Avery's house. She smoked a bowl before school in the morning like most people drank a cup of coffee. Her mom bought sandwich baggies of it in parking-lot deals while we waited in the backseat of her beat-up sedan. Back in Avery's room, to the perpetual background oeuvre of the Insane Clown Posse, she taught me how to break up the dry buds with my fingers, separating the seeds and the stems before rolling the best of it into a wrap and licking it closed. When the rolling papers ran out we smoked from anything we could find—from bongs and pipes and fruit and old homework pages ripped from school notebooks.

When high, Avery was buoyant, elevating. Sometimes, as we lay back on her mattress, listening to music with our arms folded behind our heads, she'd lean over and whisper all the corniest parts of old Beatles songs in my ear through fits of deep, flirtatious laughter. Other times we embarked on long, hot walks to this or that friend's house, stumbling around the neighborhood with loose limbs, tripping over potholes in the street and beer cans scattered in the vacant lots we cut through. But no matter what we did together, we did it high.

I'd smoked enough cigarettes to get past the nicotine head rush, but weed always made my teeth feel too big, the skin on my cheeks so tight I wanted to pull them off my face. I couldn't hold on to a single thought long enough to vocalize it, so I mostly sat back and listened, mentally swatting at the discordant ideas whizzing between my ears like horseflies. But I wanted Avery to like me, to think I was cool. If I smoked enough, maybe I'd come to enjoy it the way she did.

Dad seemed to like that I'd started smoking weed—or *pot*, as he called it. Smoking was a favorite pastime from his own teenage years, and I often brought a little back from Avery's house to share with him. One weekend afternoon, Dad and I traded a pipe on the Airstream's foldout couch while he caught me up on his latest business venture. Many of our retired neighbors, the snowbirds, were getting too old to continue traveling down to Tucson every winter season and needed a middleman to help them sell their RVs. Dad had first taken on a few of these jobs as paid favors, and was recently beginning to build something of a career of it, charging a modest fee for listing, showing, and managing the sale. Now that he'd made a little money this way, he was starting to buy a few cheaper RVs himself, with the intention of fixing them up and flipping them for a profit.

"You should see this new motorhome I picked up, Zo," Dad said, his voice stilted from holding his breath. "It's fucking disgusting, a real shithole." He exhaled, releasing a white plume into the air. I squinted at him through the haze of smoke, absently pulling on my cheeks, keenly aware how puffy and unnatural my face felt. *Shithole*, I thought. *Shithole. A real shithole.*

We took a slow walk to the RV storage row in the back of the park. A few spaces down from our family's red storage trailer, separated by another Airstream and an abandoned boat occupied by a colony of feral cats, was a boxy motorhome, its paint faded yellow from years under the desert sun. A sticker on the side pictured a kangaroo leaping over the word BOUNDER, an RV brand popular in Cactus Country. From the outside, it looked no different than the motorhomes some of our neighbors lived in. Dad hopped through the doorway and offered his hand to pull me up after him.

The place was gutted, ransacked, with cabinets missing drawers, their contents—prescription pill bottles, crushed cigarette packs, corroded batteries—strewn across the floor. Shredded magazines littered the carpet, their pornographic images interwoven with dried pieces of jumping cholla cactus that the desert rats had dragged in to build their nests. Empty beer cans and cigarette butts from dumped ashtrays stained the kitchen sink black. Rodent droppings covered the sticky bathroom floor. The toilet was unspeakably filthy. Even if I had been sober, I'm not sure I could have imagined a motorhome as far gone as this one appeared could ever be called a home again.

"Believe it or not," Dad said, as though reading my thoughts, "this one has good bones. It's just a matter of cleaning it all up." Dad had plenty of experience renovating vehicles. He'd gutted the short school bus we'd traveled in years back, removing the seats we didn't need to install a full-size foldout bed and a working kitchen. Our Airstream, too, had gone through some aesthetic changes since we'd moved to Cactus Country. Dad had ripped up the thin, dusty 1970s carpet and replaced it with wood flooring. He'd lovingly repainted the blue stripe that wrapped around the trailer and polished its aluminum exterior until it shone.

If the Bounder were cleaned and fixed up nice, Dad said, nobody would ever imagine it had once looked—or smelled—like this. Our family had had a lot of bad financial years, but with RVs like this one, he assured me, we could turn our luck around. The Bounder was our golden goose, our prize bird. Dad patted the motorhome's faded exterior as he said this, and in my high mind, I imagined the Bounder as bloated and featherless, an ugly duckling that would never make it off the ground.

IN THE FIRST hot, dry days of spring, I turned sixteen, and Avery became my girlfriend. She asked me out over the phone, presenting me with a silver-painted wire ring with a red stone the next day on the bus. The ring was part birthday present, part affirmation. Tangible proof of our relationship that I promised never to take off, not even to shower or sleep. I came home to the Airstream blushing, ecstatic, spreading my fingers to show the ring to my parents. Mom murmured appreciatively over her afternoon cup of coffee, but Dad wasn't impressed.

"That's a nice rock," he said, rubbing the stubble on his chin. "But this Avery girl. Isn't she, I don't know, kind of morose or something?"

"What makes you say that?" I asked, studying the way the stone shimmered in the light streaking through the open door. Mom shot him a sideways glance, tapped him in the ribs with her elbow. Dad shrugged.

"Nothing, I guess," he said. "Forget I mentioned it."

That summer, Avery and I sent text messages back and forth whenever we had to be apart, hundreds of them a day—romantic song lyrics, and expressions of love, and starry-eyed plans for the future. I'd take the Sun Tran to meet her in the afternoons when she finished summer school, and we'd hold hands as we waited for the bus back to the cool, dark haven of her room.

We had sleepovers every weekend night, staying up late to get high and watch movies we never remembered in the morning. Locking the door to her room, we'd shed our shirts on the floor like snakeskins and cuddle under a thin sheet on her mattress, pressing all the softest parts our bodies together. I never knew there were so many ways to kiss or be kissed. Lips and breath and tongue and teeth. But we always slowed down to smoke another joint before things got too heated. Avery insisted we should wait at least a year before having sex.

"Your first time should be perfect," she said, smoke swirling around us in bed. "Beautiful, memorable. Everything mine wasn't." Avery's plan for us sounded good to me. She was the one with relationship experience, having dated both girls and guys in the past. Though I didn't feel ready for sex, I trusted that Avery would know when the time was right. That we would have a conversation, or a series of them, beforehand. I wasn't in any hurry. If the texts we sent each other about the future were true, we would have the rest of our lives to figure it out.

Those early summer months in Avery's room felt as eternal as the desert sun outside. But as the monsoon rains precipitated a muggy fall, her mood darkened with the clouds gathering overhead. She grew increasingly sullen and withdrawn, the depth of her depression growing more apparent to me by the day. We stopped laughing together, her self-deprecating remarks about killing herself seeming less like jokes and something closer to warning signs. When Avery got upset, which happened often now, it became my job to talk her down. To drop everything and immediately respond to her text messages during a crisis—a fight with her mom, a bad day at school, an empty bag of weed—with reassurances of her worth, and of my love for her. In time, this became the currency of our relationship, the price I gladly paid to be with her.

ONE LATE NIGHT, Avery and I snuck an open bottle of wine into the dim cavern of her bedroom, locking the door behind us. We passed it back and forth on the carpeted floor, Avery growing a little quieter with each sip. She'd been in a somber mood all day and I was on edge, unsure what form her impending meltdown would take.

I took a small sip from the bottle and winced. Though I didn't like the acidic tang on my tongue, I wanted to develop a taste for it, the way adults did. The wine was warm. A drop spilled from my lips and onto my bare foot like a thin line of blood. I passed the bottle back to Avery, who accepted it, taking a much deeper drink than I had.

"I never should have done it," she began. "I wish I could go back and make it stop. He didn't deserve to take that from me." This refrain had become common for Avery in the past few months whenever she was sad, or drunk, or both. I didn't know much about the boy she'd lost her virginity to, except from the pictures she kept. His dyed black hair, round glasses, mild smile. "He was the first person I ever really loved," she continued. "Now, when I think about us together . . ." she paused, her voice cracking. "It feels like a rape, you know?"

She curled her arms around her knees and started to cry, deep sobs echoing from her body. I had worked hard throughout my boyhood to develop a stoic, masculine exterior, but I wanted to be soft for Avery, approachable and soothing and maybe even a little motherly. I placed my hand over hers and held it tight, wiped some tears from her wet face.

"I'm so sorry that happened to you," I said, hoping these might be the right words. I wrapped my arms around her shoulders. "But it's okay now," I said. "You're okay now." She slipped her hands around my waist and we rocked together, slowly, our bodies huddled on the carpet. Avery rested her forehead against mine so that we looked into each other's eyes.

"Let's just forget about this, okay?" she said. "We can still have a fun night." I nodded, eager to move away from the darkness of the previous moment.

Avery plucked a half-smoked joint from a full ashtray and held it to her lips. She pointed to the lighter by my foot. I flicked it open for her as she leaned into the flame, her blue hair sweeping forward like a curtain. Inhaling deeply, she closed her eyes and allowed the smoke to escape from her lips. It hung low, fogging the dank bedroom air.

"You want some?" she asked, holding it out to me, a smile already creeping back onto her face. I pinched the joint between my lips, breathing deep with relief. Too deep. I coughed, quickly passing it back.

"Let me try something," she said, crawling closer to me. "Close your eyes and open your mouth." I closed my eyes. I opened my mouth. I trusted her completely.

"When I breathe out, you breathe in," she said. I heard a sharp breath, then felt her lips, soft and wet as she pressed them to mine. She breathed the smoke in my mouth as I inhaled it into my lungs, and held it there.

"Now me," I heard her say. "Give it back." I blew the smoke into her mouth. When she tried to give it back again we both started hacking, laughing between coughs. Avery grinned at me.

"I fucking love you," she said. It felt so good to see her smiling again.

"I fucking love you, too," I said. I motioned to the wine bottle at her feet. "Pass me that?" Avery handed me the bottle and I drank as deeply from it as she had, its glass mouth clinking painfully against my teeth.

Soon, the seconds slowed to a crawl. My face was a monkfish, my body a heavy stone pillar, my brain a small electric bead, swiveling from one part of the universe to another as though following a circuit path on a motherboard—here, and then gone. A flash of Avery's face, then blackness, stars. A swatch of red from the STOP sign on her bedroom wall, then blackness, stars. The blinding glare of the bare lightbulb overhead, then blackness, stars.

"Do you feel," I said, staring at the backs of my outstretched hands, "like everything is starting and stopping?"

"What?" she asked, a giggle in her voice, but I couldn't think of a way to explain what I meant. It was beyond language, and anyway my arms felt so heavy. I curled up on the floor and covered my eyes, feeling suddenly dizzy, almost sick. To vomit in Avery's room would be very uncool. I wrapped my arms tightly around my head, trying to hold it—everything—in.

"We should probably go to bed," I heard Avery say. I felt her pulling off my shirt and jeans, my binder and underwear. Heaving me up to the mattress, where I flopped over onto my side. No one had ever seen my naked body this way before. My hands fumbled for a sheet but couldn't find one. The lights went out. Avery's body settled beside mine in the dark. Her hands ran through my hair, roughly massaging the back of my neck. I tensed under them. Her fingers were so cold, her grip too tight, my scalp stinging in their wake.

"Wow," her voice whispered through the darkness, coarse and stilted and so unlike the Avery I thought I knew. "You're gorgeous."

Blood beat in my ears as a hand slipped down the inside of my thigh, another sliding between my breasts. My body a kaleidoscope of nerves, every sensation howling across my bare skin like an echo. Pinching, squeezing, twisting, spreading, stretching. Splitting pain between my legs, raw and gaping like a wound. Wider, wider, until all I know is pain, all I see are stars.

I WOKE UP shivering in the early morning light, goosebumps spreading over my body like a rash. My head, throbbing. A dull ache like a punch in my stomach. A stinging soreness somewhere further down. Avery groaned as I sat up, her body curled away from me, the sheet pulled up over her sleeping face. I shuffled gingerly to the edge of the bed, where my clothes lay crumpled on the floor. Wincing as I pulled on my faded black t-shirt and jeans, I felt my way toward the mobile's tiny bathroom, immediately throwing up into the open toilet. Sickness washed over me in shivering waves, its sour taste rising in the back of my throat. I spat into the bowl a few times, flushed it all down, faint stars flickering at the edges of my vision.

I took a deep breath, tried to stand up, but the room spun around me, sending me careening back onto the floor. My body felt too heavy, my head too light. I huddled against the bathroom door until Avery came out of her room.

"What's wrong?" she asked, rubbing her eyes, her hair wild from sleep. "Come back to bed." I shook my head stiffly, muttering something about a hangover. She stared down at me a moment before awkwardly crouching on the peeling linoleum, placing her hand on my back. She rubbed it for a little while, which felt good, warm. The floor was so cold.

"Last night was a mistake," she said softly. "It was too soon. We shouldn't have done all of that." Avery spoke so gently, and it was hard then to believe the voice I'd heard in the darkness also belonged to her. "You can't tell anyone what happened, okay?" she continued. "Promise me you won't." I nodded slowly, afraid if I opened my mouth I might be sick again.

TWENTY MINUTES LATER, I waited alone on Avery's porch steps for Mom to pick me up, practicing the normal, disaffected face I'd make when the van pulled into the driveway. The morning sun hung low in the sky, and I shivered in the shadows of the Mexican fan palms dotting the edges of the mobile home park's cracked streets. When I closed my eyes, I could still hear the echo of that strange voice, the plume of Avery's breath in my ear. Her cold fingers on my leg, circling closer and closer to the place I'd never touched or been touched, never even seen in a mirror.

A sudden honk startled me back to reality. I buckled myself into the van's passenger seat, careful not to make eye contact with Mom, worried she might sense something was wrong.

"Have fun?" she asked.

"Yeah," I said. Then, preemptively, "Just a little tired. Didn't get much sleep." I tried to convince myself on the quiet drive home that how I felt was okay. Normal, even. That, maybe, this was what sex was supposed to feel like the first time—scary and secretive and uncertain.

Later that afternoon, I lay on my bed in the Airstream, staring up at my phone. Avery and I had never gone more than an hour without texting each other, and I wasn't sure how to break this new silence between us. Before I could decide, the phone vibrated in my hands. I flipped it open with my thumb to find a new message from Avery.

"We need to talk," it read. I stared at the tiny screen, my stomach starting to turn the same sick way it had earlier that morning. A second text flashed across the screen, another vibration so sudden I almost dropped the phone on my face.

"I don't think we should see each other anymore."

I stared at these words, my body buzzing but my chest strangely numb, hollow, as my thumbs tapped out a response.

"Are you breaking up with me?"

I closed the phone and waited minutes, then hours, compulsively checking the screen every few seconds for a message I might have missed. I sent more texts. I called and left messages, my voice cracking as I pleaded for her to message me back. Just one text. Please. But Avery didn't respond, her silence the answer to my question.

I DIDN'T SEE Avery at our bus stop on Monday, or again for the rest of the school year. But she wasn't really gone. Even in her absence, I woke up from nightmares I couldn't remember, weighed down by a feeling I didn't know how to name. I carried this heaviness with me through my days, wandering the hallways during my classes, pretending to be perpetually on my way to the bathroom. Images from that night flashed through my mind at random, sending me back to Avery's room while zoning out during a class lecture, or sitting on the bus, or staring down at my homework. I cried in empty classrooms and locked bathroom stalls. I couldn't tell anyone what had happened to me, because I didn't have the words to explain it, even to myself.

The week Avery disappeared, one of her friends stopped me at the crosswalk on my way to the Ronstadt Center, placing her warm hands on my shoulders as though grounding me in place. A rare overcast day in Tucson, white light shone through the clouds, imbuing the street with an otherworldly glow.

"Avery told me what happened," she said, her dark eyebrows heavy with concern. "I think it was kind of messed up of you to take advantage of her when she was drunk like that."

My shoulders stiffened under her fingers.

"That's not—" I started, glancing around to see if anyone could overhear. I lowered my voice to a whisper. "That's not true." Until this moment, I hadn't acknowledged what happened that night to a living soul. Now, in the absence of my side of the story, Avery had created her own narrative, twisting the facts to explain why she and I were no longer together. I realized, with a pang, that she didn't trust me to keep my promise. This was damage control.

"We were both drunk," I confessed. "I didn't know what was going on. I swear."

"Well, okay," she said, her face softening. "But you're the reason Avery stopped coming to school, you know. You must have done *something* wrong." I stared down at my feet, breath catching in my throat.

"I gotta catch my bus," she said, pushing past me. I stood on the sidewalk alone for what felt like a long time, blinking away tears through the soft light.

"YOU HUNGRY?" MOM asked later that night, stirring a pot of soup on the stove. I shook my head. From the corner of my eye, I could see Dad shooting her a glance from the foldout couch.

"I'm going for a walk," I said.

"Another one?" she called, but I'd already shut the door. I didn't feel the sensation of hunger anymore. The smell of food—any food—was enough to make my stomach weak. Just about everything I put in my body came back up.

I walked a lap around the park, hoping the change of scenery might offer a change of mind, but it didn't. By the time I returned home, it was dark. Standing on the porch, I could hear my parents' voices, muffled and tense, through the Airstream's aluminum walls.

"Marc, be rational," Mom pleaded.

"I'm serious, Susan," Dad said. "That girl's family did something to her. Maybe they poisoned her food, or—"

"*Poisoned* her? Marc—"

"I'm telling you, there's something *wrong* with her," he said. "This isn't normal."

I'd heard all I could stand. Covering my ears, I walked back to the empty playground and rocked gently on the swings, dragging my feet through the dirt. I felt guilty for worrying my parents, but I didn't know how to tell them what was wrong with me, why I wasn't "normal" anymore. What did you call an act like that when you and the girl who hurt you were the same age and in a relationship together? When you were too drunk and high to say anything, let alone no? I'd never read about an experience like mine in any book, seen it dramatized in any movie, heard it told in any story.

Sometimes late at night, when I woke up from nightmares struggling to breathe, I took kitchen knives from their drawers and snuck them into the Airstream's bathroom to make deep, deliberate slices in my upper arms and thighs. For hours at a time, as I felt the pain of my body opening, as I occupied myself with the secret ritual of caring for it, of bandaging it closed again with paper towels and packing tape, I could forget what happened in Avery's room. I could relax, sink into a heavy, dreamless sleep.

SOON, DAD TOOK his concern for me into his own hands, lugging home an enormous twenty-pound bulk bag of protein shake powder. Every morning before the drive to my bus stop he faithfully stirred two scoops of the powder into a glass of milk. He took a deep swig and smacked his lips exaggeratedly before handing me the glass, as though offering me a treat.

"Delicious," he said. "The rest is yours." I accepted the glass reluctantly, grimacing as I pressed it to my lips. The powder always clumped together at the bottom, the color and consistency of something a baby might spit up. I took a few tiny sips until Dad turned his back, then poured the rest anywhere I could—down the kitchen drain, into a potted plant, out the window—pretending I'd finished it all. On days I couldn't find a way to throw it out, I was obstinate. I would not drink the shake. He could not make me.

Dad quickly lost his patience with me. We fought bitterly about the protein shakes almost every morning for weeks on our drive to the bus stop. In addition to preparing the shake for me, Dad had taken to brewing a morning tea for himself. He drove the van into town with a full pot balanced precariously on the dash, pouring cups into a ceramic mug at stoplights. On one particularly tense morning, Dad promised to ground me for a month if I didn't finish the shake. No internet, no cell phone, no leaving the Airstream. I'd never backed down from a threat.

Without a word, I gripped the full glass in one hand and held it from the open window of the moving van, staring him defiantly in the eyes.

"Zoë!" he warned. "Don't you dare!"

I tipped the glass, its contents pouring thickly out onto the road. He slammed on the brakes. The teapot flew from the dash, scalding liquid spraying over his torso. Dad screamed in pain and rage, tea dripping from his curled fingers. He punched the steering wheel, slammed his purple fists down on the dash, howling like a wounded animal.

"Get the fuck out of my car!" he managed to yelp. Fine by me. I slammed the door as hard as I could on the way out. Dad hurled his empty mug through the open window after me, smashing it to bits on the road.

"Bitch!" he shouted, driving off. My face flushed red, throat tightening with fury. After months of feeling nothing, the anger had been waiting for me all along, and it was stronger than ever, blazing hot in my chest like fire. I gritted my teeth, hating Dad even more than I hated myself.

"I hope you fucking *die*!" I screamed, my voice cracking. When the last ripple of my echo had dissipated from the surrounding trailers, I turned to find an old woman out walking a little white dog. She adjusted her glasses, staring at me with wide, gaping eyes. Ashamed, I looked away and trudged back to the Airstream. I didn't go to school that day.

LATER, WHEN DAD returned from wherever he'd been, he stepped into the Airstream slowly, the spring groaning as he pulled the door open and then gently shut. He hesitated a moment before sitting down on the fold-out couch beside me, one hand rubbing the stubble on his chin, eyes fixed on the wooden floor. He cleared his throat and apologized for throwing the mug. I folded my arms tightly across my chest, refusing to look at him. Dad bit his lip and acknowledged the dashboard was probably a stupid place to put a pot of tea. His leg bounced on the floor as he said this.

"Throwing shit at your kid when you're mad is not normal," I said. "That snowbird saw everything. What if she reports us to the management and we get kicked out of the park?"

Dad scoffed at this hypothetical scenario, waving one of his hands through the air. "She's probably raised kids of her own," he said. "That's just how families talk sometimes. You know that." I shook my head.

"You're wrong," I said. "That's not how families talk. *You* have an anger problem."

I'd never acknowledged it aloud before. Dad stared down at the Airstream floor with his hands clasped together. But as much as I wanted to blame him, I knew this wasn't just Dad's problem. I could see the anger all around us, in the eyes of the men we called our neighbors. The anger grew like a culture in the heart of every desert boy I'd ever known. It was in the hot air we breathed, and in the sharp sting of cactus needles piercing the tender soles of our feet, and in the mangled bodies of the palo verde beetles we slaughtered. The anger was here, in the desert, and it was a part of us all, even as I wanted so much for it not to be. I was still furious, but what I said next was measured, calm.

"If you throw anything at me ever again I will leave this place and I will never come back. You will never see me again. I will never speak to you again," I said. "Do you understand?"

Dad looked up at me then, my fierce eyes shining in the reflection of his. I was my father's child, and he had always been proudest when he could see himself in me. But he was not proud, I hoped, of the anger we shared, of the rage that threatened to destroy us both. Dad nodded slowly.

"I won't," he said. "I can promise you that."

THE NEXT AFTERNOON, Dad and I drove home from the bus stop, tensely watching a wide plume of smoke rise and spread over the desert, blackening the sky.

"Did a train get derailed or something?" I asked, peering over the railroad bridge at the tracks as we crossed. Dad shook his head.

"Looks like it's coming from Cactus Country," he said. We parked the van at our campsite, jogging to the back of the park to locate the source of the smoke. When we saw the Bounder burning, we broke into a sprint, Dad cursing under his breath.

Heat stung the whites of my eyes as I watched fire curl around the Bounder's kangaroo sticker, bright flames licking it clean off the motorhome's charred sides. Windowpanes cracked and buckled, shards of glass exploding from their frames. The fire quickly overtook another motorhome in the back row, then a utility trailer, the other Airstream, and the abandoned boat, its stray cats fleeing into the desert. Dad and I hustled with park staff and our neighbors to remove the trailers' propane canisters before the fire could reach them in case there were any traces of gas left inside. I heard some of the onlookers say it was a gasoline fire, that fighting it with water wouldn't do any good. With the canisters a safe distance away, there was nothing for us to do but hang back and watch the destruction until help arrived.

The story of the fire went like this: earlier that day, a man had come to buy the Bounder. When the deal was done, Dad asked how he planned to haul it away. The man insisted he could get the RV running again. He would start working on the motor while Dad drove out to pick me up from the bus stop. The Bounder's engine compartment was still covered in dried cholla, its parts buried in tinder. The man's attempt to jump the battery, the turn of the key in the ignition, sparked a fire underneath the motorhome. Within minutes, the flames had spread to the roof. No one was hurt, but just like that, our prize bird, our golden goose, was gone.

When Dad and I ran toward the fire, I'd heard him cursing the man's name. But now, watching the firefighters douse the flames, he was silent. The fire finally out, all that remained of the Bounder and the RVs beside it were several blackened, smoking husks. He watched the cinders smolder with his hands in the pockets of his shorts, calmer than I'd seen him in years. Dad sighed.

"Could have been a lot worse," he said, finally. "Nothing to do now but pick up the pieces and try to move on."

I nodded. "We'll get through this, motherfucker," I said, echoing what had become his—our—favorite adage, a prickly inside joke that had budded and flowered into a mutual term of affection. "Just you wait and see."

Dad screwed his mouth up to one side in a half smile. He put a broad arm around my shoulders, pulling me tight, and together we watched steam rise from the Bounder's frame in the harsh afternoon sunlight. The wind swept away the white ashes of what remained, dusting them over the surrounding desert like snowflakes.

THE CURSE

MARK WAS THE FIRST OF my neighbors to die that season. A retired mechanic who took pride in his Harley-Davidson, Mark had injured his back on the job years ago and lived on a combination of workers' comp and disability. He was quick-tempered on a good day and known to self-medicate his chronic pain with cases of cheap beer. On a cool fall night, Mark had a drunken argument with his longtime girlfriend. In the middle of their fight he stormed into the trailer's back bedroom and shot a bullet through the roof of his mouth. The next morning, his suicide would become the talk of the park.

Death in Cactus Country wasn't unusual. Each winter, I recognized fewer returning faces as the oldest snowbirds became too sick to travel or passed away over the summer in their home states. Ambulances crept through the park with the sirens off a few times every year, paramedics quietly pulling a sheet-wrapped body out of the trailer on a stretcher. But the violence of Mark's death made it different, reducing the suicide from tragedy to a new, morbid brand of the usual park gossip. Neighbors clicked their tongues around the picnic tables, saying it was a shame, but Mark had always been a hothead. Within weeks, his girlfriend would get their bedroom cleaned and adopt two dogs. She paid me to walk them on nights she worked late, and I was always wary of that dark back room, trying hard not to think about what had happened there.

Not long after Mark's death, a snowbird crept outside early one morning when the desert sunlight was streaking and soft. He sat alone at his campsite's picnic table and composed a short note to his wife. Later that morning, park staff found him slumped over the table, a gun at his feet. The neighbors called it a "copycat suicide." Some expressed indignation that the man had killed himself outside where, they said, anyone could have found his body—even one of the little boys roaming the park. The cleanup was extensive and messy. His picnic table would need to be repainted. Everyone seemed to agree that he should've had the decency to walk a few yards out into the desert first. That this would have been the considerate thing to do.

Though I hadn't known either man well, I didn't like to think about how they'd suffered before making the choice to pull the trigger. As their neighbor, my proximity to their deaths made them feel heavy, almost personal. So when the speculation going around the picnic tables devolved into the macabre, as it often seemed to, I excused myself to take a long, slow walk across the park, passing each man's campsite to pay my private respects.

Months later, just as the suicides were beginning to recede in Cactus Country's collective memory, another man, Roy, was killed in a gruesome accident. Roy had always been quiet and stoic. We called him "Cowboy" because of the broad-brimmed hats, thick mustache, and leather boots he wore. The story going around the next morning went like this: Cowboy Roy's friend had driven him back home to the park after a long night at the bar. Roy lost his footing on the way out of the pickup truck, and his body slipped onto the road. It was dark. They were both drunk. His friend didn't see him fall and accidentally backed the truck's front tire over Roy's head. He was airlifted to a hospital but didn't survive the trip. Blood stained the place where it happened for weeks, baked into the asphalt by the sun.

On the same late night as Roy's fall, my next-door campsite neighbor, Butch, rushed his partner, Hank, to the emergency room. Hank was diagnosed with sepsis and died that night in the ICU of complications from HIV. Of all the recent deaths in Cactus Country, I had the hardest time coming to terms with his. Butch and Hank felt like uncles. Butch reminded me of an older version of Angel, with his scruffy beard and a propensity toward the fabulous. Hank, by contrast, was more centered, a calming presence. They'd sit outside their motorhome together, smoking and holding hands as they listened to the birdsong from the mesquite branches above. I always felt welcome to come over and hang out with them at their picnic table. Hank would offer me a snack as Butch asked questions about what I was learning in school.

Hank had seemed perfectly healthy to me the afternoon before he died. That day, he brought out the brand-new instant camera he'd just bought, excited to show me how it worked. He had grinned, stubbly chin just visible behind the lens he held up to his eye. There was a click, a flash of light, a blank square protruding from the camera like a glossy tongue.

"Isn't that neat?" Hank said, shaking the photo between his fingers. "I don't know why, but I find a lot of pleasure in little things like this." He handed me the picture. I watched color bleed onto the white square. My black hoodie and shoulder-length hair. A silver piercing shining from the side of my lower lip. The gaunt circles under my closed eyes, dark from lack of sleep.

After Butch returned from the hospital alone, he didn't come out of their motorhome again for days. From the Airstream window, I watched a stream of neighbors drop off cards and flowers and hot meals on his picnic table. Sometimes at night I could hear muffled sobs through the thin walls as I lay on the foldout couch, squinting at the tiny picture Hank had taken of me, trying hard to preserve the memory of what he had looked like that day on the other side of the camera.

Hank had been my neighbor, my friend. Now he was gone. I knew Butch and Hank took medications to manage their HIV, but I didn't understand how or why the disease could take him so suddenly. I'd read about the AIDS crisis, how the virus had decimated gay populations across the country and the world. My parents had told me devastating stories about friends, and friends of friends, who'd died during the initial waves of the pandemic in the '80s and early '90s. But HIV was supposed to be a survivable condition now. Hank had been generous and compassionate, a loving partner to Butch and a good neighbor. Unlike so many of the other men I knew in Cactus Country, Hank wasn't an alcoholic. He wasn't violent. He didn't own a gun. And still, the desert had taken him. The cosmic unfairness of his loss felt too enormous to express, a chasm between the thoughts I had and my inability to speak them aloud that made my bones ache.

IN THE SLOW year since my breakup with Avery, I'd started making progress in the weekly therapy sessions my school counselor had referred me to. I could eat without feeling sick again. I could pay attention in my classes. I could do my homework. But I still couldn't talk about what happened that night in Avery's bedroom. Every time I tried, the words became tangled and knotted in my throat. I didn't know how to describe it, what words to use or where to begin. So instead, I recounted everything that had come before and after to my therapist, an unfailingly upbeat woman with a head of tight curls that bounced when she walked. I told her about the shoplifting. The weed we smoked. The wine we drank. The blackness and stars. How I'd thrown up the next morning, shaking like I would never stop. She listened intently, leaning forward in her seat with two fingers of her slim hand pressed against one cheek.

"It sounds like you were raped," she said, and I flinched as though the word were a raised fist. I shook my head no, that this didn't feel like the right word. To me, rape was what strange men did to young girls in dark alleyways. Rape was a violent altercation between victim and aggressor, an act involving a struggle, an attempted escape. One had to resist, to scream, to cry out for help. I continued shaking my head, lips tight until my therapist changed the subject.

"Let's take a break from this," she said. "How else are things going?"

AT HOME IN Cactus Country, death permeated the air, made it thick with grief. Even the most casual conversations seemed to circle back to the grisly circumstances of our neighbors' demise. Partners and friends mourned them with funeral services in the recreation hall and memorials out in the desert. Some tried to make light of it, joking the park was cursed, calling it "Cactus Cemetery," and I began to believe them. Intrusive images of my neighbors' final moments pervaded my thoughts, keeping me awake late into the night. I couldn't get their faces out of my head, imagining their ghosts walking along the dark roads outside my window, their souls doomed to wander the desert after such violent departures from the world of the living.

I slept restlessly, haunted by recurring dreams about running as far away from Cactus Country, from its curse, as I could. But in these dreams, no matter how fast I ran, something always prevented me from leaving the park. A thick wall of saguaro cacti would stretch from the ground into the sky, impossible to climb or penetrate. Other times, my own legs weighed me down, each step like trudging through waist-deep sand. I'd wake in a sweaty panic, feeling that same dark presence I'd feared during the time of the javelina lurking just outside the Airstream window. The fates of these men, my neighbors, seemed prophetic, warning of what was to come. The specters of depression, disability, alcoholism, addiction, chronic illness, anger, and poverty lived on in almost everyone I knew. Any one of us could be the next to succumb to their pull.

WITH A CLOSET full of band t-shirts and a thick black beard framing his pudgy face, Roger looked much younger than forty years old. His battered Southwind motorhome was packed with toys—a seventy-two-inch flatscreen TV, a surround sound speaker system, an Xbox and all the latest video games. Roger drove a sleek black Pontiac convertible with custom subwoofers that took up the entire backseat. He blared heavy metal albums at full volume with the top down, turning heads and drawing derision from the neighbors every time he cruised through Cactus Country.

But while Roger might have acted like a rock star, he had a tragic backstory. His left arm had been ripped open in a motorcycle accident years before. The accident effectively ended his career as a drummer in a local band, dashing his dreams of musical fame and fortune. His injury also meant he couldn't reach higher than his shoulder, or lift anything heavier than a TV remote.

Roger paid me five dollars an hour to help him clean and organize his motorhome on the weekends. I liked having a new job to do in addition to my usual dog walking, another distraction from the grief and the sleepless nights. Roger had moved into the park after our neighbors' deaths, so he was one of the few who didn't have much to say about them. I threaded stereo wires around the ceiling like Christmas lights, plugging things in and testing equipment while he sat back on the couch with his fat Dalmatian, Misty, and told long stories about the good old days in the band.

"We could've been big time," Roger said, wincing as he rubbed the bicep scars on his bad arm. "We were amazing. Until, well, you know." I nodded and he smiled, appreciative of the commiseration.

Roger didn't have a job. He never said where his money came from, but he seemed to have a lot of it, handing me a crisp twenty after only a couple hours of work. There was always something at Roger's place that required my attention and care. Supposedly, he paid me to look after the things he couldn't. But I had a feeling Roger might have been exaggerating his need for that kind of help. What he really needed, I thought, was a friend. And my company came cheap.

ONE SATURDAY AFTERNOON, while searching for an aux cable Roger said might be in the closet, I spied a small black case tucked away on a low shelf. Curious, I opened it to find a gleaming semiautomatic pistol and several rounds of ammunition. I froze. Lots of our neighbors kept guns in their trailers, but Roger didn't strike me as the Second Amendment type.

"Why do you have this, Roger?" I asked.

"For protection," he said, vaguely. He took the gun out of its case and offered it to me. I recoiled. I'd never liked guns and had become even more wary of them since the suicides. Nothing good ever seemed to come from passing a pistol around in a trailer park.

"It's not loaded," Roger said. "Look." He released the magazine from the bottom of the gun's grip, revealing three bullets nestled inside.

"Oh, shit," he said. "Hang on a second." He knocked the bullets loose into his hand, tossed them back into the case.

"Now it's safe," he said. I shook my head in disbelief.

"You almost handed me a loaded gun?"

He held it out again, but I still didn't want to hold it. I found the cable Roger needed in the back of the closet and tossed it to him, muttering something about having to get back to the Airstream for lunch. I didn't even wait for him to reach for his wallet.

MOM AND DAD knew I was seeing a therapist about my breakup with Avery, but they'd never been the kind of parents to ask too many prying questions. Dad continued to renovate and resell RVs despite the Bounder fire setback and had recently used some of the profits to buy a park model—a small trailer similar to a mobile home—from a neighbor. My parents moved from the Airstream into the park model in the hope that having some space to myself might help me process whatever I'd been going through. Though only a year ago there was nothing I'd wanted more than a room of my own, I found the solitude this new arrangement brought disquieting.

Now that family meals were prepared and eaten in the park model, the Airstream fridge became storage for the half-empty cases of beer our neighbors brought over for cookouts and left there. My parents never drank them. I knew they wouldn't be missed. The beer was thin and bitter, the way I guessed the water that collected in the dry riverbeds during monsoon season might taste. But I held my nose and drank them anyway, drifting off on the foldout couch with the TV on. If I drank quickly enough and fell asleep fast enough, I wouldn't have to be alone with the stories of the men who died, or what happened in Avery's room, or the tempting release of a blade sliding against my skin.

All my clothes had become tight and long-sleeved and dark. I didn't want to be touched, even for a haircut, and my hair grew long enough to hide behind. In the Airstream's kitchen sink, I dyed it with the blackest shades I could find. I pierced my lower lip, steel ring glinting like the end of a rattlesnake's tail as I gnashed it between my teeth. Gradually, I stopped binding my chest and correcting people on my pronouns. I stopped caring how others perceived my gender, or didn't; what happened to me next, or didn't. Mostly, I wanted to disappear. For the person inside my body to become no one and my gender to become nothing. But despite my efforts to be invisible, without actively cultivating an androgynous appearance I looked more feminine than I ever had before.

It wasn't long before my new gender presentation started attracting the attention of boys at City High. I accepted their invitations to hang out after school, sitting in the passenger seats of their shitty cars, laughing as they swerved dangerously around hairpin turns. We loitered outside empty buildings downtown, talking about everything and nothing as we traded cigarettes and tiny bottles of booze. Boys felt safe, a known quantity. I didn't say that, until recently, I'd been just like them. That, in some ways, I still was. Instead, I smiled when they told me I wasn't like other girls, which was much truer than they realized.

A few of them became my boyfriends, or something like it. They caught rides across town at all hours to help me drink the beer in the Airstream's fridge. I could feel their eyes wandering over my body when they thought I wasn't looking, tracing the length of my legs, the curve of my hips. I followed their gaze, trying to see myself how they did, to appreciate the feminine side of my body the way I might if it didn't belong to me. I didn't desire the boys so much as I desired their desire; I wanted to chart the dimensions of their erotic imagination, to map it inversely onto mine. When the boys asked to kiss me, and sometimes more, I always said yes.

AFTER THE GUN incident, I stopped coming around to Roger's place for a few weeks. I felt uneasy. Roger had never professed enthusiasm for guns or gun culture, the way a lot of boys and men in the park did. He never went to the shooting range or out hunting in the desert. I found it hard to believe he was really afraid someone might attack him in sleepy little Cactus Country, a trailer park miles away from town where nobody ever bothered to lock their doors. I worried about heading to his motorhome some morning to find that Roger had snapped, shooting the dog and then himself in some twisted interspecies murder-suicide.

Roger must have been wise to my discomfort, because he brought over a handwritten letter apologizing for trying to hand me a loaded weapon.

I watched him through the Airstream window as he awkwardly handed it to Dad. He stood like a nervous teenager, arm extended, eyes on his feet, brushing a big hand through his thick, chin-length beard.

"Can you tell her I'm really sorry?" Roger mumbled. Dad nodded, visibly biting his tongue to keep from laughing. I hadn't told him or anyone else about the gun or why I'd stopped going over to Roger's place. No one had asked. In Cactus Country's tight-knit community, kids were encouraged to be sympathetic to people like Roger. He was disabled and lonely. A little off, sure, but not dangerous. When Dad gave me the envelope, I opened it to find a note written on the inside of a sappy greeting card in loopy, childish letters.

I'm very sorry for being such an idiot, it read. *I promise to never do such a stupid thing ever again and I hope my behavior will not in any way change our friendship. Sincerely, Rog.*

"This is weird, right?" I asked, holding the card up for Dad to see.

"Oh, give him another chance," he advised. "You're making good money."

Dad had a point. I *was* making good money helping Roger—money I couldn't have earned otherwise. Work in Tucson was impossible to find for a teenager without wheels. I was saving up for my first car, and walking dogs after school wasn't bringing in the kind of cash I needed quickly enough to make any significant progress toward that goal. I stuffed the card back in its envelope, quietly deciding to accept Roger's apology and give working for him another shot.

ONE MORNING, AVERY suddenly reappeared downtown. The sight of her casually walking with her friends—as though she'd been there all along—rendered me mute, my mind blank, hands shaking. Avery saw me from across the street and smiled, waved. My limbs went cold. She started toward me, and I pressed myself into the crowd of students heading for City High. I ducked into the school counselor's nook, breathing hard. The counselor was out, but I peeked from her window through the curtain, watching Avery look for me, like a perverse game of hide and seek. I watched until she gave up and walked away, my breath held tight in my chest like a fist.

Avery tried approaching me on the street several more times that week. Whenever I heard her voice, I turned and walked in the opposite direction. As in my dreams about running from Cactus Country, it didn't matter where I was going, so long as it was away from her. I begged my parents to pick me up from school so I wouldn't have to take the bus. On days this was impossible, I sat in the farthest open seat from Avery's, surrounded by strangers, refusing to turn around and meet her gaze, knowing her eyes would be searching for mine. I could feel she wanted something from me, something more than what she had already taken, and I had nothing left to give.

To keep my mind occupied on the bus, I would search for a guy—any guy—walking on the sidewalk at stoplights. I'd catch his eye through the window and nod at him the way I'd learned as a boy to acknowledge other men. The first time I did this had been from force of habit. But instead of returning the nod, the man's face had broken into a wide smile. He lifted his chin toward me, tipped the rim of his ballcap. The man seemed to walk a little straighter, his chest up, a renewed energy to his gait. Bewildered, I tried nodding at another man at the next light. Again, he smiled at me, his stoic demeanor melting like ice in the sun.

From a feminine body, the nod, it seemed, had an entirely different effect—even a kind of strange power. One tilt of the head and these men thought I was flirting with them. Maybe I was. It was quietly thrilling to elicit such a strong reaction in them from a safe distance. To study it and then, just as quickly, speed away without having to face the consequences of whatever the men might expect to happen next.

When nodding at guys on the street wasn't distracting enough, I made bets with myself about how many cars would be parked that day at the Party House, a store on 22nd Street advertising DVD rentals and something called an "adult arcade." Once or twice, I'd even glimpsed a man slipping in through the door as my bus rushed passed. I was endlessly curious about the Party House and the alluring mystery of what it held inside, but its unassuming brick exterior offered frustratingly few clues. Was the Party House dark and dingy, I wondered, a dungeon lit by lava lamps and glowsticks? Or maybe it was an exclusive, members-only club with a DJ and live music? I imagined a dance floor with an adjacent bar, a dedicated bouncer at the front door. Pressing my face against the window, I wanted to know what kind of people spent their time in the Party House, and what drew them there.

THAT WEEKEND, ROGER paid me double to help move some boxes from his father's house in Tucson to his motorhome in Cactus Country. Roger's dad, a shriveled old man wearing a bathrobe and compression socks, spent the entire visit in a recliner, making crude remarks about "jailbait" under his breath. There really wasn't much to move—just some speakers and boxes of assorted electronics, a crate of record albums, a few loose cassette tapes. Nothing, I thought, that Roger couldn't have handled himself. But he seemed to be enjoying my company, and I appreciated any excuse to get out of the park for a few hours.

Roger blasted music in the Pontiac with the top down and drove way too fast down a neighborhood street with his aviator sunglasses on, hot wind blowing through our hair. We rolled up next to the Party House, waiting at the stoplight for our turn to pull back onto 22nd Street and head home.

"Have you ever been in there?" I asked, gesturing toward the building with my thumb.

"What, the porn shop?" he said, smirking. "Sure. Lots of times."

"What's it like inside?" I asked. "I mean, is it dark?"

Roger looked at me, his eyebrows crooked over his sunglasses. I pictured an amused expression under them.

"Do you want to see for yourself?" he asked, trying to call my bluff.

"You're serious?" I said. "Cause I'm totally serious. I'll go if you go." Roger paused.

"Okay, let's try it," he said, finally. "Worst they can do is kick us out."

He pulled into the parking lot. A prominent sign screamed NO MINORS in bolded red letters. I held my breath as we stepped across the threshold into a blast of cold air. The bright overhead fluorescent lights imbued our skin with a sickly electric glow. From behind the counter, a wiry man with bushy white hair shot me a suspicious glance. I avoided eye contact, and he didn't ask for my ID. A customer in an ill-fitting business suit perused the rows of VHS tapes and DVDs for rent, holding the back of each case close to his glasses to read them. The Party House was much quieter than I expected. There were no women in the store, except those plastered naked in unlikely poses on posters and in display cases. No flashing strobe lights or costumed daytime revelers. No music, just the humming of an A/C unit and some muffled moans coming from behind a theater curtain in the back of the shop.

"You definitely don't want to go back there," Roger said, noticing the direction of my gaze. I turned my attention to an alcove left of the entrance, a room of floor-to-ceiling toys in every shape, size, color, and texture. The collection was overwhelming, a shock of copious, synthetic sex. Above it all, an enormous purple dildo jutted from the wall like a hunting trophy.

"That can't be real," I whispered. "Is that real?"

"Oh, I think it's real all right," Roger laughed. He seemed strangely at ease in the Party House, moving with a fluidity and confidence I'd never seen in him in Cactus Country. He bounced on his toes, giggling as he pointed at some of the more outlandish toys on the wall.

"Can you guess what this is for?" he asked, gesturing to what looked like a glittery, hot-pink feather duster. I shook my head, realizing this might be the first time in our friendship that Roger felt like he had something to teach me. Most of the time, I thought of him as more or less another teenager, an equal. But here, his apparent sexual knowledge and experience starkly exposed the more than twenty years between us—how, though he looked and acted like one, Roger wasn't really a kid.

AVERY KNEW I was avoiding her. She cried whenever I walked within earshot, screaming after me in the street, sobbing as her friends rushed to comfort her. Avery told anyone who would listen that our relationship ended because I'd cheated on her with one of the boys I was seeing. Downtown Tucson was like a small town. The rumors flew quickly, whispers following me through the hallways of City High as I trudged to class, my head down, headphones in my ears, hands in my pockets. A few girls tried to intervene on Avery's behalf, imploring me to give her another chance.

"She's going to kill herself if you don't talk to her," one hissed at me from behind a pre-calculus book. "You owe her that, at least." I didn't answer her, staring through the nonsensical problems our teacher had scrawled across the whiteboard with my head in my hands. Even if I'd wanted to, I couldn't have brought myself to speak to Avery any more than I could have solved these equations. Nobody knew the truth about what happened, and there was nothing I could do to change that. From my years living in Cactus Country, I knew even the most salacious stories died out in time, as people ran out of ways to talk about them. For now, I tried not to care what Avery told other kids about me. As my therapist had once said, she couldn't hurt me anymore if I didn't give her a way in.

EMBOLDENED BY OUR excursion to the Party House, Roger began exploring new ways to test the elasticity of our friendship. One Saturday, I knelt on the floor in his motorhome, attempting to alphabetize the haphazard stacks of CDs surrounding me. Roger sat at his kitchen table with Misty asleep at his feet, sorting through a massive pile of unopened mail.

"So, who was that guy at your trailer last night?" Roger asked in what he must have thought was a casual tone. I dismissed his question, shrugging my shoulders up to my ears. Roger tried again.

"No, but seriously, was he like your boyfriend or something?" he said. "I've never seen him around before."

"I don't know," I said, looking up from the CDs. "Why do you care?"

"I don't, it's just—you must be pretty loose if you let random guys come over," he said. "I mean, if he's not even your boyfriend or anything."

"Shut the fuck up, Roger," I said. He rolled his eyes.

"Guess it must be that time of the month," he muttered. Anger rose hot in my chest, flickering like a freshly lit match. Without a word, I threw the CDs in my hands onto the floor and stormed out, slamming the door of his Southwind behind me.

Roger slipped a card under the Airstream door the next morning. The note apologized for his crassness, but said that he'd only been concerned for my safety. He hoped we could still be friends. Though I didn't buy this explanation, I returned the next Saturday on the explicit condition that he stop asking me about boys. But Roger always seemed to find new ways to make me uncomfortable, with probing questions about my bra size or speculative remarks about how far I'd probably gone in bed.

With each new incident I kept my distance a few days longer, wondering all the while if I was being unreasonable. After all, he'd never asked me on a date or tried to kiss me. I couldn't be sure where to draw the line, and I was so damn close to having enough cash to buy a car. Before long, I'd rationalize myself back into Roger's motorhome again, assisting him with a never-ending laundry list of tasks until his next remark, when the cycle would continue.

During our breaks, I'd find letters from Roger stuffed into the doorjamb of the Airstream or pinned onto the windshield of the family van. Notes with candy taped to the outside or written in alternating colored pencil, each letter of every word a different shade of the rainbow. I opened them to lengthy, stream of consciousness–style lamentations about his "stupid, idiotic" behavior and how his injury kept him from becoming the rich, famous drummer he was supposed to be. They insisted Roger only wanted to be a good friend to me. That he was trying so hard. That he was sorry.

Roger's letters came to an abrupt end the day I saw him drinking a beer with a girl at his campsite, the two of them leaning against the hood of his Pontiac. She was about a year older than me, slender with dyed-black hair, a spiked dog collar, fishnet stockings, and a tight band t-shirt.

"Meet my new girlfriend," Roger called. I started to laugh, but stopped when I saw her fingers laced with his. She half-waved with her free hand, a bottle cap between her teeth. Roger had drawn the line for me. His relationship quickly became the latest gossip among the neighbors, eclipsing any lingering talk about the park curse. Some insisted they'd always had a feeling Roger was dangerous, even predatory. Others just shrugged, said the girl was probably in it for his money. So long as she was eighteen—or "legal," as they called her—it wasn't any of their business what Roger did in the privacy of his bedroom.

"He never tried anything with you, did he?" neighbors asked me, over and over. There was a lot I could tell them about Roger: about our trip to the Party House, his many crude comments and handwritten apology notes. But all my life I'd seen how stories like these lost their meanings around the picnic tables, the nuance stripped with each retelling the way a body decayed in the desert, sun-dried and picked clean until all that remained was a pile of parched bones in the sand. The neighbors might blame me for Roger's advances, or else begin to imagine I'd welcomed his attention, even led him on. I shook my head, not wanting to become the subject of their next round of rumors.

ABOUT A MONTH after her reappearance, Avery once more vanished like a ghost. I never saw her again and, in time, this is what she became to me. Almost overnight, the rumors following me disappeared, everyone moving on to other gossip, as I knew they would. The only external reminder now of what had happened were the scarring lines on my skin, gradually fading from red to pink to the faintest white. I bought a dark green 1997 Saturn coupe with the money I'd saved working for Roger and drove myself to school instead of taking the Sun Tran. I applied for jobs and landed a part-time position at a thrift store in town. I spent more and more time away from home, staying with friends who lived in Tucson, closer to City High. When I was in the park, I mostly ignored Roger, returning the occasional wave as he walked by with Misty.

ONE NIGHT, ROGER approached me on the Cactus Country playground to say that he'd just broken up with his girlfriend. They'd been fighting all day, he explained. Roger took her to dinner, then to a concert venue to meet up with a group of her girlfriends. She said something disparaging about his penis in front of them, and they laughed. Then he spat on her.

"You *spat* on her?" I asked from my place on the swing. Roger leaned against the monkey bars, arms folded, shaking his head.

"That's all I could think to do," he said.

"Jesus, Roger," I said. "Don't you see how that's wrong?" Roger didn't try to argue with me. He stared at his shoes a minute before turning around and lumbering back to his motorhome, hands in his pockets, his body slow like a sigh.

Later that week, Roger moved out of Cactus Country and onto his father's property in Tucson. Most of the neighbors seemed to forget about him until almost a year later, when I heard the latest story going around the picnic tables. Roger had shot himself. Nobody knew exactly why he did it. In the final months of his life, he'd been deep in debt. Bill collectors forced him to relinquish his assets—the Southwind, the Pontiac, the seventy-two-inch TV, the surround sound speaker system, even the Xbox. But the rumor was that his dog, Misty, had died of old age. That Roger had buried her, alone, in the overgrown backyard at his father's house, where I'd once helped him move some boxes. He drove the shovel into a pile of freshly dug earth under the yard's lone ironwood tree, went into his childhood home, and didn't come out again. Apparently he left a note, though I never found out what it said.

DISPATCHES

"WHAT DO YOU WANT TO do with yourself, Zoë?" she asked, sweeping her brown hair to one side of her face. Lucinda was a local NPR journalist volunteering with City High School's radio program, helping me get my recorded audio essays to a place she called "radio-ready." That day, Lucinda and I worked on a short spoken diary I'd written reflecting on the trauma of the previous year. With the help of my therapist, I hadn't hurt myself in more than six months before recording it, a fact I was proud of. Lucinda thought the story had potential to get picked up by a radio station, but I was just glad to have someone to share it with.

Lucinda had a comforting way of focusing her keen, dark eyes completely on you, nodding with a small half-lipped smile as you spoke like you were sharing something of great personal interest to her. I looked up to the ceiling. Adults seemed to ask me versions of this question—who did I want to become?—all the time. But I was never sure what to tell them. Now a high school senior, I still had trouble picturing myself as an adult: where the person I would grow into might go after graduation, or what they might do once they got there. I thought back to a conversation with a friend from earlier in the day.

"Hey, so whatever happened with that whole androgyny thing?" she'd asked, a piece of hard candy clicking behind her teeth. I shrugged, tapping my pencil against the desk. In the past year, I'd fallen into an uneasy femininity as a girl who didn't feel much like a girl. But even if I cut my hair short again, traded in my new tight clothes for baggier ones and snapped my binder back on, my voice was now as soft as my body had become, with strangers forever asking me to *please speak up, Miss*. I didn't want to try to pass as androgynous anymore, because trying and failing felt worse than giving up, worse than letting people see whatever they wanted to see in me. So whenever anyone asked about my gender now, I kept the conversation light.

"I only tell people I'm androgynous when I need to get out of things I don't want to do," I said. In perfect comedic timing, an assistant teacher approached us with fliers promoting an afterschool Grrls Literary Activists workshop.

"Oh, I'm sorry," I said. "I can't go. I'm not a girl." My friend laughed, candy dancing on her tongue. The teacher insisted I would still be welcome. I accepted a flyer from her, though I wouldn't have been caught dead at a grrls workshop, however cool "literary activism" might've sounded. Over the years in Cactus Country, I'd picked up on the casual misogyny men espoused around the picnic tables, admonishing us boys not to throw, fight, or cry like girls. I still struggled to understand how anyone could take pride in a gender so often perceived as less strong, courageous, intelligent, and capable than another, even when it wasn't true.

I returned to Lucinda's question—*what did I want to do with myself*—aware she was still looking at me, patiently waiting for an answer.

In addition to working part time at the thrift store after school and walking the neighbors' dogs on weekends, I did some babysitting in Cactus Country to make a little extra cash. Not just for older kids like Aiden, but also babies and toddlers. I loved tending to their bumped heads and scraped knees, and reading stories to them from picture books. On the park's playground, I pushed them on the swing set and helped them across the monkey bars, cheering when they learned to do it themselves. The responsibility of their care gave me a focus I found calming, centering. On babysitting days, I could forget about my body, and my trauma, and my desire to leave the park behind; all that mattered for those hours was being present with the children, making sure they were happy and safe.

"I don't really know," I said. "But I like kids. Maybe I could be a teacher one day." Lucinda thought about this for a minute, tapping a finger to her cheek.

"You know, my friend's kids go to this amazing preschool," she said. "I think they're looking for community volunteers. Any chance you'd be interested in something like that?"

"Definitely!" I said, grinning. Lucinda nodded, the corner of her lip turning up into her signature smile.

"I'll look into it," she said.

MY FIRST MORNING at Second Street School, I arrived thirty minutes early to find the yard already full of children. A group of curious three-year-olds stalked a pair of chickens pecking for grubs in the community garden. The four-year-olds sped around a circular path on tricycles while the kindergartners used miniature shovels and a hose to dig a muddy river for the sailboats they'd folded out of paper. A row of the youngest children raced down a hill, holding hands like a paper-doll chain. Kids crawled through tunnels and climbed on top of hay bales and leapt from tree stumps. They screamed in delight as they chased each other around the schoolyard, laughing, calling, singing. Never before had I felt so calm with so much activity buzzing around me.

I quickly grew to like the pace and structure of the days at Second Street, with designated times for snacking and reading and resting. Even their crises felt manageable in their own way—a heated disagreement over a particular toy, a cry after saying goodbye to a parent at morning drop-off, a scraped elbow from tripping on a run down the hill. Despite my fondness for the work, though, caretaking was the most challenging job I'd ever had. A good teacher needed to be vigilant, to keep their attention on the comings and goings of multiple children in the background without losing focus on the child in front of them. By afternoon pick-up, I felt even more exhausted than I had after a long day washing windows or shoveling after horses in the heat. But working with children gave me a sense of purpose, and I wanted to do it well.

My new co-teachers were glad to help me learn. Following their examples, I learned to speak Second Street's shared pedagogical language, to cultivate the child-centered sensibility that guided everything we did, from the daily activities we planned to the spontaneous fun a child's question might inspire. But my co-teachers also taught me how to move by feel. Knowing when to stand back and let kids figure out how to solve a problem on their own was a skill, I discovered, as important as choosing the right moment to intervene. Teachers at Second Street worked in teams of two, and I got to learn from all of them, spending most of my time supporting each classroom on an as-needed basis—thirty minutes at snack time here, a couple hours on the playground there—until I knew the names and personalities of every teacher and child in the school.

My co-teachers also taught me to appreciate femininity in ways I'd never experienced before. Everyone on staff was female, and the gentle energy at Second Street couldn't have been more different from the rough shows of masculinity I'd grown up with in Cactus Country. During monthly team meetings, we sat together in a circle on the floor, sharing a meal from a tray of assorted cheeses, fruit, and wine. Our director, a fiercely ambitious woman named Jenny Douglas, would tap a resounding gong to begin the meeting, where we practiced deep-breathing exercises and yoga poses and selected fortune cards to ruminate over before discussing the month's announcements, initiatives, curricula, and concerns. When these conversations became emotional, warmth and support were freely given—a sympathetic smile, the light touch of a hand. More than once, one of the teachers would break into unexpected tears, and I would find myself crying with them. The nuances of good caregiving—to care and accept care in return—were still new to me, but I wanted to learn, and this was enough for the women to accept me into their fold, to call me their co-teacher.

The children, for their part, were curious about me, their new volunteer student-teacher. With a metal ring through my pierced lip, my dyed-black shoulder-length hair, my band t-shirts and homemade cut-off shorts, I didn't embody the same kind of femininity their other teachers did. The adults at Second Street all regarded me as another woman, and no one had ever hesitated over my pronouns or called my gender into question. Somehow, though, the children were not convinced.

"Are you a boy or a girl?" they asked me again and again, no matter what answer I gave them, all of us making a game of the question. I never knew how to explain my complicated relationship with my gender identity to adults, let alone in a way kids might understand. So instead I'd shrug good-naturedly, smile at them the way Lucinda had smiled at me.

"Maybe it's not important," I would say, and for a moment the answer would actually feel that simple: that maybe how I felt today didn't mean I had to feel the same way tomorrow. That I would be the same teacher, the same person, whether I looked like a woman, or a man, or somewhere in between. That this uncertainty itself, this fluidity, could be part of me even if I didn't yet know what to call it. But just as quickly the moment would pass, the children moving on from their inquiries to play, and the question of my gender would go back to feeling as unanswerable as ever.

"YOU NEED TO look at this," Mom said, her eyes wide at the piece of paper in her hands. I had just returned to Cactus Country from volunteering at Second Street, and was helping prepare eggs and toast for lunch in the park model when Dad brought in the mail. She handed me the letter. A congratulations. I had been accepted to the University of Arizona—and there was more. *"We at the Arizona Assurance Program are pleased to inform you . . ."*

"I don't understand," I said, holding up the letter. "What does this mean?"

"It's a scholarship," Mom said, her voice hushed in an awed whisper. "They want to pay for your tuition, all four years." I glanced back down at the paper, fighting a strange wave of disappointment. The University of Arizona was the one college I'd applied to, and only because it had been a requirement for graduating City High seniors. I never considered the possibility I might actually get in, let alone receive any kind of financial aid to go.

Soon I would be turning eighteen, with graduation just a few months away. Second Street's director, Jenny, had offered me a paid position at the school for next year. A few of my co-teachers were students pursuing early childhood education degrees, and in our meeting, Jenny had praised my talent and enthusiasm for the field, suggesting I join them to become qualified as a lead teacher. I held Jenny's opinion in high esteem, but I didn't feel ready to take on that kind of responsibility. Maybe I would go to Pima, the local community college, in a year or two. For now, I just wanted to teach at Second Street, the place I felt most at peace, while I sorted out the next stage of my life. The university, with all of its big unknowns, didn't fit into the plan.

"I don't want to go," I said, trying to stuff the letter and its generous offer back into the envelope, but Mom persisted. This was the opportunity of a lifetime. One too good to pass up.

"You're going to that school," she said sternly, her hands on her hips. I looked to Dad.

"She's right, Zo," he said from his place on the couch. "Hell, it's a free college education. You'd have to be stupid to throw that away." I sighed, reading over the letter again.

Few of my friends, whether at City High or in Cactus Country, planned to attend even community college next year, let alone a school prestigious enough to call itself a university. They wrote off higher education as too expensive, a waste of time and money when you could be out working. We all knew the teachers and guidance counselors who persuaded us to apply were full of shit; college couldn't prepare you for real life in a place like Tucson. I'd visited UA's campus once or twice on school field trips and had joined my friends in making fun of the students kicking hacky sacks back and forth on the mall and running into one another in the rush to their next class. They seemed to belong to a different world than us, one more like the Rita Ranch kids of my childhood had inhabited.

Encouraging me to join that world seemed to contradict what Dad had always told me about retaining my imagination and vision, a sense of life's rich possibilities. But he had also been firm about the necessity of my education, from shaking his head on the nights I begged to be homeschooled to enrolling me in City High when my grades and morale suffered at Empire. Somehow, he'd seemed to know a day like this one might come. I folded the letter into my back pocket. My parents were right. This would likely be my only chance to go to college, even if I didn't yet feel I had a good reason to be there. My heart heavy with dread, I agreed to attend the University of Arizona in the fall.

OVER THE SUMMER before my first year at UA, I reconnected with Sage through social media. She sent a message inviting me back to her place in Rita Ranch. On the drive over, I wondered how it might feel to hang out with her again after all this time apart. Whether I would experience the same seasick rush of giddy terror that I'd associated with Sage's house since our middle school sleepovers.

When she answered the door, Sage looked more or less exactly as I remembered her, only taller. She still had that same long hair, those same wayfarer-style glasses. The resemblance to her younger self was so uncanny I worried, momentarily, that I might still have feelings for her. But as we grabbed sodas from the kitchen and settled into her bedroom to chat, the feeling quickly passed. We sat on the floor, catching each other up on the last five years of our lives and reminiscing about old times, both of us dancing around the pricklier aspects of our friendship, just as we always had.

"Your house looks different than I remember," I said.

"That's because it *is* different," Sage said. "We moved!" That I'd thought her old house and this new one were the same place was a testament to the ubiquity of Rita Ranch's signature beige stucco exteriors.

"Anyway, you look different, too!" she exclaimed. "Almost like a girl."

"Thanks a lot," I said, grinning. Sage cackled, revealing a set of straight, unbraced teeth. "It's good to see you again."

"I'm actually surprised we didn't hang out sooner," she said. "Like in high school, I mean."

"Yeah, Empire was just closer to Cactus Country," I said, staring down at the carpet. "And then I transferred to City High, so we probably wouldn't have seen each other much anyway." We sipped our sodas, an awkward pause hanging between us.

"Listen," she said. "About all that. I know I wasn't always a good friend to you. Like the end of our last year at Desert Sky . . ."

My face grew hot as I tugged at the laces on my high-top sneakers. I never thought Sage had a clue how I'd felt at the awards ceremony. In retrospect, though, it was probably obvious. I had always been dreaming up grand romantic gestures to show Sage what she meant to me, like standing up for us when we'd been falsely accused by the bully box. Back then I would have done anything to be the boy Sage wanted to kiss in front of a crowd. But in the end, I wasn't the one she chose.

"And—Zoë?" I looked up, met her eyes.

"I'm sorry," she said. "I hope we can start over." I brushed it off, said it was okay. I'd learned a few things about reconnecting with people from living in Cactus Country, where friends came and went with the seasons. Certain friendships, even after lying dormant for a year or two, seemed to pick up right where they left off. Other times, a different way of relating to each other would emerge from the remnants of the old, like new growth budding from a felled cactus stalk. Just as I was no longer the boy Sage had known in middle school, she had grown into a woman who was almost nothing like the girl I remembered.

When we were kids, Sage had been a tomboy who was vocal about her ever-changing obsessions, from her favorite fanfiction series to her latest crush at school. By contrast, the older Sage was quieter and more subdued. She wore makeup on nights out and had a wardrobe of new, more feminine clothes: lacey skirts and short shorts and frilly button-ups. I'd experimented with skirts on and off during high school, but I had trouble with the nuanced mannerisms—crossing your legs when sitting on a chair, legs to the side when sitting on the ground, checking, always checking, that the back wasn't riding up—that went along with a garment seemingly designed to embarrass the wearer. I felt certain I would never be comfortable wearing a dress in the effortless way some of my co-teachers at Second Street seemed to.

Sage took on my fashion reticence as her personal project, pushing me to try out as many feminine styles as she could think of, from modeling outfits in her closet to shopping for new clothes together. The novelty of seeing me dressed as a woman never seemed to wear off.

"Oh my god, you'd be so pretty in this," she insisted, stuffing the garments she'd picked out under the dressing room door. "C'mon, just try it and see how you feel." I humored her. Most of Sage's clothing choices made me feel overdressed, like I was wearing a costume, but occasionally I appreciated her vision: the flattering silhouette of a tight pair of "boyfriend" jeans, the hang of a high-cropped sweatshirt I otherwise would've never thought to try on my own.

While I still looked back wistfully on the easy companionship I'd shared with the Cactus Country boys, my new friendship with Sage helped me recognize how lonely I'd sometimes felt in boyhood, too. How we boys had displayed our affection for one another through the limited emotional outlets of play fighting or good-natured ribbing. A firm slap on the back, a sharp knuckle to the chin, our love just one or two beats removed from the violence of the adult masculinities we emulated. I'd never opened up to my guy friends the way I could with Sage.

The girl I'd found inscrutable in boyhood had, it turned out, grown into one of the easiest people for me to talk to. So long as we didn't delve too deeply into the past, our conversations flowed like water in a parched riverbed. Whenever I slept over now, we'd throw on a rented movie and toss popcorn into each other's mouths, chatting about everything from our mutual anxiety about menstrual cups to the guys we were currently crushing on.

Sometimes on weekends we'd drive to house parties around Sage's neighborhood as each other's "date"—an unspoken but ironic twist on our childhood dynamic—so the boys wouldn't hit on us as much. I never got over how surreal it felt to see the kids I remembered from Desert Sky suddenly all grown up, their cheeks thick with stubble and bodies covered in tattoos. They drank warm beers, sucking smoke from homemade gravity bongs and swallowing bright tablets of ecstasy.

Sage and I watched them play drinking games into the early morning, regaling us and each other with all their big plans for the future, showing off their new school colors with pride. They talked about the majors they'd already declared, the internships and specialty programs they'd already applied to. I listened politely, feeling stupid that I didn't understand what these words meant but too afraid of reminding the Rita Ranch kids where I'd come from to ask. Whenever anyone asked what I was studying in the fall, I just shrugged, taking a deep drink as though the answer might be at the bottom of my cup.

THAT AUGUST, I circled Old Main on the University of Arizona campus, searching in vain for my next class. I clutched my backpack straps, unable to shake the uncanny feeling that there must have been some mistake—that, any minute, an admissions officer would leap out from behind one of the giant agave plants in the cactus garden and announce that I hadn't actually been accepted into the school after all. I didn't recognize anyone on campus and was surprised to learn that many of the other students in my classes came from California. They'd chosen UA because out-of-state tuition here was cheaper than in-state tuition in the wealthy cities they'd grown up. Almost nobody I knew in Tucson outside of Rita Ranch could afford to go to the university, and certainly none of my high school friends.

I'd never felt more alone anywhere than during that first year at UA. Neither Mom or Dad had a college degree. They didn't know much about navigating a university campus and struggled to help me when I had questions. I didn't understand how to register for classes on my own, or what other students meant when they asked what I was majoring in. I didn't know how to read a syllabus or what office hours were for. I didn't know how to find the campus resources available to me—where to go if I got sick, who to ask if I needed help with my coursework, or how to check out books from the school library. I wandered, adrift, on the university's vast campus, stumbling my way through a current of students from one class to the next, most of them so large the teachers never knew my name. Through it all, I couldn't shake the feeling that I didn't deserve to be here.

That I wasn't smart enough to study at a university. That everyone could see the evidence of the trailer park I'd grown up in on my face.

Still, I was determined to leave Cactus Country behind and understood, in my vague adolescent way, that a college education might allow me to do that. Jenny had been so excited when I told her I'd been accepted to UA on full scholarship. She and the other teachers celebrated me at that month's team meeting, raising their glasses as I flushed with warmth. I wasn't sure then whether I wanted to be a preschool teacher forever, but I knew I wanted to be as good at my job—at any job—as Jenny was at hers. When school felt too hard, when I wanted to give up, I thought about the chance she and the other teachers had taken on me at Second Street, their trust in me and faith that I would succeed. I thought about what Mom and Dad had said when I got my scholarship letter—*You'd have to be stupid to throw that away*—and resolved to stick with it, if only to prove to myself I could.

BY THE SPRING, I'd saved enough money to move out of Cactus Country and into a student apartment complex on the north side of town, a newly gentrifying area not far from the Catalina Foothills, where the wealthiest Tucsonans lived. I'd never been to this part of Tucson as a child. There were no Check Into Cash stores here, no broken windows or boarded-up shop fronts or even that much litter. Northside was a shopper's paradise with an expansive indoor mall, its entrance flanked with invasive species of palm trees. Big-box stores stretched into one another in vast strip malls as far as the eye could see, and every fast-food chain restaurant had its own drive-thru line of cars wrapped around the building at all hours of the day and night. If not for the landscaped cactus gardens and the sun's brutal heat on the short walk between the car and the overly air-conditioned stores, I might not have recognized the north side as Tucson at all.

I lived in a complex called Northpointe, but everyone I knew called it "knifepoint"—the dark joke a holdout from the years before the complex had hired onsite security and enacted a strict no-guns policy. Though Northpointe was safer now, apartment parties still raged every night of the week. Cheap alcohol abounded, and petty fights over drunken misunderstandings, romantic betrayals, and drug deals gone wrong were common. I didn't mind Northpointe's parties, or even its drama, much of which felt tame compared to what I'd seen in Cactus Country. The noise was a small price to pay for the proximity to Tucson's nightlife. Living in the park had meant driving a half hour or more to get anywhere farther than Rita Ranch. Now, I was minutes away from all kinds of midnight misadventures—from meeting up with my City High friends, to tracking down cases of beer for a party, to getting into whatever new shit was going down.

My friends met me at Northpointe for house parties every weekend night, drinking well into dawn the next day. We were eighteen, nineteen, twenty, and had nothing else to do. With high school behind us, we'd begun to make a game of watching each other slowly waste away, finding ourselves on drugs, or pregnant with unwanted babies, or stuck at dead-end jobs because work was hard to find and we took what we could get. Because, despite living close enough to see Tucson's gleaming monuments to economic progress on the horizon, we knew that they were not built in our names. That the coming waves of gentrification would drown the city we knew, and us along with it. Escape was not an option. Every kid we'd ever known who tried to leave Tucson eventually found their way back home, prodigal sons falling prey to the desert's pull. My friends and I stared down the flood, joking about how shitty it all was, how shitty we all were. About how much we wanted from life and how little we would actually get.

I got comfortable with this narrative and consoled myself with it whenever I felt overwhelmed by my new responsibilities. But even as I laughed along with my friends, we all knew my story would be different. At the University of Arizona, I had a chance to work toward something else, something better. Something that might allow me to leave Tucson, to become the one kid who did not return. The longer I stayed in school, the harder it became to relate to my high school friends, some of whom I suspected might be quietly resentful of my scholarship. Though I didn't feel any closer to answering Lucinda's question about what I wanted to do with my life, I came home to Northpointe in the evenings already counting down the hours until the next day, when I could return to work at Second Street and my classes at UA.

IN MY SOPHOMORE year at the university, I took a nonfiction writing workshop where I read essays by women writers like Joan Didion, Mary Ruefle, and Maggie Nelson. I loved the way these writers sought big truths about the world through the small details of everyday life—in the vibrations of the Hoover Dam, the cold prickle of snow against bare skin, and the sublime melancholia of the color blue. In the spirit of these works, I wrote a serious essay—my first—waxing philosophic about the vacuity of house parties, about drugs and the kids who did them, about feeling isolated from my old friends, about the vastness of the world and my uncertain place within it. I stayed up all night writing and brought copies to class the next day with bleary eyes.

Anxiety buzzed through my pen on the morning of my workshop as I sat silently at the table, listening to the group discuss my essay. I took copious notes of their observations, their praise, their suggestions and critique as a heated argument erupted about the significance of the essay's ending. Some insisted the final paragraphs should remain as they were, while others lobbied hard for a revision. I scribbled their comments furiously, trying not to miss a word. The arguing became so loud and contentious that our teacher, a graduate student named Daisy Pitkin, stepped in to regain control of the situation, pausing the workshop to guide the class through several deep breaths. I sat with my pen hovering over my notebook, awed. I had written something that stirred passion in other people. Something, it seemed, poignant and affecting and maybe even a little *good*. They'd fought for its integrity, and had to be calmed.

When the hour ended, I gathered the feedback letters from my classmates, holding the stack against my chest. I wandered from the classroom in a daze, pacing the halls of the Modern Languages building and thinking back to a different class I'd taken the previous semester, a survey course taught by the writer Ander Monson. While I'd been a passable student in his class at best, I remembered an offhand remark he'd made one afternoon, that his office door was always open if we ever wanted to talk about something we'd written.

Ander's office was down the hall. I sprinted there, my arms still full of papers. The door was indeed open. Ander sat inside, reading a book at his desk. He was a stocky man in his late thirties with sparse, wispy hair and a prominent forehead who resembled a wizard, or maybe a gnome. I knocked on the doorframe and he looked up, invited me in. Breathlessly, I explained about the workshop and the arguing and the passion.

"So—" I finished, holding out a copy of my essay. "Would you please read this and tell me what you think?" Ander nodded, accepting it. I leaned back in a low armchair as he read, glancing around at his overflowing floor-to-ceiling bookshelves. His desktop was hidden under messy stacks of papers, books, and toys—a Barbie makeup head, Spice Girls action figures, and, most bizarrely, a row of disembodied doll parts. Ander finished my essay in only a few minutes. He held the paper in one hand, glancing up at me. We stared silently across the desk at each other for a moment.

"It's okay," he said. Not unkindly or dismissively, but as though stating a simple fact. The essay was not good or bad, but a decent first attempt.

"It's okay?" I repeated, a little incredulously. What about the argument that broke out in my class? How upset and excited everyone seemed to get?

"Yeah," he said.

I took a breath. "Well," I said, "what can I do to make it better than okay?"

Ander glanced back down at the page and began to list a few preliminary thoughts as I grabbed a notebook. He flipped through my essay, pointing to specific scenes, character portrayals, and quotations, asking open-ended questions about each. As we talked, I wrote his suggestions down with my earlier notes from the workshop.

"You should bring me a revision sometime," he said, handing the essay back to me. "I'd like to see it." I thanked him and promised I would keep working at it.

I left Ander's office with a sense of elation. In my essay, I had the seed of something with potential. Something to work on, to get better at. From that afternoon on, I sunk hours into my writing practice every day after coming home from Second Street. I read the essay collections and memoirs my teachers recommended, studying them for what I learned to call "craft." I took every creative nonfiction class offered to undergraduate students—some of them twice—and attended office hours whenever my teachers held them to talk about how I could improve my essays. Writing became a welcome discipline in my drifting, unmoored life, the creative writing program a shining beacon amid an overwhelming university sea. I clung to it as one would a life raft. There was no letting go if I wanted to succeed. I would be a writer, or I would be no one at all.

WHENEVER I MADE the drive back to Cactus Country to visit my parents, I always stopped by Rita Ranch to catch up with Sage. While we still went on the occasional night out together, Sage preferred spending the evening in with fistfuls of sour candy and a horror movie. We'd stay up late, chatting about the people we were dating or wanted to date, swapping the latest Facebook gossip about the kids we'd gone to middle school with—the same ones who only two years ago had seemed so confident about their plans for the future. Some of them had since dropped out of college and moved back in with their parents, working retail by day and battling addiction by night. When we ran into them at house parties now, they never had much to talk about.

One night toward the end of my sophomore year at the university, Sage and I sat on opposite ends of the couch, watching a rented DVD—something about a contagion that turned infected people into bloodthirsty zombies. My fingers drummed distractedly against my knee. Earlier that day, I'd been to Ander's office with the promised revision of my essay. We'd met regularly for the last several months to discuss the possibility of a more formal mentorship centered around a manuscript project. Ander sat at his desk with the paperwork and asked if I had any questions for him. I thought for a moment.

"How did you get here?" I said. "I mean, how did you become a writing professor?"

"I learned to teach in grad school," he said, running two fingers over a new mustache. "I got my MFA. Then I published my first book and applied for teaching jobs." I considered this, training my eyes on the doll heads lining his desk.

"Why, is that something you're thinking about?" he asked.

"I don't know," I said. "Maybe." Until that moment, I hadn't considered what I might do with my degree, other than continue to write. Becoming a writing teacher sounded like the ideal manifestation of my two great passions, the first and only clear answer I'd ever had to the question of what I wanted to do with my life.

"If you're serious about teaching, you should consider graduate school," Ander said. "Happy to talk more about it sometime if you're interested." I nodded, and we moved on to the terms of the mentorship.

Ours had been a short talk, no more than a passing thought, really. But I couldn't get it out of my head. Graduate school would mean moving to a new state, a new city, the prospect as exciting as it was terrifying. The desert was what I knew best, and as often as I dreamed about leaving it, I couldn't imagine what life outside of Tucson might look like for me. Back in Sage's living room, I stared at the TV without really seeing it.

"If you could move away from this city," I asked, "where would you want to go?" Sage tapped a finger against her chin, eyes still locked on the screen. A swarm of zombies dragged a woman to the ground, feasting on her entrails as she screamed for help.

"I guess I wouldn't go anywhere," she said, finally.

"Haven't you ever wanted to leave?" I asked. Sage chewed thoughtfully on a gummy worm. Light from the TV beamed across her face as she turned to look at me.

"No, not really," she said. "Tucson is my home. I like it here."

Her answer shouldn't have surprised me. Even as a kid, Sage had always been a homebody who didn't like to leave Rita Ranch much, or for too long. When we were younger, I used to fall asleep to a fantasy about rescuing Sage like the heroic boys in the stories I wrote might do for one of their maidens—to sweep her off to a more prosperous land far away from her dark house and dreary desert town. Back then I never considered the possibility that she might not want—or need—that kind of saving. That she might be content right here, on her couch, with her parents and friends and life as it was.

The new version of our friendship operated under the assumption that we'd both grown into more-or-less straight women, a role that seemed to suit Sage, but that I couldn't quite pull off, no matter how many of her clothes I wore. I still didn't know what to call myself, how to reconcile the boy I'd been with the not-quite-feminine, not-quite-masculine person I had become. I'd spent years asking myself this question, tracing it from every angle within my reach, and felt sure its answer couldn't be here in Tucson. But I also had no reason to think I would find it anywhere else.

We returned our attention to the movie in time to watch the protagonist succumb to the virus, taking his wife down with him in one last bloody expression of rage. Sage covered her eyes with her hands and I laughed, gently poking fun at her squeamishness. We microwaved a bag of popcorn and settled back into the couch for another movie, another quiet evening in Rita Ranch like yesterday, like tomorrow, like now, like then, our pasts and futures stretching ahead and behind and around us as countless nights like this one had before, as many more would again.

BODY OF LIGHT

RHYS'S TATTOO WAS THICKLY OUTLINED in black, its striking detail covering the entire top of his shaved head. The last two people awake after a house party, we sat on the front porch, watching the sun come up over the distant mountain range. He bowed so I could trace my finger around the sly snake, mouth open to reveal a pair of sharp white fangs, saliva dripping from its forked tongue like the villain in a fairy tale. The snake's thirsty eyes and slender body curved toward its prey, a desert mouse, itself running toward the snake's tail, a chronic half step ahead. The snake would not catch the mouse. The mouse would not outwit the snake. The two spun together endlessly in a kind of eternal danse macabre.

When Rhys lifted his head, I asked him about the design, what it meant. He shrugged playfully, moved his lips closer to mine. Whispered, "Not everything has to mean something."

AN ASPIRING MUSIC producer, Rhys mixed hip-hop tracks from old record samples in his spare time. He was tall and beguiling, with a lean face and a set of long, gleaming teeth that contorted into something like a snarl when he laughed. His sunbeaten skin was covered in the stick-and-poke tattoos he'd given himself with a sewing needle and black ink collected from a ballpoint pen, contrasting the professional style of the snake and mouse circling his scalp. I loved running my hands over Rhys's tattoos, trying to decipher the stories he was adamant they didn't tell.

Since Avery, I'd been too guarded to date women, even those who I liked and felt reasonably certain might like me back. But I'd gone out with a few men since high school, mostly townies I met through mutual friends, and the occasional guy from my classes at the university. There was the straight-edge gamer who followed punk rock like a religion, the baby-faced cocaine dealer who got high on his own supply, the card-playing business major who spent too much time on red-pill forums. In each of these relationships, I'd tried and failed to play the role of the quiet, patient girlfriend, feeling too much like a footnote in someone else's fucked-up story. But Rhys had a feral quality I liked, a wayward streak that reminded me of the boys I'd grown up with in the desert—of the kind of man I might have once grown into.

We met in the summer at a party in downtown Tucson, a season so hot the asphalt can melt the soles of your shoes, each step threatening to grab hold and never let you go. The kind of heat that sparks wildfires. We talked all night and never stopped. Words seemed to come more easily talking to Rhys than they had with my previous partners. His disarming way of sharing vulnerable stories from a troubled childhood made me feel I could open up, too. He'd lay on his side, head cradled in his elbow as he told me about doing hard drugs too early and failing school until it was too late. In return, I told him stories about growing up in Cactus Country. About cutting my hair short and living as a boy, my unwelcome puberty and uneasy androgyny.

"And then one day," I said, "I just . . . stopped trying with all the gender stuff. I didn't feel like I was anything anymore. Or maybe it's more like I didn't *want* to be anything anymore."

"But then you went back to being a woman, right?" he asked.

"Yeah," I said. "Something like that, I guess." It felt strange to say I'd *gone back* to a gender I never really identified with in the first place. But I didn't know what else to call myself. No one had stumbled over my pronouns in years. Even in clothing designed for men, my body was unquestionably feminine. I had come to accept, even appreciate, having the kind of smooth, angular face I'd found attractive on the girls I crushed on, noticing men look at me the way I looked at women. Observing myself through their eyes, and liking what I saw. The implications of being seen this way weren't all new to me. But still, womanhood so often felt like the sudden gusts of desert wind that would occasionally burst through Cactus

Country, ripping awnings from trailers and branches from trees. Like a force of nature beyond my control, something I never felt quite ready for, whether I braced myself for it or not.

Rhys and I fell for each other in a week. Shared a bed within two. Split the rent just shy of six. In our new duplex, the stifling summer days seeped through the windows like a fog, lingering into the night. Cockroaches larger than human thumbs emerged from the kitchen sink and settled between our bedsheets, crawling over our legs as we slept. Winter evenings blew freezing winds under the front door. Our yard was littered with trash the wind brushed into the rows of prickly pears that served as our garden, chip bags and candy wrappers sticking to their needles like ornaments on the world's shittiest Christmas tree. The duplex was more a hovel than a home, but it was affordable and close enough for me to walk to school. We settled in, made it our own.

THAT WINTER, I took an intermediate creative nonfiction course. My professor, a tall, soft-spoken man named Fenton Johnson, drew a line across the board, labeling one end "self" and the other "world." The personal essay, he explained, fell somewhere in the middle of these two points, with other nonfiction modes—reportage, research essays, memoirs, diaries and journals—scattered out toward either end. The trick to a good personal essay was to record your experiences in service of something greater than yourself. To write about big things through the examination of something small—a dying moth, say, or a single piece of chalk.

He told us about the poet William Carlos Williams. The red wheelbarrow so much depended upon, and his sweet, cold, delicious plums. The belief that the abstract is always hiding in plain sight. In a good essay, Fenton said, ideas must be anchored to the speaker's tangible reality. Ideas, he said, cannot be conjured from an empty room. That semester we students would be tasked with finding things close to the self and connecting them to the big ideas of the world through our writing.

After class, I walked back to the duplex on 8th Street, across from Tucson High School. Rhys and I were just twenty, still too young to go out to the local dives, so we drank on our front porch, watching kids stream in and out of the school like the ants that paraded in little black lines over our kitchen countertop. He chain-smoked American Spirits as I read one of the books from the stack that served as my bedside table, mentally underlining the metaphors each writer employed. A migraine headache, a lost diamondback terrapin, a monstrous child. I wanted to understand the meaning of these things. To pick the symbols out of my daily life and write them for my professor in a way that felt like truth.

On my days off from Second Street School I'd pace back and forth through the doorways connecting the three rooms of our tiny abode—our three little boxcars—noting how the sun streaked across the linoleum floor in the kitchen and the number of steps it took to move from one end of the house to the other (forty-six). The way Rhys and I had organized the layout was all wrong. Our Craigslist couch sat in the back room where a bed was supposed to be. We'd stationed our estate-sale box spring and mattress in front of the fireplace in the room closest to the front porch. Our kitchen was devoted not to cooking, but to making music, the table covered with machines Rhys had picked up at pawn shops around town: MIDI controllers, turntables, and speakers, their thick black wires tangled like tails in a desert rat king.

"What do you think?" Rhys asked one afternoon, bare-chested and breathless from hours mixing music in the heat. His broad shoulders glistened with sweat as he gestured to the machines spread out on the table before him, beckoning me closer with an excited wave of his hand. I didn't know anything about making music, but I stopped pacing to press his damp headphone pads against my ears and listen to the rhythm of the back beat, the screaming skip of warped vinyl, the tinny vocals laid over an unlike track. I nodded along to Rhys's beat at what I thought would seem like the right pace. But the music was loud and uproarious, an unending cacophony of noise on more noise, like the teenagers hollering across the street on their way home from school. The longer I listened, the less sense it seemed to make. The beat was beyond me.

"It's really good," I said when the song was finished, removing the headphones to shrug the sweat from my ears onto my shirtsleeve.

"But *how* is it good?" Rhys asked. "What did you like about it, specifically?" My mind froze, blank, as though his question were a test I hadn't studied for. We'd lived together six months now, and the long summer's afterglow had begun to set, the easy conversations we used to share fading along with it. Despite knowing how I'd grown up, Rhys didn't seem to consider me different from the women he usually dated. I could sense he wanted something from me—a kind of careful attentiveness to his feelings, or unconditional faith in his abilities, or fawning praise that as a boy I'd never learned to give. I didn't know how to speak the language he seemed to expect. So much was lost in translation, the words between us coming out stilted and strange.

"I don't know," I said, slowly. "I just thought it sounded good."

"Whatever," he huffed, his eyes rolling. He snatched the headphones from me, put them back over his own ears, and was gone to the music. I sighed, retreating from the kitchen to my writing desk, back to my quest to find the meaning of things. Scanning the near-empty room, I saw a mattress covered with a single stained sheet. A growing pile of dirty clothes strewn across the floor. The desk in front of me, a notebook open on top of it, the pencil in my hand. What big ideas could I find here, in these things? I couldn't focus, feeling almost dizzy as repetitive MIDI noise suddenly blasted from the kitchen, drowning out anything my professor might call "writerly" thoughts.

Sharing the duplex with Rhys was nothing like living at Northpointe had been. Here, I had no onsite laundry facilities, no handyman when things broke down, no carefree party-all-the-time lifestyle. I sat at my desk, thinking circles around the ideas I couldn't escape, didn't dare to write: I was incapable of dealing with the pests that scurried across our filthy floors; I couldn't cook a decent meal or remember to wash the dishes every night or get the recycling out on time; I didn't have the first clue what to buy when I walked into the grocery store, gaping down its gleaming domestic aisles like a goldfish. Our kitchen cabinets were always empty. The fridge housed cold ketchup packets and the six-packs Rhys's dad occasionally brought over—Pabst or Steel Reserve. We lived like children, eating sheet cake for dinner with our bare hands and rinsing them clean in the sink.

Adulthood seemed full of problems I didn't know how to solve. I watched as a baby cockroach flattened its body and scooted into one of the lightning bolt cracks raining from the ceiling, worrying about getting enough to eat tomorrow and making next month's rent and whether maybe, someday, I would write something worthwhile. I felt so overwhelmed by the idea of failure that, often, I wrote nothing at all.

ONE EARLY MORNING midway through the semester, I woke up to find the ceiling moving in slow circles. I turned my head, and the room turned with it, my eyes rolling to keep up. With difficulty, I pulled myself from bed. I stumbled to the bathroom, reaching the toilet just in time, heaving until there was nothing left. Exhausted, I rolled onto the carpet. Slept there until my world slowed.

When I woke again, I don't know how many hours later, Rhys stood over me, a blank, vaguely confused expression on his face. Light streamed in from a nearby window onto the gleaming gaze of the snake on his scalp.

"What's wrong?" he asked. "Are you sick?" I began to shake my head, but the dizziness was returning so I stopped, held it in place with my hands. Managed, weakly, "No." He stared down at me, his eyes narrowing.

"Pregnant?" he asked quietly.

"Don't think so," I said, closing my eyes again. I was still so tired.

"You should probably sleep it off, then," Rhys said. He brought me a pillow and some water, placing the glass on the bathroom tile near my head, and went back in the kitchen to work on a new beat. I couldn't look up at the glass without getting dizzy all over again. As his music flooded the room, I curled into myself, plugging my ears, closing my eyes tight. Willing it to stop.

In a few more hours the spinning had ceased and I was able to sit up, keep down a little of the water Rhys had left. I felt better so long as I kept my head straight and took care not to turn over or stand up too quickly. That night in bed, while Rhys slept, I studied the hungry way the snake eyed the mouse. How the mouse seemed to understand that look, knew to fear it, yet continued to pursue the snake. I wondered again what it meant, what the animals stood for.

Some nights, when I came home from my classes, Rhys seemed out of breath, as though he'd just taken a lap around the duplex. There were too many beer bottles in the recycling bin. Long strands of hair in the shower that belonged to neither of us. Books of mine continually going missing from the pile next to our bed.

"I'm sure they'll turn up," Rhys always said, though they never did.

I watched the mouse's feet kick as Rhys opened his eyes and blinked, returning my gaze with a scowl. "Why are you staring at me?" he asked.

"I'm not staring," I said. He rolled his eyes, rolled over in bed, taking the sheets with him. I turned to the ceiling, blinking back the dizziness that followed. A quick internet search had pointed to stress and poor nutrition as the source of my sudden vertigo, but the minutiae of seeing a doctor—of finding affordable care, of making an appointment, of dealing with co-pays and prescriptions—felt too daunting to merit real consideration. Besides, the website had assured me the symptoms would clear up on their own within a few months. I stared up at the patchy green paint on our duplex's high ceiling and sighed, wishing I could make time go forward, or backward, or something. Anywhere but here and now.

THE NEXT EVENING after class, I found an unfamiliar baseball cap lying abandoned near the duplex's front steps. I picked up the cap, turning it over in my hands under the porchlight. Someone had bent its blue bill up so that the underside faced out, a style popular among the local Tucsonan punks we hung out with. I knew it didn't belong to Rhys, didn't belong to me. A quiet rage began to build in my throat as I thought about the extra beer bottles and my missing books. About the secrets Rhys seemed to be keeping from me for reasons I didn't understand. I threw open the front door, tossed my backpack to the ground.

"Who's coming over here when I'm not home?" I demanded, holding up the cap.

"What?" Rhys called over the noise blaring from his speakers. I leaned into the doorway between the living room and the kitchen. Repeated myself, louder. The record skipped to silence. He turned away from the computer to face me, his handsome features blank, innocent.

"Nobody," he said. "What makes you think that?"

"Don't lie to me," I said, folding my arms, cap tight against my chest.

"Fine," he said, eyeing the cap. "I had some guys over to hear my new track. We had a couple beers on the porch and they left. That's it."

"Why try to hide that, then?" I asked. He shrugged.

"Didn't want you to be mad," he said, pulling another record off the shelf.

"Why would—" I began to ask, but my voice was engulfed in the blare of the music, one sound now among all the others. There were so many things I wanted to talk to Rhys about. Really talk, the way we used to, about why he didn't have a job or go to school. How his dad paid his half of the rent. How he never bothered to clean, or take out the trash, or do half the things he said he was going to. The only thing I could count on was his continual presence in our kitchen, making fresh beats on his MIDI machines. After countless nights coming home to find the dishes molding in the sink, the garbage bin overflowing with rotting food scraps, and cockroaches scurrying along the linoleum, I couldn't keep these thoughts to myself anymore.

"You didn't wash the dishes again," I called, my voice breaking through the noise a second time. Rhys tore his eyes from the computer screen, paused the music.

"Yeah, sorry. I forgot," he said. "I'll do them tonight. I promise."

"That's what you always say," I said. "What are we supposed to cook with? What are we supposed to eat on?" Rhys shrugged, flipping through some records stacked in a milk crate.

"I'll figure it out later," he said.

"Right," I said. "Like you always do, huh?" Rhys glared at me, but didn't respond. His jaw tightened and squared the way it did whenever he was upset. I wanted him to say something, anything, that might help us reach a place of mutual understanding. But knowing he wouldn't just made me angrier.

"You're a fucking deadbeat!" I shouted. "All you do is make shitty music!"

I'd gone too far, but I couldn't stop. A slew of insults spewed from my mouth like bile. I called him a burnout, a loser. Said I didn't care about him or the duplex or anything else. Rhys screamed at me to *shut the fuck up*. He punched a dent in the thick plaster wall, blood spackling his knuckles. Grabbed me by the arms and shook me until I was so dizzy I could see bright stars circling the water stains on our ceiling.

"Don't you fucking say that shit to me!" he spat through clenched teeth. "Don't you *ever* fucking say that!" His grip left angry red welts, frustrated purple bruises that faded to green and then yellow in the days following our fight. The marks were a lesson, a warning. I had tried to live the role Rhys seemed to think a girlfriend was meant to play, but in my heart I was still a desert boy, conditioned since my first day in Cactus Country never to back down from a threat. The next time we argued, and the time after that, and every time from then on, I fought back. We covered each other in every shade of bruise until it became difficult to tell who was the mouse and who was the snake, what that metaphor was even supposed to mean.

ONE EVENING ON the way home from my last writing class of the semester, I passed an old man lying on his back at a bus stop. The smell hit me first. A sweet, coppery stench that hung low in the air. The man's long, scraggly white beard was stained with weather and age, his coat torn and ragged. Piles of smudged plastic grocery bags surrounded him, tied together in a bundle. I could see the man's eyelids fluttering in the corner of my vision, and what looked like a gash on the top of his head, exposing something pink and fleshy. He moaned softly as I passed, dark blood pooling on the sidewalk under him, trickling into the street.

I kept walking, not fully comprehending what I'd seen until I crossed Euclid toward Tucson High School, halfway to the duplex. *That man needed help*, I thought. *I should go back and help him. I should go back.* I knew that. I knew it. But I didn't go back. I kept walking. I went home.

Earlier that day, in my writing class, Fenton had returned to William Carlos Williams, the course ending—as I'd learned all good essays should—with a nod to where it began. He read to us aloud from *Paterson*, and I closed my eyes, picturing Williams's faceless houses, not unlike the houses in my neighborhood, among a forest of his beleaguered trees, tangled and gnarled like the cacti growing in my front yard. For months, I'd been attempting to deconstruct and distill the things in my own life—the tattoo, the music, the duplex—down to their most essential ideas. To write a personal essay worthy of the significance I knew each of them to secretly hold. I had tried to bring them into the light, to give them a narrative body like this one, and I had failed, their answers beyond me—circling overhead, perpetually out of reach.

When I got back to the duplex, Rhys sat smoking on our porch as usual, bopping his head along to his latest beat. I needed to tell him what I had seen. The old man was hurt. I opened my mouth. Tears rolled down my face and onto the chapped dirt of our front yard. The old man needed our help. I stammered incoherently through hiccups. My nose ran freely over my upper lip. We needed to go back and help the man. There wasn't much time. Hurriedly wiping my face against my sleeve, I took a shaky breath. Tried again, my words trapped and stilted.

Rhys stood up from his chair, cigarette hanging from his mouth. "What's the matter, babe?" he asked. "Are you sick again?" I shook my head, immediately feeling dizzy. Rhys bowed as he came down the porch steps into the yard, his tattoo swirling, the snake chasing the mouse chasing the snake chasing the mouse on and on endlessly forever and suddenly I did feel very sick, just as he had said. I needed to tell him about the old man, but none of it was making any sense now and Rhys's voice was so sickeningly sweet, like the stench of blood baking against asphalt in the sun, and the smoke from his cigarette was billowing into my face and I couldn't breathe. I opened my eyes to find myself on the ground, the prickly pears and their ornaments spinning around me.

"Why don't you come inside and lie down," the snake said, pulling the mouse up by the arm, guiding it up the stairs and into the cool darkness of the duplex. "Just lie down and sleep."

GUY FRIENDS

"I'M NOT GONNA LIE," HE said. "That's a pretty crazy story."

Gavin and I sat on the threadbare couch in my new living room. From the floor, his beloved old dog, Marnie, sighed in her sleep. We were up late, way past her bedtime. I could overhear a few of our friends laughing as they lined up another round of shots in the kitchen. Outside, my roommates drank beer around a backyard bonfire, stoking the flames with creosote brush. This was supposed to be my housewarming party, but I didn't feel much like celebrating.

I described the last time I'd stepped into the duplex I shared with Rhys on 8th Street. How I'd come home after a summer trip to find his music machines gone, the bills left unpaid. The empty beer bottles covering every surface, shattered dishes stuffed into an overflowing recycling bin. The dead cockroaches littering the kitchen linoleum, legs up as though in surrender. I'd salvaged what little Rhys had left of my things and moved here, into a house one street over, with some friends of friends. Gavin was technically my neighbor. He'd lived in the 9th Street house previously, but his new place didn't have a washing machine or "anybody dope" living there, so Gavin still came over all the time, an honorary roommate with his own key.

"Damn. You sure you don't want a drink or anything?" he asked, patting me gently on the back. I shook my head and thanked him for the commiseration, wiping tears on my sleeve.

Gavin was a big boy of a man with short, sun-bleached blond hair, a wide-cheeked smile always present on his face. The only thing I knew about him was that he was gay, and famous in our circle for showing off the enormous, hyper-realistic dick portrait tattooed on his bicep. From where I sat on the couch, I could see its shaded tip peeking out from the bottom of his sleeve. I'd heard all the stories about "Big Gay Gavin" from our mutual friends but never expected him to be such a good listener. He had a comforting way of nodding as I spoke, urging me to go on. Rolling his eyes and shaking his head in all the right places.

"Well, you don't have to worry anymore," he said when I finished, gesturing grandly out to the room. "This is your home now. Welcome to it."

THE 9TH STREET house was a crumbling adobe-style rental where several of my high school friends had landed over the years, crashing with its ever-rotating occupants. Its beat-up furniture belonged to everyone and no one. Two small bedrooms sandwiched the one shared bathroom, with an extra bedroom tacked onto the back of the house. While only three of us actually paid rent, we shared the space as best we could with everyone who came over, whether to hang with us for the night or to sleep on our couches for a couple of weeks. To use the toilet or take a shower, our guests had to cut through my room, often early in the morning or the middle of the night. I didn't mind the intrusions, for the most part. They were easy enough to tune out. I faced the window at my desk with headphones in my ears, writing on my laptop for hours.

I felt a sense of ease on 9th Street I hadn't enjoyed in a long time. My vertigo resolved the week I moved in as I began eating more regular meals and sharing the responsibility of chores with my roommates, falling into an easy routine. But shit always seemed to be going down at our place. I'd get up from my writing desk to find guys in our living room from out of town, from Tucson's southside, from across the street, partying until they collapsed on our dusty floors. They held naked wrestling matches in the muddy backyard, roasted cactus at barbecue cookouts, took mushrooms and raced through the house like a pack of wild javelina. They lied about their pasts, slept with one another's girlfriends, developed addictions and mental illnesses. Following the drama of their lives was as exhausting as it was exciting, and the 9th Street house seemed to be at the center of it all.

On quieter days, Gavin would wander into the house and vent about his managerial job at the grocery store or pass along a rumor he'd heard about someone we knew. Gavin didn't tell a story so much as cultivate it: reveling in the dirty details, tilling over the minutiae again and again until it germinated into something containing only a sliver of the original seed. As a result, he was an exceptional storyteller, albeit notorious for his ability to twist a secret. But I didn't mind; I had nothing to hide.

Gavin smiled a lot, laughed easily, and was always free to walk with me a couple blocks down to the Taco Shop for a two-dollar burrito. While we ate, we'd swap stories about growing up queer in Tucson. Gavin told me how he'd struggled through school as a gay kid with Asperger's syndrome. In exchange, I told him how I'd grown up as a boy in Cactus Country and about my conflicted gender feelings. How I wasn't sure what words to use to describe myself anymore, but that I was trying to be okay with not knowing. I liked the way Gavin would nod and say what I told him made sense, even when I knew it didn't.

SOME AFTERNOONS, WHEN the latest hijinks at the 9th Street house distracted me too much to write, I walked the few blocks across Broadway Boulevard to Anthony's place on Cherry Avenue. Anthony was in his mid-twenties, short but toned, with a goatee and long black dreadlocks that hung down his back. He worked from home, making custom jewelry with stones he bought wholesale at Tucson's annual Gem Show and growing marijuana from a complex hydroponics system he built in his closet. Anthony's weed was popular, and among our friends he'd become the reluctant neighborhood dealer.

Though I'd stopped smoking after breaking up with Avery, I liked hanging out with Anthony because he never participated in drama and didn't have the patience to entertain even the most lurid rumors about our mutual friends. His house was reliably quiet, and I was always welcome, day or night, to chill on the couch and watch his collection of BBC nature documentaries. But best of all, I liked coming over to play with his affectionate, coffee-colored pit bull, Baby. Anthony didn't seem to mind my company, either. He appreciated that I never asked to smoke his weed, unlike most of our friends.

"Fuckin' moochers," he said. "They come over here all, 'Oh, Anthony, you got that good?' like, 'Oh, Anthony, can you smoke me out?'" He pressed some sticky leaves into a glass pipe, flattening them with his thumb. "Psh. Fuck that shit, man."

I nodded along to his complaints, massaging Baby's ears as he pressed his enormous head into my lap like a cat. Baby was excitable, the kind of dog who greeted you by wagging his entire body. Lately, I'd been taking him on walks whenever Anthony was out of town, usually just a few days or a week at a time. In return, he always slipped me a couple of folded twenties or bought me a cart of groceries when he got back from wherever he'd been. I never asked too many questions, and Anthony liked that about me, too.

ONE LATE NIGHT toward the end of my senior year at UA, Gavin invited some friends into our backyard for a drink. The sky was a deep, sobering black, lit only by the stars and the occasional beam of a helicopter searchlight. Some of us had to work in the morning, while others had just clocked out from a day shift. We huddled around a dying fire, our conversation punctuated with long pauses and loud sighs. Where most nights at the 9th Street house were characterized by a kind of collective mania, a celebratory contact high, I'd learned to dread the tired, hungover times like these, when discontent hung over and around us like smoke from the fire.

A late arrival hopped the low fence to join us, collapsing into an open folding chair. Gavin tossed him a beer. A wiry kid with thin, shoulder-length hair, Javier worked afternoons at Axis Food Mart, the convenience store where we bought our alcohol.

"One day closer to death," Javi said. "If I don't get around to it first." He mimed shooting himself in the head with a finger gun. No one laughed.

"Are you being facetious?" I asked.

"Am I what?" he said, scrunching up his face. Four years out of high school, I was the only one of my old friends on track to finish college. Some had gone a semester or two before dropping out. Others were chronically underemployed, saving what little money they had by living with their parents or crashing with friends. Those who did have steady jobs mostly worked at coffee shops, convenience stores, and call centers. Everyone wanted something better than what they had.

"Like, kidding," I clarified. "Are you kidding?"

"Shit, just say that then," he said, rolling his eyes. "You think you're fucking smart or something?" Javier took a long rip from his vape pen as a few guys snickered around the fire.

"No," I muttered, curling my toes into the dirt. Gavin shot me a sympathetic glance. In hanging out with the guys at the 9th Street house, I sought to recapture the camaraderie I'd had with the Cactus Country boys, joining them on frenetic midnight romps through an endless rotation of house parties, dive bars, and Sonora dog carts. Though I didn't feel like a woman, exactly, to most guys who hung around the house I was girlfriend material, a potential hookup. In the gap between their expectations and my reality, I'd quickly gained a reputation.

The guys rarely talked shit to my face, but they didn't have to. Gavin told me everything they said when I wasn't around to hear it. Like most rumors, their implications weren't strictly true. But, as Gavin pointed out, the evidence was all against me. Our friends talked about how I'd let guys who would have otherwise slept on the floor at the 9th Street house crash in my bed instead. How I'd strip down in front of anyone—guy or girl—to go skinny-dipping at night in backyard swimming pools. How much time I'd spent alone with Anthony at his place, and nobody believed it was to play with Baby: word on the street said I was trading his weed for sex.

"I tell them you're *not*, of course," Gavin sighed, "but you know how guys are."

I did know how guys were; I remembered being one of them. My friends seemed to share everything with one another, from six-packs to futons to girlfriends. They hung out with whoever they wanted as long as they wanted, no matter how early in the morning or late at night. I had seen every one of them, whether showering or swimming or shitfaced, in various stages of undress. Somehow, none of this was worthy of conversation around the campfire. But when I behaved the same way, I became a tease, an attention-seeker, a slut.

I appreciated that Gavin stood up for me. But whatever he said to our friends didn't seem to make an impact, because he always had more to report the next time he came over. Hearing what the guys said behind my back always made me feel less at home in the 9th Street house, and in myself. Though Gavin knew how I felt, he couldn't seem to help himself. Every other day he came into my room with some new social bombshell he was bursting to share. While Gavin's recounting seemed to come from a genuine place—telling me what *he* would want to know in my position—I couldn't shake the sense that he might've also enjoyed these rumors, especially as the only one with the scoop on either end of the story.

THAT SPRING, I graduated from the University of Arizona. Mom and Dad clapped in the audience as I climbed onstage to receive a certificate from the English department. They beamed, each of them wrapping an arm around my shoulders as we walked back to the van from the ceremony.

"So, what's next?" Dad asked. He meant for the day, but I couldn't help thinking back to my most recent conversation with Ander about graduate school. For the last two years, we'd been meeting on a monthly basis to discuss the dozens of books he'd assigned and the short collection of essays I'd written. Several of my other writing professors had assumed I would be applying to programs post-graduation and were surprised when I told them I hadn't decided yet. A couple of weeks before the ceremony, I'd met with Ander on a bench outside of the Modern Languages building to talk it over.

"You don't *need* a master's degree to be a writer," he said. "But it can be hard to keep up a writing practice without the structure of a program. Life shit gets in the way."

So far, I'd managed to follow a loose schedule outside of what was required for my classes, writing in the afternoons when I got home from

Second Street and on the weekends in coffee shops around town. But I worried about what might happen when I lost access to the resources on UA's campus—to the teachers, classes, and events that tethered me to its community.

"What do you think I should do?" I asked. Ander leaned back on the bench and shrugged.

"I don't think you have to do anything right now," he said. "Plenty of writers wait years before they apply, until they have more material to write about and good, clear reasons to go."

I nodded, wondering whether a desire to leave Tucson qualified as a good enough reason to apply. My picture of the writing world outside of the university was still nebulous, largely constructed from overheard conversations among UA grad students in the hallways between classes and in the stray back copies of literary magazines I scavenged from the boxes of free books lying around Modern Languages. Though the connection between entering this world and "making it" as a writer was unclear to me, I could sense that graduate school might be a crucial next step, just as getting a college education had once been to leaving Cactus Country. But the prospect of living so far from home was scary, too.

Later that night, at the 9th Street house, I hashed out what Ander had said with Gavin. I sat up in my bed while he sprawled his long arms out along the couch, listening in his all-encompassing way.

"What if I can't do it?" I said. "What if I have to come back?"

"My question is, why would you want to stay *here*—" Gavin said, casting his hand around in the air, "and waste your time wondering, when you could go and find out for yourself?"

I didn't have an answer for him, but I understood what Gavin was getting at. Over the years, we'd heard so many friends talk about leaving the desert to pursue their dreams in cities like Los Angeles, Portland, and Seattle, even though we all knew they never would. Some were breadwinners, the sole providers for aging parents and young children on a meager minimum wage. Others didn't have the resources they needed—a bachelor's degree, a nest egg, a reliable car—to establish themselves in a new city. Not everyone in Tucson had the chance to leave it, even if they desperately wanted to. In a few more years, the same could be true for me.

"You're better than this place," Gavin said.

"We all are," I laughed. "But thanks, man. You're a good friend."

"For you?" he said, smiling. "Always."

I LAY IN bed, my head throbbing, limbs aching, stomach churning. I had been home almost a week with the debilitating summer flu going around Second Street and was now quietly praying for the release of death. Gavin gently knocked on my door before pushing it open and shuffling into view. Something seemed off. He scratched the back of his head, staring fixedly at the wood-paneled floor.

"Heard you weren't feeling well," he said. "Mind if I sit with you for a bit?" I nodded weakly. Gavin lowered himself onto the foot of the bed. He tucked his hands between his thighs, as though bracing himself to tell me something. I worried it might be about his dog, Marnie. Lately, she'd been ambling around the yard slower than usual. Her legs were stiff with arthritis, and Gavin had started to carry her up the few stairs into his house after her walks.

Gavin took a breath. He reminisced about all the adventures we'd had since I moved to 9th Street, recounting the night a group of us played a drunken game of baseball in the street, taking off like a pack of kids when the ball shattered a neighbor's window. The time he and I and some friends went running barefoot through an afternoon storm until our clothes were heavy with rain. Our many hours-long conversations about our childhoods. I closed my eyes and followed loosely along to Gavin's stream of consciousness, slowly drifting away from his words and into sleep.

"The truth is I kind of, well—" he said, "I like you, Zoë. More than a friend." My eyes snapped open. I stared at him, certain I must be hallucinating. Nothing about me in this moment was attractive. I was covered in fever sweat. My lips were chapped and bleeding, my nose red from sneezing into an old t-shirt I kept bunched up by the bed for this purpose. And anyway—

"I thought you were gay," I wheezed.

"I know," he said. "I know it doesn't make sense. But it's how I feel." He looked down at his clasped hands, a nervous half smile spreading across his cheek. The pounding in my head now had nothing to do with my cold. Because our friends saw me as a woman, I'd always assumed that Gavin did, too. That his loud-and-proud identity as a gay man precluded any possibility that he viewed me in the same romantic light they did. The uncomplicated nature of our friendship, its freedom from the sexual tension that characterized so many of my other relationships with men at the 9th Street house, was part of why I'd always liked hanging out with Gavin, the reason I sought out his company and trusted his counsel.

"Are you sure?" I asked. Gavin nodded. He recounted how Javier had crossed a line one night, saying something about me that Gavin, uncharacteristically, refused to repeat.

"All I can tell you is it was bad," he said. "Javi really pissed me off." He told me how the encounter had devolved into a shouting match that ended with Gavin storming home, leaving Javier and the other guys in the backyard to sit around the fire in stunned silence. At first, Gavin said, he didn't understand why he was so worked up, and later came to the realization that he had feelings for me.

I wrapped myself in another blanket, my body shivering as much from the chills as my disappointment. Any appreciation I might have had for Gavin's defense of me to the group was overshadowed by the reason he'd done it. That stupid "bros before hoes" maxim was popular for a reason. I'd spent enough time among boys and men to know that in a conflict between a guy friend and a crush on a girl, the other guy always won out in the end. Nothing Javi said about me could endanger their friendship, no matter how mad Gavin might have been with him in the moment. Guys never got in any permanent trouble for what they said about women.

I rubbed my hands hard on my face. With just a few words, Gavin had complicated everything. I wanted to shake him back in time, to long before he thought to confess these feelings. Back to our conversation on the couch my first night at the 9th Street house. To our Taco Shop burritos and all the stories we'd told when we were just getting to know each other. I wanted us to be two friends with queer experiences in common, to confide in one another without the expectation of anything between us becoming more than what it was. I wanted that to be enough.

"Gavin, I'm really sorry, but I don't feel the same way," I said.

"I understand," he said quickly, getting up from the bed. "And that's fine. I just needed to tell you." He disappeared behind the door, leaving me to stare at the ceiling, wishing the whole thing had been a fever dream.

THE DAY BEFORE he left, Anthony gave me a key and some specific instructions.

"Don't let nobody in this house while I'm gone, you understand?" he said. "I don't trust these motherfuckers with nothing." Anthony was going to work on a farm in California for a month and couldn't take Baby with him. I didn't know the details, but he promised to pay me a couple hundred bucks for my help when he got back. This would be the longest Anthony had ever left Baby in my care, but it was the middle of summer and I had the time.

"Remember, just you," he said, pointing at me, "and *him*." He pointed to Baby, who licked Anthony's extended finger. I nodded.

"Of course," I said. "You can trust me."

"Oh, shit, almost forgot," Anthony said. He pulled two quart-sized mason jars full of dried weed from his closet and set them on the coffee table. "Can you keep these at your place for me?" I stared at them. I'd never seen so much marijuana at one time.

"Can't they stay here?" I asked. Anthony shook his head.

"Everybody knows I grow it," he explained. "Someone might break in and steal them."

I hesitated. Knowing our friends, Anthony was probably right. But I didn't relish the idea of holding his drugs for him.

"What if I get in trouble?" I said, feeling uncool before the words even left my mouth.

"Psh, c'mon," he said, grinning. "Pretty white girl like you?"

I sighed. He had a point. Cops never got called to the 9th Street house, no matter how loud we were or how late our parties stretched into the night. Even on the chance they did, my room would probably be the last one they searched. I stuffed the jars into my backpack and fast-walked home with Baby on a leash, hyperaware of every car and person we passed. Standing on a chair, I pushed the weed into the farthest corner of my bedroom closet shelf and hid them from view behind some old blankets.

Marnie took immediate offense to Baby's presence. She growled, snapping at him as he thumped his tail against the floor, oblivious to her aggression. He bounced around her like a puppy, leaning down on his front paws, trying to entice her into play. Marnie snarled.

"This is your house," Gavin said, pulling Marnie onto his lap. "Isn't it, old girl?"

It wasn't. But at Gavin's insistence, I reluctantly brought Baby back to Anthony's place, knowing that living there with him full time was a no-go. Anthony's bed was a dusty mattress without pillows or blankets. He had no hot water or eating utensils. I'd run over to let Baby out quickly in the mornings before work and then take him for long, sprawling walks around the neighborhood in the evenings when I got home.

Baby was strong, but I knew from my dog-walking days in Cactus Country how to wrap the leash around my wrist so that he couldn't rip it away at the first sight of a desert mouse zipping across the street. I threw stick after stick for Baby to fetch in Anthony's barren backyard until colors streaked across the sky and it became too dark to see, like those long sunsets of my adolescence, back when all I wanted was to catch a train with Chyna and leave Cactus Country behind. Back when things seemed simpler, even though they weren't.

By the time I headed out from Anthony's, the streetlamps were on, their faint orange glow guiding me home. I turned my key to find Javier holding court in the living room, a card game spread out on the coffee table amid a pyramid of crushed beer cans.

"How much of a slut do you have to be to turn a gay guy straight?" he was saying. He turned around in the armchair to face me as I came in, his teeth clicking on a beer tab. "Oh, sorry," he called, "didn't realize you were home." He laughed harder than he should have, the other guys laughing with him, a chorus of voices deep enough to drown in.

"Fuck off, Javi," I said, my cheeks burning. "You know it's not like that."

"C'mon, it was a *joke*," he groaned. "Why are girls always so fucking sensitive?"

Javier and the guys finished their beers and moved on to another house. I sat alone on the couch, tossing their empty cans into a garbage bag as I tried to work through my fury with Gavin. Why did he have to go and tell our friends about his feelings for me, especially a jerk like Javi? I'd figured Gavin, as a fellow queer person, would know nothing good could possibly come from blabbing about his crush to a bunch of straight guys. Maybe he'd just needed to confide in someone and the story got away from him, as stories at the 9th Street house often did. But I also knew how much Gavin loved to talk. How many times had I listened as he told a particularly juicy tale to the next person who hadn't yet heard it? How many times had that person been me? He liked to watch the intrigue spread over our faces, to entertain all of our follow-up questions. Maybe the commiseration he got from wearing a broken heart on his sleeve had been too good to pass up.

Whatever his reasons, I was left to deal with the consequences. For weeks after Gavin's confession, whenever I texted our friends to hang out, they blew me off, said they were too busy. But inevitably I'd catch them at the house later that same night, on their way somewhere I wasn't invited to go. Other guys were suddenly much more available than they'd ever been, texting me invitations to "come chill" at their places at odd hours of the night. There was nothing I could do but ignore them and wait for the drama to pass. Confronting Gavin would only give everyone more to talk about, prolonging the spectacle. In time, I hoped, his feelings would wane, and we could go back to being friends like we'd been before.

ONE LATE SUMMER afternoon at Second Street, I heard my phone vibrating in my bag as I slathered the children with sunscreen. It buzzed and buzzed and wouldn't stop. As soon as I could, I took a bathroom break to a barrage of missed calls and texts from Gavin.

"You need to get home ASAP," he wrote. "Someone broke into the house."

I rushed to 9th Street to find a policewoman already taking Gavin's statement in the living room. She wore blue latex gloves and held a clipboard, all business.

"Mind if I look around?" she asked, and I nodded, too shocked to respond.

Gavin had contacted all of my roommates, but I was the first one home to assess the damage. The communal TV and video game systems had vanished from the console, a pile of dusty cords left in their wake. In my room, clothes and books were strewn over the floor. My laptop was missing from its spot on my desk. I searched frantically, hoping it had been knocked down and buried under the mess. No such luck. I dug my bare toes into the wood floor and ran my hands hard over my face to keep from screaming. All of my writing, gone in an instant. I could only pray that my most important projects were backed up on an internet cloud somewhere.

The only place left untouched was my closet, where Anthony's mason jars were still safely stashed behind the blankets. I pulled them down from their hiding place, keenly aware that a police officer was here, in our house, rifling through our cabinets and drawers. How could I ever explain this much marijuana away? She probably heard the "only holding it for a friend" excuse all the time. I wrapped the jars in a blanket. Climbed out my bedroom window. Hands shaking, I fumbled my phone out of my pocket and called Javier. He worked a block away from 9th Street and was the only person I knew who might be able to come over on such short notice.

"Got it," he said before I finished explaining the situation. "On my way." Within minutes, Javi arrived from Axis Mart to pick up the mason jars. Without a word between us, he transferred them into his backpack and slipped into the street. I climbed back into my room, clutching the empty blanket against my chest to muffle the sound of my heart, which was beating so loud I worried the policewoman might hear it. I'd barely made it over my desk and onto the floor when she burst into the room, startling me.

"Do you have renter's insurance?" she asked, her hand on the doorknob.

"Renter's what?" I stammered. She sighed heavily.

"Nothing you can do but report what was stolen," she said, ripping a blank form from her notepad and handing it to me. "Hope you kept your serial numbers." This inventorying was a waste of time. I'd heard enough about break-ins at other friends' houses to know the police wouldn't help us. But I wasn't sure what else to do. I filled out the form as best I could, and she left.

"Gavin," I said, trying to keep my voice steady. "What the fuck happened, man?"

Gavin stared at his feet, explaining that he'd gone home to feed Marnie. He forgot to lock the back door when he left. The thieves entered through the unlocked door and plundered every room in the house, dumping our laundry onto the floor and filling the baskets with everything of value. Gavin had come back with the dog to find our front door swinging ominously open. This kind of operation wasn't uncommon in our poor downtown neighborhood, where most rentals didn't come equipped with alarms and security systems. Our house didn't even have bars on the windows or a barking dog roaming the backyard.

"I was gone thirty minutes, tops," Gavin said. "I'm really sorry." I couldn't even look at him. Who knows what would've happened if the cops had found Anthony's weed. As it was, I would need to save up for a new laptop and find a way to recover the writing I'd lost. But though I was furious, I knew the break-in wasn't entirely Gavin's fault. This was

Tucson, where I'd had half-empty bags of candy stolen from the backseat of my car, filthy pairs of shoes swiped from my front porch. I'd learned long ago that in this city, holding tight to the important things wasn't always enough to keep them safe.

THE NEXT DAY, I brought Baby to the 9th Street house to stay. Gavin was still too apologetic about the burglary to object. I was tired of waking up early to run over to Anthony's place before work, and anyway, I didn't feel safe at home anymore. Baby was gentle, but he had a deep, intimidating bark that caused strangers to cross the street when I took him out for walks. At night, he curled up next to me in bed, resting his wide head on my chest while I slept.

Anthony had been gone now a total of three months. The timeframe for his return seemed to stretch longer every time I spoke to him, which wasn't often. He didn't answer most of my texts, and his spotty pay-as-you-go cell service meant he'd had to change his number a few times. When I did manage to get him on the phone, he was evasive.

"Man, when are you coming home?" I asked. "Baby's running out of food again."

"Soon," he said, his voice staticky, distant. We always seemed to have a bad connection. "Two more weeks, I promise. Just need to save enough cash to catch a ride. I'll get you back for whatever he needs."

The two weeks came and went without another word from Anthony. I brought Baby along to hang out one evening on Javier's front stoop. Guys milled in and out of his apartment, crowding into the back bedroom to smoke what I hoped wasn't Anthony's weed. They laughed when I complained about paying for Baby's food, teasing me that Anthony was never coming back.

"At this point, that dog is basically yours," Javi said, taking a sip from his tall can. I sat on a milk crate, stroking Baby's back as he lay on the dusty ground at my side. Though Marnie had grown more accepting of his presence in the house, she still barked at him whenever he strayed too close. I couldn't trust them alone together. Feeling bad that Baby was cooped up in my room all day, I'd started taking him along with me everywhere I could—to friends' houses and on errands around town and to visit my parents in Cactus Country. Over our months together, Baby had become part of my routine, and I had grown to love him. But his care required a lot of my time and a substantial portion of my paycheck. I watched as Baby sniffed intently at a spot between his paws, hoping I didn't have to keep him forever, but knowing if Anthony never came back, I would care for the dog like he was mine.

THAT FALL, GAVIN announced he was going on a rafting trip. He'd be completely unreachable, without cell service, for at least a week while on the river. I agreed to take care of Marnie while he was away, no charge. To thank me, Gavin left a large basket full of snacks in my room. When I moved the treats to the kitchen, I found an envelope buried under a bag of homemade rice crispy bars. My heart slumped into my stomach. We hadn't talked about Gavin's confession since before the break-in, and as the months passed the incident had finally begun to recede from the 9th Street house's collective consciousness. Javier and the guys had since moved on to other scandals, and I'd quietly hoped Gavin had forgotten about it, too.

I examined the letter, running my thumbs over its thick envelope. Gavin had spared no expense; the brown, faux-aged paper bulged, its contents sealed with stamped red wax. For a moment, I considered whether to open the letter at all. I had already turned Gavin down once and couldn't imagine anything he'd written would change my answer. But not reading the letter wouldn't make whatever might be waiting inside any less consequential. Gathering my courage, I took a breath and ripped open the envelope to a pages-long handwritten appeal.

In the letter, Gavin described his appreciation of our friendship, taking every opportunity to praise, in great detail, my boyish features, the soft tone of my voice, my androgynous style, my anarchist spirit, my sense of humor, my zeal for adventure, the way I danced, how I ate cereal, the quality and depth of my writing, and more, on and on for pages. Gavin implored me to take a chance on a relationship with him. He said that we belonged together. That he knew I was destined to leave Tucson and that he would follow me anywhere I desired to go.

As I read and reread his words, the lump in my stomach grew hard and inflamed. Gavin's was the kindest, most earnest, heartbreaking, devastating letter I'd ever read or received. I had no doubt every word he'd written was sincere. Under the right circumstances, his confession might have been a beautiful expression of queer sexuality. After all, Gavin, "Big Gay Gavin," was the only man I'd ever known who was attracted to me because of my masculinity rather than in spite of it. But however he perceived my gender, here, we were surrounded by guys who saw me not as friend, but as female. To Gavin, I'd become the same object of desire that had precluded me from genuine friendship with the men of the 9th Street house. I knew I couldn't return his feelings.

I dreaded facing another awkward conversation where I would try to let Gavin down gently. Our friends would hear about the letter, that I'd rejected him a second time. All of the teasing, the jokes, the harassment that had died down over the past few months would spring back to life with renewed vigor. Even if my friendship with Gavin somehow survived the backlash, I'd never stop wondering when I might have to endure it all over again. As I stared at the letter in my hands, the room began to spin around me the way it had when I'd lived in the duplex with Rhys.

I felt suddenly claustrophobic, an urgent sense that if I didn't get away now—right now—I never would. Not only from Gavin and Javier and the rest of my friends, but from shitty, chaotic houses like this one, forever burdened with the care of other people's animals, other people's drugs, other people's problems. From living with and among men who called me a friend to my face but a slut behind my back. The dogs followed me as I paced the house with Gavin's letter, an escape plan forming more clearly with each step. I would leave the 9th Street house. I would apply to graduate schools. I would get the hell out of Tucson. But first, I would text Anthony.

"I'm leaving," I wrote, "and I'm taking Baby with me unless you come back for him. You have one week."

I scoured the house with bleach until my knuckles burned and showed my room to prospective subletters in the evenings after I came home from Second Street, lighting scented candles to give the place a cozy ambiance. By the end of the week, a young man with scruffy brown hair and a goatee agreed to take over my portion of the lease. He wasn't part of our friend circle but seemed trustworthy enough—and anyway, I thought, since the burglary we had nothing left in the house to steal.

Anthony finally showed up on my last night at the house while I was deep in the midst of packing my car, boxes piled high on the front porch. Baby seemed glad to see him again, whipping his frenzied tail against our legs. Anthony was mad at me for threatening to run away with his dog, but even more pissed that I'd handed his weed over to Javier.

"The fuckers smoked it all," he seethed. "Both jars. Man, I left my shit with you so this wouldn't happen."

"You think I *wanted* the cops to come sniffing around here?" I said, arms crossed over my chest. "What the fuck was I supposed to do, Anthony?"

"They wouldn't have found it," he insisted. "You should've just left it where it was at."

"Maybe you should have come back when you said you would," I countered. Anthony glared down at the floor, shook his head. He hooked Baby's collar onto his leash and turned to go.

"Thanks for taking care of my dog," he muttered coldly. "I don't have any cash on me right now. I'll have to hit you back later."

"Whatever," I said. I knew I'd never see any of the money Anthony had promised, and I didn't have time to argue with him—Gavin would be home from his trip in less than an hour.

Leaving now, I knew, would mean the end of my friendships on 9th Street. Gavin would tell everyone his side of the story, where I ghosted him without so much as a note goodbye. Our friends would be outraged on Gavin's behalf. They'd sit around the campfire and talk their shit. None of it mattered anymore. Whoever Gavin and the guys saw in me, whatever they expected from her, I couldn't be that person for them. I would take some time away. Wait for the anger, theirs and mine, to pass. Maybe someday, with the benefit of distance, I could reach out to Gavin again with the right words to explain why I felt I had to go. But until then, I needed to be alone.

I packed the last of my belongings into the car, giving Marnie a quick head scratch on my way out the door. As I drove away, I tried hard not to imagine Gavin's face when he stepped into the 9th Street house to pick up his dog, only to find his letter gone, my room empty, the whole place quieter than either of us had ever seen it.

THE HOUSE GHOST

THE RENTAL STRUCK me as unusually tall for Tucson, especially on a shitty street like Park Avenue. At three stories high, it towered over surrounding houses, casting a shadow that stretched all the way across the road. Along either side of its cracked facade grew rows of sharp, leafless trees, their branches gnarled and mean. I knocked again on its great wooden door. From where I stood on the porch, I could see into a neighbor's fenced yard—their pit bull rolling around in something long dead. I looked out over the roofs lining Park Ave all the way to the University of Arizona campus, just visible in the distance, thinking it was a little like standing on the turret of a castle.

Eli was late. I waited twenty minutes on the porch, then thirty. Just as I was about to forget the whole thing, he rolled up in a dusty white Honda, sipping on a thirty-two-ounce chalice of Diet Pepsi. I'd only spoken to him over the phone, but seeing Eli for the first time, I guessed he was in his early forties, his hair all salt and pepper. He offered me an unsatisfying handshake, unlocked the massive front door with a skeleton key, and immediately sank into one of the three overstuffed armchairs dominating the living room. I perched myself on the chair opposite his as Eli laid out the house rules. No drugs, no house parties, and most of all, no—

"Drama," Eli muttered, drumming his fingers against the arm of his throne-like chair. "I get enough of that shit down at the bar."

I told him I knew what he meant. He nodded and took another gulp of his gigantic soda. Eli, I learned, worked nights bartending at a local gay dive. He rented the house from our landlords, who lived above us on a second level only accessible via a flight of stairs outside.

"And if they ask," Eli said, pointing at the ceiling, "you don't live here."

He got up to show me around. Other than the overstuffed chairs in the living room, the four-bedroom house was eerily devoid of furniture, our voices echoing against its bare floors and empty walls. Eli was looking for three roommates, but so far I was the only person who'd answered his ad. I surveyed the bedrooms, ultimately choosing the one behind the kitchen, located in the recesses of what had once probably been a broom cupboard. The door to my new room was obscured by a tiny, L-shaped hallway. I liked that a person could easily pass it by, never realizing it was there. My space was private, hidden; a room you had to believe in to find. I handed Eli a wad of cash and agreed to move in. We shook on it.

LATER THAT NIGHT, Eli introduced me to Jack, a kid visiting him from Phoenix, the sprawling capital city two hours north of Tucson. Jack was twenty, just a couple years younger than me. Stocky and athletic, thick arms hung from his broad shoulders like barbells. Since Eli was still showing the bare guest rooms to potential renters, he and Jack bunked together in his room, sharing a bed. This arrangement was curious, I thought, but not really my business. I began stacking boxes and shuffling furniture around my hidden room. Eli went to work for the night, leaving Jack, too young to hang out at the bar, alone in the living room. He sat enveloped by one of the massive chairs, listening to music on his cell phone's speakers.

Each time I walked by to gather more boxes from the car, Jack peppered me with questions—how old was I, where did I work, what was my sign. On the sixth or seventh trip he asked, "So, you got a boyfriend?" I think he thought he was being conversational. My silence as I weighed the implications of answering either way must have troubled him, because he hastened to add, "Just so you know, me and Eli aren't, like, involved or anything."

I nodded but didn't look at him, busy wrestling with a stuffed javelina head I intended to bring into my room. I'd seen it at Bookmans, Tucson's local bookstore and more, and couldn't resist taking it home. It reminded me of the javelina roaming the desert around Cactus Country. How they traveled in packs through the warm winter months, eating the seed neighbors put out for birds and attacking dogs left outside on chains. I liked the idea of sharing space with an animal that had once made me afraid to go walking alone at night. Of mounting fear on the wall and calling it mine.

The javelina head was heavy and awkward. I had to hold it carefully from the wooden base it was mounted to, otherwise its rough, prickly hair would turn my arms red and itchy. Care had to be taken, too, not to look directly at the creature's face. Something about its expression, those glistening, black eyes, that mouth molded into a snarl, made it hard for me to separate the spirit of the animal from the inanimate object I now held against my chest. Even with the pig safely hung on the wall, I was scared to touch it, as though the animal might come alive and bite.

"Sometimes Eli tries to, like, spoon with me," Jack said. "Which is weird cause I'm not gay or anything." He forced a laugh. Lost in my javelina thoughts, I had forgotten he was speaking to me.

THE FALLOUT OF my sudden disappearance from the 9th Street house came swiftly. Two days and several unanswered calls from Gavin later, my phone flooded with texts and voice messages from Javier and other mutual friends who'd heard only his side of the story. What kind of fucked-up person would just vanish without saying anything? I was a bitch, a whore, a selfish cunt. They'd always known I was a shitty friend, that I thought I was too good for them, and this proved it.

I couldn't bring myself to answer their messages, but I read them all, their edges sharp like knives. No explanation on my part would change what my friends thought of me now—or rather, what I was now able to acknowledge, too late, that they'd thought all along. When I moved into the Park Ave house, I'd thought I just needed some space—from Gavin and the 9th Street house, yes, but also from the struggle to survive in a hardscrabble desert town like Tucson among the kind of company we kept. From the despair that shadowed every late-night conversation about the future, which only became bleaker as more of our friends dropped out of colleges and technical schools, got addicted to drugs of one kind or another, succumbed to untreated mental illnesses, toiled at the same dead-end jobs they'd been working since high school.

But now, as their messages flashed on the screen, illuminating my face in the darkness of my hidden room, I understood that no amount of space would ever be enough. I had found my reason, the clarity I needed to let Tucson go.

THE PARK AVE house was haunted. Eli waited until after I'd gotten settled to tell me this, the first month's rent paid and the javelina head firmly mounted to my bedroom wall. The house was possessed, he said, by the spirit of a ghostly woman. He'd heard her whispering unintelligible things through the walls. She watched him from the windows in the living room, and at night he could see the shadow of her feet standing at the front door.

"Just so, you know, you're aware," he muttered.

I'd been fascinated by the supernatural since childhood, drawn to the ghost stories boys told around late-night campfires in Cactus Country. But I'd never lived in a haunted house before. Eli crossed his legs, chewing on the straw of his afternoon diet soda as I posed my questions: Could her presence cause physical harm, or was she more like an apparition? How did one protect themself from the advances of a ghostly woman? Was it pointless to try? Eli just shrugged, said she'd never tried anything with him.

Just in case, I took to locking my bedroom door at night and sleeping with a baseball bat. I carried a small hand mirror in my back pocket, using it to peek around the L-shaped hallway between my bedroom and the kitchen before turning into it. But after several days of the ghostly woman failing to appear, I grew dubious. Eli said that I didn't have "the sight." That if I were patient, the ghostly woman would reveal herself to me. He invited me to wait for her.

That night, Eli, Jack, and I sat in the living room, staring out from the cushy armchairs until my vision began to blur, shadows flickering across our motionless bodies. Everything in the dark appears to move.

"There!" Eli whispered, pointing at some obscure shape on the ceiling, or a beam of light from a passing car. "Did you see that?"

I tried, I really did. I wanted so much to believe him, to see the ghostly woman with my own eyes. In the week since I moved in, after the initial alarm subsided, I'd started to develop a strange empathy for her. If the ghostly woman existed, I thought, maybe we had misinterpreted her watchful gaze. Maybe standing vigil at the front door was her way of protecting the house, acting as a benevolent guardian to those who inhabited it. Or maybe she hid from us out of fear, as haunted by our presence as we felt by hers.

On nights when Eli and Jack went out, I wedged myself between two of the overstuffed chairs and waited for her in the dark. During one of these stakeouts, I noticed a hole in the living room floor. The hole was about the size of my open palm, and over it I could feel cool air rising from the crawl space under the house. According to Eli, the hole was made by the previous tenants, a group of loud college boys who played beer pong and inhaled Whip-It! canisters. I knew this to be true because if I laid flat on the floor and shone a light into its crevice, I could make out several ping pong balls, a smattering of cigarette butts, too many bottle caps and empties to count. They lay in a pile, glistening like pearls in the beam of light, their secrets well beyond my reach.

"I HAVE TO get out of here, Ander," I said, staring into a mug of tea. "If I can't leave soon I don't know what I'll do." He and I sat at a table in Caffe Luce, a coffee house at the edge of campus. Briefly, I told him about my friends' angry messages and Gavin's confession. Ander snorted when I described the ornate handwritten letter he'd left for me.

"A wax seal?" he said, taking a sip of his coffee. "That's pretty intense."

"Creepy, even," I said.

"But unrequited love is always a little creepy, isn't it?" he said. I laughed. It felt good to make light of a situation that had weighed so heavily on my conscience. To be at the university again, in the company of another writer. I'd finally saved up enough cash to buy a new-to-me laptop on Craigslist, and had slowly eased back into a writing routine at the Park Ave house. But, as Ander had once cautioned me, life shit was definitely starting to get in the way.

"So I've been thinking about graduate school," I said. "I'm ready to go."

"Sounds like the time is right," he agreed.

I took notes as Ander talked me through submission materials and program requirements. We were just two months away from application deadlines. In that time, I would need to write statements—of purpose, of interest, of intention—and put together packets of my best writing, much of it retyped from printed copies after my old laptop was stolen from the 9th Street house. I'd need to sit for the GRE exam, request official transcripts from UA, collect recommendation letters from my professors, and research dozens of programs, looking for ones that offered tuition waivers and teaching assistantships.

"Only apply to programs that'll pay you to teach," Ander said. "That's my best advice."

I envisioned what it might be like to teach writing classes. Standing in front of a classroom in a blazer, leading workshop discussions full of the kind of ardent, hungry students I'd once been. For the last four years, teachers like Ander and Fenton had supported me in my impossible ambition to become a writer. Collectively, they'd read dozens of drafts from my fledgling writing projects and met with me for countless hours, inside their offices and out. They'd invited me to campus literary events and introduced me to my favorite books. But most importantly, they'd taken me seriously and made me feel that I belonged at the university, that I would be a writer. I could think of nothing I wanted more than to follow their example and become that person for someone else.

"What if I don't get in anywhere?" I asked. Ander looked up at the ceiling for a moment.

"Yeah, you might not," he said thoughtfully. "But you won't know until you apply. Either way, it might be smart to get more involved in the local literary scene."

That fall, I would volunteer with *Sonora Review*, UA's MFA student-run literary magazine, where I'd work along with graduate students to evaluate submissions as part of the editorial team. Ander would put me in touch with Katherine Standefer, a recent graduate from the program who held writing groups around her kitchen table. Once a week I'd walk to Kati's house from Park Ave to talk about books and generate new material for my essays. I'd spend my evenings researching application requirements and going out to see visiting writers read their work at UA's Poetry Center. When I listened to other writers tell their stories, the far-flung places and unlikely circumstances they had come to writing from, I would begin to trust that I might succeed in leaving Tucson. That I could start again somewhere new, as my family had when we first moved to Cactus Country all those years ago.

MEANWHILE, JACK WAS becoming a fixture as permanent in the Park Ave house's living room as Eli's enormous chairs. Between staring into space and listening to Hot 98.3's Top 40 mix on blast, Jack complained that Eli wouldn't drive him home to Phoenix. That he was stuck here, in this house, with us and the ghostly woman.

"Eli won't take you back?" I asked. "Why not?" Jack shrugged, eyes locked to an indeterminate spot on the ceiling.

"Too tired from working at the bar, I guess," he said. "He tells me, 'Tomorrow, man, I'll take you tomorrow.' But then tomorrow never comes."

I couldn't quite figure out why Jack had come to stay at the house in the first place, or how he and Eli knew each other. But though I hadn't lived with Eli long, I'd already noticed his tendency to let things fester. He'd leave kettles boiling on the stove until I could hear them screaming through the wall dividing my room from the kitchen. Dishes piled up in the sink, left to soak and stink under our bare cupboards. Dirty laundry congregated on the floor until we had trouble opening doors. Eli never seemed to mind the mess until, all at once, he descended upon it—typically overnight—with a focus and attention to detail I assumed had something to do with drugs, unable to stop until every surface was rank with the scent of citrus cleaning solution. Eli would take Jack home eventually, I figured, but it would be in his own time.

Jack said he heard noises in the house at night. Too spooked to fall asleep until Eli came home from the bar, Jack invited himself into my room whenever I stayed up late working on my application materials, sitting on my bed and asking questions about the boyfriend I said I had. Jack liked to tell long, impossible stories. To brag about unlikely encounters with celebrities and performing Olympian-level feats of athleticism. I never listened to his tall tales very carefully. But the later it got, the more implausible they seemed to become. He spoke quickly, pacing the narrow space between my bed and the wall, the javelina head jutting over him like a gargoyle. Even after kicking him out for the night, I'd still hear him restlessly creaking around the living room.

It's hard to explain, but the house did have a certain animating energy at night. I found it difficult to sleep myself unless I crept out for a long walk along Park Avenue. On my walks, I would fantasize about running past the downtown city limits, on and on until I reached the same set of railroad tracks that cut across the desert surrounding Cactus Country. In these daydreams, I'd climb into an open boxcar and ride it to California, or New Mexico, or Utah. Anywhere. But after a few hours of walking, my legs would grow tired and achy, telling me the time had come to turn around. No matter how far I went, I could always look back and find the house. A castle looming above its lowly neighbors, sharp against black sky, reminding me where I'd been and where I would inevitably return.

Some nights on the way home I distracted myself by looking for things to collect along the roadside. Pennies and marbles and empty Whip-It! canisters: anything shiny and round. I brought these objects to the hole in the living room floor and rolled them in, one by one. They made a smooth sound against the wood, a satisfying clink as they landed in the pile under the house, where I suspected the ghostly woman might also be lurking. But no matter how many gifts I brought, she never appeared for me. I wanted to ask her what she was hiding from, and how she learned to do it so well.

THE DAYS IN the Park Ave house ticked by, my phone continuing to ring like clockwork. I'd wait for the vibration to stop before pressing the phone to my ear, listening to the recorded voices of former friends asking where I was, telling me I couldn't hide forever. Some cursed me for not answering their calls. Others wondered if I might be dead. They made up all kinds of stories to explain to one another where I'd gone and why I never picked up the phone. No matter what they said about me, the messages they left just reaffirmed what I already knew: I'd made the decision to leave Tucson, and getting caught up trying to untangle their webs—to separate fact from fiction—would only ensure that I never did.

Sometimes, reading over their texts at night, I felt a twinge in my neck, an uncanny sense that I wasn't alone. I'd look up, glancing around my room—at my desk, bookshelf, and dresser—eventually locking eyes with the javelina head glaring out from its place on the wall. I told myself this feeling was silly. My bed was a mattress on the floor. The door was locked. There was nowhere for anyone, even the ghostly woman, to hide. Yet the feeling remained. The sensation was unsettling, reminiscent of the presence I'd once felt watching me from the desert in Cactus Country as I walked along the fence with Max. But I had been a boy then, and was an adult now.

I'd sit up, straining to listen for the footsteps of any potential intruders as I reached for the baseball bat leaning against my mattress. But the house was always quiet. Lately, Eli had been spending less and less time at home, leaving Jack alone for most of the night, as well as for part of the day while he slept. The two used to seem inseparable, always on their way out the door to a breakfast joint or to catch a matinee at the movie theater. Now, Jack had fallen uncharacteristically silent. He'd stopped pacing, stopped sleeping, stopped listening to his music. He'd stare up at the ceiling for hours, his body blending into the fabric of his favorite chair.

"Just thinking," Jack would say, though I never asked.

ONE NIGHT ALMOST a month after moving into the house, I went out for a long walk. The roads had flooded from a day of heavy rain. I took care to avoid stepping in the deep puddles refused by the chapped desert earth, water that would stand until the morning's heat soaked it back into the sky. The full moon drenched the street in a soft light. Rounding the corner on a neighborhood sidewalk, I saw a wild javelina separated from its herd. The creature and I stopped, staring at each other, its eyes sparkling in the reflection of moonlit puddles.

I felt vulnerable, exposed, with no way to defend myself if the animal chose to attack. But I was curious, too. I'd never seen a javelina on its own this far into town. In stark contrast to the ferocious head mounted in my room, the bloodthirsty monsters of my childhood imagination, this javelina seemed apprehensive, its nose wet and twitching in fear. All at once, it turned and ran, taking cover in the riverbed, leaving me alone on the street.

THE NEXT MORNING, I awoke early to a soft knocking on my bedroom door. A voice whispering my name. Eyes closed, still dreaming, I could hear the knob twisting, slowly—first one way, then the other. *Open the door*, the voice called. The ghostly woman. She had appeared to me at last. I wanted to open my eyes, to get up, but I couldn't move, my mind awake but my body still deep in sleep, a weight on my chest like an arm pinning me to the mattress.

The knocking grew louder. *Let me in*, she urged. Her voice was raspy, inhuman, like the wolf in so many children's stories. Sharp fear stabbed at my heart as I realized that, maybe, I'd had it backward: Maybe all this time it was not I who had been looking for the ghostly woman, but she who had been searching for me.

Let me in! she shrieked, pounding against the door with her fists. I wanted to cry out for someone to save me. To run into the cover of darkness, as I'd seen the javelina do the night before. But I couldn't move, couldn't open my mouth, couldn't scream.

All at once, the pounding and shrieking quieted. As quickly as she had appeared, the ghostly woman retreated to her place under the house. I slipped back into a tense, dreamless sleep until I heard another knock, this time sharp and authoritative.

"Tucson Police!" a woman's voice called. "Please unlock this door!" I snapped awake, sheets tangling around my legs as I pulled myself from bed, tripping me onto the floor. The policewoman came in slowly, one hand on her gun. She eyed the javelina head on the wall before turning to me. I sat on the edge of my mattress, still unable to speak, as the woman knelt to meet my gaze. She apologized for the intrusion, said she hadn't realized anyone else was still in the house. My room was so well hidden.

Jack had a psychotic episode during the night. He'd paced the living room wielding a kitchen knife, believing the house was under siege. He heard gunshots, a woman screaming. He thought our landlords upstairs had been murdered. The officer asked whether I'd heard anything strange. I told her about the whispering, the knocking at my door, unsure now which parts, if any, had been a dream. She asked me to follow her out into the living room, where another three officers hovered over Jack, who rocked, cradling his head, in one of the overstuffed chairs. His shirt lay torn and abandoned on the floor.

"I told you all before," he wailed through his hands, "I forgot my medicine in Phoenix." Eli stood back uneasily, watching the scene with his arms folded from the open front door. Our landlady came downstairs, apparently unharmed, asking Eli why the hell were there cops in her goddamn yard. He waved her away, said everything was fine, fine.

"I didn't know Jack was sick," Eli muttered after she stormed back upstairs. "Did he ever say anything to you?"

Jack had said lots of things to me, I just hadn't been listening. I looked at him, naked from the waist up and crying in our living room. My eyes wandered to the place in the floor where the hole was, wondering if the ghostly woman might be watching us. I shook my head.

"I think he just wants to go home," I said.

HOBOLAND

THE SILENCE IN THE HOUSE that night was broken only by the occasional swish of a passing car, the lonely howling of a distant dog. No creaking floorboards or blaring cell phone music now, just me home alone for what felt like the first time since I'd moved to Park Avenue, packing my hidden room into boxes as Eli drove Jack back to Phoenix. In the hours since the cops had gone, our landlords wasted little time grilling Eli about what, exactly, had been going on down here. Not only with Jack, but also with me, and who was I, and why wasn't my name on the lease? Eli didn't have good answers for them. I would need to sign on to continue living in the Park Ave house or leave at the end of the month.

Later that week I would unceremoniously sell off my furniture, my mattress and writing desk, stowing a few remaining possessions in my car for safekeeping—a couple bags of clothing, a small collection of books. But as I reached up to take the javelina head down from the wall, I hesitated, craning my neck to study my reflection in its shining black eyes. Moving it felt wrong, somehow, as though the javelina belonged here, in this house. The head had become a part of its story as I knew it, like the Whip-It! canisters and ping pong balls beneath the floorboards, or the watchful gaze of the ghostly woman. I put my arms down again, deciding to leave the head as an offering to the house, a kind of prayer for safe passage into the unknown.

The air was sticky with humidity from the previous night's storm. I wiped the sweat from my forehead, taking a break from packing to cool off on the house's great, turret-like porch. A distant train rolled through Tucson's downtown, its forlorn whistle echoing against the Park Ave houses. I sat on the porch steps, remembering the days in Cactus

Country when the boys and I would hike out into the desert to lay pennies on the railroad tracks. While waiting for the next train to flatten them, we'd go spelunking in the concrete tunnels underneath, digging for hidden treasure in the piles of trash that teenagers and vagrants had left behind—aluminum cans, clothing scraps, and near-empty cylinders of spray paint.

We called this place Hoboland, named for the stories Dad told me about the men who hitched rides on cargo trains during the Great Depression in search of better prospects elsewhere. While desperation might have led the hoboes to the tracks, he said, the freedom of the open rails is what kept them riding. They weren't homeless, but nomadic, chasing seasonal work around the country, never laying root in one place for too long. According to lore, hoboes had a spoken code of honor and a complex set of symbols they scrawled on street corners and railroad signs to help guide others traveling the same path. Under the tracks we boys emulated the railriders of the past, pretending the spray-painted graffiti on the tunnel walls were runes left behind for our safe travels.

SHORTLY BEFORE JACK'S episode, I'd started submitting applications to graduate programs across the country, and now didn't expect to hear back from schools for the next two or three months, at least. I couldn't find another rental in town for such a short stay, and, since the incident with Gavin, no longer had friends I could reliably crash with. Instead, I left Park Ave and returned to Cactus Country, moving in with my parents until I could figure out what to do next.

"Happy to be back?" Dad asked as we lugged boxes from my car into the Airstream. I shrugged. I'd been back to the park plenty of times over the years, making the long drive for family dinners and holidays, or to do the occasional basket of laundry. But this was a true homecoming, with no end in sight. I'd come full circle, and it was depressing.

"Well, it's good to have you back, at least," he offered, pulling my shoulders into a tight squeeze. "It won't be forever."

I hoped not. Returning to the park felt more uncanny than comforting, like going back to the house you'd grown up in to find it occupied by another family. Now under new ownership, Cactus Country seemed so different from the place I was raised. Yes, there were still the sprawling cactus gardens, the public restrooms where I'd once been banished from using the men's toilets, the park store where the boys and I used to buy popsicles on hot days. But the neighbors I'd known had long since moved on, replaced by weekend vacationers and cross-country road-trippers. Even my favorite palo verde had been chopped back to its most essential branches, encouraging the tree to grow upward instead of out. This made it less likely to be hit by passing motorhomes, but also impossible for children to climb.

Dad said Cactus Country's new owners were in the process of rebranding the park as a "destination getaway." Over the past year, the annual campsite rental price had nearly doubled. Management had become more selective about what kinds of vehicles would be allowed into the park, knowing that the older, sun-bleached trailers with missing hubcaps that used to populate much of Cactus Country, especially in the summertime, would likely house poorer families with the kind of wild, unwashed children I had once been. They made exceptions for certain "classic" or "vintage" trailer makes, such as the Airstream, but my parents' aging van had recently garnered some scrutiny, and they faced mounting pressure to make their campsite of ten years look "less lived in."

For as long as we'd called Cactus Country our home, there had always been community rules to follow. But for full-time residents, like my parents, these new restrictions made living in the park feel more like a homeowners' association than the untamed desert of my youth. By Dad's estimation, they now paid as much in rent to stay in Cactus Country as they'd spend on a mortgage for a small house in town.

"And at least then we could do what we wanted with the place," he said, shaking his head at the latest notice management had pressed into the Airstream's doorjamb detailing a new ban on semipermanent structures like decks and porches. "I swear, the park is feeling more and more like Rita Ranch by the day."

At dusk, my parents and I gathered outside the Airstream in folding chairs, watching the sunset's fading hues as Mom and Dad sipped their wine. We discussed all the recent changes to the park and the surrounding desert. Rita Ranch developers had plans for a shopping complex just across the railroad tracks—a strip mall with sprawling superstores, quick-service tire shops, and drive-up coffee chains. In other parts of our desert, construction had already begun, paving the way for bus routes connecting Tucson's suburbs to its newly revitalized downtown. We marveled over how much the land had changed in ten years and made bets about whether the park would still be out here after ten more.

Growing up, Cactus Country had always felt so remote, a desert safe haven and an arid hellscape miles from where the rest of the world began. I'd sat in front of the Airstream with my parents on so many evenings like this one since the day we'd moved to Tucson, back when I was still learning what it meant to live as a boy, and how to survive in this strange, hostile place—not only under its dry, relentless heat but also among the rough characters who populated its landscape. The desert felt so much smaller to me now, the anger I'd felt permeating the air in those days beginning to fade along with the faces of the boys and men I'd grown up with. I knew I'd never be content to live in Cactus Country again, this home that didn't feel like home anymore. But neither could I continue living in Tucson, where I'd learned life was just as harsh as in the desert, the disillusionments there just as real as they'd ever been out here.

Before I submitted my materials, Ander had warned me that sometimes writers took multiple application seasons—years—to be accepted into the right graduate program. I felt I needed an exit strategy, a plan to leave the city behind in case the writing life didn't work out the way I hoped. Recently, I'd been paying close attention to the folks who rode into town on the rails, known colloquially as "train kids" no matter how young or old they were. Fourth Avenue, Tucson's funkiest downtown street, was a popular pit stop. There, train kids busked with guitars on street corners and crashed on friends' living room floors and danced in circle pits at local punk shows. Most lived simply, carrying only a small pack and the faded black clothes on their backs, maybe a road dog on a rope leash. The idea of starting over with only the open rails ahead had long appealed to me. As a child, I'd wondered whether railriders could see us boys waving up at the boxcars speeding past Hoboland, secretly dreaming about hopping on board to ride with them.

Once, on a dare, I had run up to a slow train rumbling along the tracks, standing just feet from where its metal wheels ground against the rails, waiting for the last boxcar to pass. I grabbed hold of a handle at the back of the caboose and clung, pulling my bare feet up to its metal step. Holding on with one hand, I waved a theatrical goodbye to my friends as they laughed and cheered, running alongside me. Suddenly, the train lurched forward. I fumbled to grasp the handle with both hands. As the engine picked up speed, the boys' expressions turned to alarm. They waved their arms, unable to keep pace with the train.

"*Let go!*" they shouted, their voices growing more distant by the second. "*Let go!*"

Wind tore against my face, the wooden planks under my feet speeding to a blur. Panic coursed through my aching fingers as I struggled to maintain my grip on the handle. With adrenaline roaring in my ears I leapt backward, landing hard on the wooden planks, my head just missing the steel rail. The train rushed away from me, rails hissing as it quickly became a speck in the distance. My elbows and t-shirt were sticky and stained black from the tar I'd landed in. I sat up and winced, a little banged up, but otherwise okay. The boys caught up to me, breathing hard.

"You're brave, man," one said, shaking his head as he offered his hand. I took it, flushing with pride as he helped pull me to my feet, feeling like a real hobo, a man among boys.

That night, I made the mistake of recounting this adventure to my parents over dinner.

"Not cool, Zo," Dad said, pointing at me with his fork. "That could've ended very badly." Mom didn't say anything at first, but I could tell she was furious by the way her jaw tightened as she jabbed at the mess of spaghetti on her plate. Didn't I know people got killed that way every day? What if I hadn't jumped off in time?

"It was *fine*," I insisted. "Really." She shook her head.

"Promise me you will never do that again," she said sharply.

"But Mom—"

"Promise me." I stared down at my plate and nodded. Since our move to Cactus Country, Mom had been more than a little wary of the train tracks. My fascination with the hoboes seemed to worry her, as though she thought I was liable to run away and join them. Whenever I voiced my fantasies of riding the rails, she swiftly discouraged me.

"You could never do that, sweetie," she said. "You'd get taken advantage of." I glowered at her, wondering whether Mom would say the same thing if she thought of me as a son rather than her daughter. "Girl, boy, doesn't matter," she continued, as though reading my mind. "Enough crazy-ass people out there for everyone."

But despite her warnings, still I was drawn to the trains, to the romance of them and their promise of adventure. I loved the way we boys could feel a train coming long before we saw it, the rails tingling with an electric hum. How we'd rush out from the tunnels under the tracks as it charged toward us, closer and faster and louder until it roared past, the conductor blowing its long, sad horn with such volume you couldn't hear yourself scream. And we screamed. We threw rocks against the boxcars, shoved each other to the ground, beat our chests until we were hoarse, until the train had consumed us in a rush of excitement unlike any other. It was an ecstatic, almost religious experience, to lose control in a force so much bigger and stronger than ourselves, a mechanical beast with the power to take life, or to make life worth living. We lived for those damn trains. Sitting on the Airstream porch more than ten years and so many sunsets later, I wanted to live for something like that again.

APART FROM VOLUNTEERING as an editor with *Sonora Review* at UA, the only remaining link to my undergraduate life was teaching at Second Street School, where I'd now been working with children for six years.

During that time I had grown confident in my abilities as a caretaker, progressing from a floating aide to a co-teacher in the afternoon program. Though I'd never taken a formal course on early childhood education, as my director, Jenny, had once encouraged me to do, through my teaching experiences I was well-versed in the play-based, child-centered philosophies Second Street abided, from the styles of Reggio Emilia, Montessori, and Waldorf to the theories of Jean Piaget and Lev Vygotsky.

My favorite children to work with also tended to be some of the angriest. There was the girl who drew dozens of family portraits while her parents were in the midst of a contentious divorce. Or the little boy who methodically tore pages from picture books that reminded him of his mother, who had passed away the year before. The source of the anger didn't matter so much as helping the children learn to feel their big emotions without being consumed by them. Their rage was fierce, the way mine had once been. They hit their teachers, bit their classmates, ripped artwork from the walls, screamed until their faces flushed.

Most of the angry children didn't allow themselves to be held or consoled. So when their emotions boiled over, I brought them outside. We went for jogs around the playground to burn off the tension in their bodies and took turns shooting balls into a low hoop to refocus their energy toward a goal. Later, when they were calm, the children drew pictures to illustrate their frustrations, and I helped them write letters, putting their feelings into words on the page.

As their teacher, I tried to impart the same lessons in survival I'd learned from the hot, angry days of my boyhood in the desert: how to run fast and play hard, how to render the big, inexpressible ways I felt in my body through art. I could teach these children to ground themselves, to weather their internal storms, even as I felt caught in the changing winds myself.

ON MY WEEKENDS off, I met Dad and Mom in town to help with their latest project, fixing up the small, four-room casita they'd purchased with a decade's worth of savings cobbled together from washing windows and selling RVs. We toasted their new home, drinking cheap champagne in the mismatched chairs they'd picked up from the roadside, surrounded by a mess of tools, building materials, and dusty housewares. As a gutted foreclosure, the casita needed a lot of love, but my parents took pleasure in the work, the idea of a homestead all their own without the petty politics and headaches of trailer park life.

Working on the casita helped allay the suspense of waiting to hear back from graduate schools, an anxiety which had compounded over the months into something like depression. No matter how much I slept, I woke up exhausted from restless dreamscapes of labyrinthian trailer parks and miles upon miles of inescapable desert. If I didn't receive an acceptance letter by the spring, I was resolved to leave Tucson on the rails that summer.

I'd begun preparing supplies for a bindle, packing my childhood pocketknife, an ultra-thin sleeping bag, a metal canteen, and a book called *The Rail Rider's Reference Guide* into a small canvas backpack. When sleep eluded me, I went online to plot out the best freight train routes into the Pacific Northwest, a landscape as far away from the desert as I could think of. I read up on train safety—from the best way to hitch a ride on slow-moving boxcars, to dodging railroad workers at the train yards, to defending yourself from other riders who might do you harm. There was a lot to learn, but I figured most of what I needed to know I could pick up on the tracks.

One day, my parents and I took a break from working on the house for lunch. We sat in the shade of an Arizona cypress tree whose branches hung over the casita's front porch like heavy monsoon clouds. Dad fanned himself with his hat as I helped Mom spread mayonnaise on sliced bread with the back of a spoon. My phone buzzed in my pocket, an unknown number, and I leapt up, hoping it might be an acceptance from one of the programs I'd applied to. But it was only a robocall. I shoved the phone back into my jeans, sighing.

"I hate to ask," Dad said, "but what's the plan if you don't get into one of your schools?" I paused, staring at my sandwich and wondering whether I should tell the truth.

"I was actually thinking of hopping a train and getting the hell out of here," I said. He chuckled. Mom rolled her eyes.

"No, I mean it," I said. "That's really what I want to do. I've been looking at routes and everything. I can't stay here in Tucson another year, no matter what it takes. This place is like death." Dad squinted at me, a serious expression on his face.

"Hopping a train, though?" he asked. "That sounds pretty dangerous."

"You don't want to live that life," Mom said, putting her sandwich down on the napkin in her lap. She'd worked in Seattle's Pike Place market as a young woman and befriended many of the tramps and drifters who hitchhiked into the city to gather there. "Sleeping on the street is so hard on the body. It changes you, and not in a good way."

I didn't need my parents to tell me riding trains was a dangerous proposition, especially traveling alone as a person others perceived to be female. Though my gender was amorphous, still somewhere on the spectrum of woman-but-not, I knew my semi-androgynous appearance—my short, pixie-style haircut, flipped-bill baseball caps, and grungy cut-off shorts—didn't preclude me from violence at the hands of men. I'd heard about close encounters with the unpredictable kinds of characters who rode. Drugs and alcohol use on the rails abounded, and gruesome accidents were common. An acquaintance had broken her leg jumping from a moving boxcar. Friends of friends lost lives and limbs trying to chase down too-fast trains. But the journey, risks and all, was a fallback plan I could get excited about, the kind of story I would have relished as a boy. If I couldn't leave Tucson the sensible way, I would go out the spectacular way, charging into the adulthood I'd never been able to envision on a freight train.

"I guess we'd better hope I get into graduate school then," I joked. My parents didn't laugh.

ONE LATE AFTERNOON as I was driving back to Cactus Country from work, Dad called asking me to meet him on Fourth Avenue.

"Are you free?" he said. "I met a couple of oogles here who—"

"You didn't call them that to their faces, did you?" I asked. An *oogle* was a derisive term for a train kid from a wealthy background who only pretended to be destitute, a poser who wanted to be part of the street scene because they liked the gritty aesthetic, rather than someone with legitimate reasons to ride.

"Well they seem like nice kids, and I'm going to buy them some sandwiches if you want to join us," Dad said. "Maybe you could ask them a few questions about your trip."

Dusty and Cricket were a little older than me, in their mid-twenties with sunburned noses, soot-brushed skin, and sweat-stained bandanas tied around their necks. This time around, they'd come into Tucson from Texas, but they had previously taken trains all over the country. The pair were anarchists, hopping freight as a means to cheaply travel where they needed to go and meet interesting, like-minded people along the way. Cricket showed me a train tracking app on her phone, which she used to determine where in the country a given train was heading and plot all its scheduled stops. Dusty wrote down the names of a few people and places that had been kind to them. After lunch, Dad and I watched them take their packs and walk hand in hand toward the rail station, on toward California.

Once they left, I turned to Dad.

"Why are you helping me?" I asked. "I mean, I know you don't really want me to do this." Dad was quiet for a while, chewing on his tongue with his hands in his pockets. Nearby, a street musician beat on a drum outside a thrift shop. A tattoo artist smoked a cigarette stub outside his parlor, and a bartender swept a splintery porch in anticipation of that night's bar scene.

"Do you remember," he said finally, "the time you snuck out from our apartment in Virginia? Back when you were, what, like two or three years old?"

I nodded, though I didn't really. Of course I knew the story, but my memory of the incident had been shaped by years of hearing my parents tell and retell it. Over time, I had formed a muddy picture of the narrow hall in our Virginia apartment. Myself as a small, barefooted child with wild blond hair padding across the darkness of the apartment's foyer. The child reached up to turn a brass knob, slowly pushing the heavy door with two open hands before climbing the stairs one by one, each a step closer to the sun casting through the windows.

"I remember going out through the front door," I said. "And following a bright light at the top of the stairs." Dad shook his head.

"No, you went through the sliding door in the back. I'll never forget the terror of finding it wide open. The wind was blowing and you were gone." Getting to the playground, where my parents eventually found me, would have meant I had walked around the complex, traversed a busy parking lot, and combed my way through a thicket of bushes.

"Mom and I were beside ourselves. But when we found you, you weren't distressed about it at all," Dad said. "I thought that was pretty remarkable for a kid so young. You knew exactly where you wanted to be, and what you had to do to get there."

"Yeah?" I asked.

"Yeah," he said. "Mom and I would rather you didn't hop trains, of course, but we trust you to find your own path. You taught us that from the beginning."

"Thanks, Dad," I said. "Maybe you guys showed me that." Preparing to leave town on a freight train mirrored many of my parents' past inclinations to go boldly into the unknown. Isn't that why we'd traveled west with the Airstream in the first place—not so much toward the promise of a new life as away from the inevitability of our old one? Uncertainty was its own kind of adventure, an echo I'd felt rippling in my blood from the day I asked for the haircut that allowed me to pass as a boy, to now, just weeks away from a decision to leave the desert that shaped me. Dad put a warm, heavy hand on my shoulder. "Let's get back to it, huh?"

AFTER MONTHS OF work, my parents' casita had begun to resemble a real home. Together, we'd fixed appliances and dug trenches for new pipes and hauled in furniture from estate sales around town. We'd gradually filled the front yard with all the vehicles Dad had acquired and stored in Cactus Country over the years—the red storage trailer with its windows warped from the fire, VW buses in various states of disrepair, and more old cars and trucks than I ever realized we owned. Finally, the day came to move the Airstream, our last tether to Cactus Country, onto the property from the place where it had sat in the park for the last ten years.

We prepared the trailer for the journey, packing away dishes and anything likely to break while we were on the road. Mom and I battened down the cabinet doors with bungee cords and Dad disconnected the sewage and water lines before carefully lowering the Airstream down to the hitch on his truck. We didn't have far to go, but still it was strange to see the Airstream in motion. Although a travel trailer, one my parents had so many plans for when Dad bought it more than a decade ago, we'd never actually taken it anywhere. Instead, the Airstream had been a permanent presence in the desert we'd pointed to and called our home.

We drove on, hot wind blowing into our faces on the highway. I leaned my head out the truck's window to squint at the Airstream's aluminum surface shimmering in the rearview. Dad steered the trailer north on I-10, "City of New Orleans" crooning from the speakers. He tapped his fingers on the dashboard in time with the beat as Mom hummed along to the melody. When we'd moved to Cactus Country, my parents and I had been chasing our big dreams the way coyotes chase the moon. The desert, we told ourselves, would grant us the freedom to live life on our own terms, to embody the kind of people we most wanted to become. We had lived that life. We had become those people. Now here we were again, the three of us, at the beginning of new dreams.

Dad pulled the Airstream into the casita's front yard. The trailer would function as a guest house, as a place for me to stay until I left Tucson, whether for grad school or the open rails. We made quick work of leveling it with wood shims and cinderblocks. From the outside, in this completely new context, the Airstream almost seemed like a different vehicle. But when I stepped inside, the trailer looked just as I'd always known it, a time capsule amid a new era of our lives. I stood thinking about the years we'd spent sleeping on its foldout couch and tiny, twin-size bed. The meals we'd eaten as a family at the folding table. The hushed conversations about our Cactus Country neighbors and the showdowns that extended to the Airstream's plywood porch and the laughter that shook the trailer on its axles. All the living we had done here, and would do no more. I stood and thought for a long time. Then, as I turned to go, the phone in my back pocket began to buzz. An unknown caller from Oregon. I held the phone's glow to my face, pressed it against my ear.

IN THE COMING weeks, my phone would ring with an offer from a program in California. Another in Tennessee. North Carolina. Minnesota. Indiana. All of these states across the country, and I wouldn't need to hop a train to see any of them. I would say goodbye to Ander and my professors at UA, thanking them for their faith in me, for their encouragement and letters of recommendation. I would hand in my notice at Second Street, where a few months later Jenny and my co-teachers and the children would hug me goodbye. I would put away my bindle and pack a new bag for a future in Oregon, at the university I'd chosen, in part, to honor my plan to ride up to the Pacific Northwest on the rails.

Merging onto I-10 that summer, I was careful not to look back at the city that had loomed large in my spirit for so long now shrinking in my rearview. The road ahead would take me through the Sonoran Desert and the Mojave, up into the evergreen California forests and a thousand miles north, farther from Tucson than I'd ever lived alone. After many days and nights on the road, the engine would tick as it cooled from the long drive, gentle rain flitting across my windshield. Balancing moving boxes in my arms, I'd climb the stairs into a small apartment above a convenience store overlooking a forest of thick-trunked trees.

On days I didn't bike to campus for classes, I would explore the lush woods and open fields surrounding my new apartment, where farmers raised dairy cows, alpacas, goats, and sheep. Wild turkeys larger than I'd ever imagined birds could be would cross the walking trails in loud flocks, leaving behind feathers longer than my spread hands. Each day I'd find a new shady place to sit and read, taking in lungfuls of crisp dewy air and pleasant musty earth.

Over the months, the soles of my feet, once hard and callused from hazarding searing asphalt and stray cactus needles, would become smooth and supple. No matter how many times I took off my shoes, burying my toes in the cool, always-wet soil, I thought how strange it felt to find myself in a landscape where everything I touched was soft, where nothing waited for me in the darkness. To call anywhere but the desert home.

HOW IT ENDS

HONESTLY, I STILL DON'T KNOW what to say when people ask about my childhood. Where to begin, how to thread the right words into a narrative that ties the boy I was to the woman it seems like he has become. More often than not, I choose the wrong ones. The boy's story doesn't make sense to the person I'm telling it to, the answers I give only inviting more questions. I explain and explain myself until the asker understands nothing about who I am or am not, who the boy was or wasn't, what having a gender is supposed to mean when you look one way but feel another.

So I talk about Tucson, what a gritty kind of place it is. What, by extension, a gritty kind of person I am. This is the story I've always been good at telling. I romanticize the desert's grit like the cowboys at the horse corral whenever they talked about the Old West, how things out there used to be. But their characterizations of that time and that place and themselves weren't all true. I guess mine can't be all true, either. It's just easier to remember the desert in this light now that I'm so far away from the place I grew up, no longer stuck picking cactus needles from my fingertips and wondering whether, one day, I might be able to leave it behind.

For a long time I thought I'd never go back. I sat at my desk in Oregon, writing about anything other than Tucson, and Cactus Country, and the boy I used to be. Back when my old friends and I were on better terms, we used to laugh at the futility of trying to escape the desert's pull over warm beers in one of our sparse, underwatered backyards. *People go*, we said, *but they always come back*. Now, by some accidental magic, some sleight of the divine, I had slipped through the cracks of fate into a life elsewhere. I didn't want to risk looking back, as though remembering the past might apprise the desert of my absence and return me to it.

In the intervening years, I graduated from my writing program in Oregon and applied to another one in Ohio. I taught writing classes to hundreds of students. I found a place in the literary world as a writer, a podcast host, and a magazine editor. I met the person who would become my partner on the dance floor at a writing conference. Gradually, my life began to encompass so much more than the city I came from. Whole weeks and months could go by, teaching, editing, even writing without thinking about the desert or my boyhood at all.

But of course, the specters of our past are always one or two steps behind us, patiently waiting for their chance to catch up, even take the lead.

When I first left home, I believed those old ghosts were dead and tried to bury them. To live as though they did not haunt my present. But the farther I wandered from the desert, the longer I lived beyond its reach, the more those memories seemed to find their way above ground again, like tarantulas flushed from their burrows during the monsoon rains. They echoed across Oregon's verdant wilds, shadowed me as I traversed the snaking brick paths to the university campus in Ohio. Wherever I went, the wind carried the voices of those I left behind, of the boy searching for answers, their cadence soft and low, an echo only I could hear.

I could tell you about graduate school, a paragraph or two about how I limited the time spent reckoning with the past by packing my schedule with as many workshops, editorial gigs, and assistantships as I was allowed to take. I could tell you how I observed my professors for clues about speaking their coded academic language and standing with confidence in front of a classroom. How making friends with the women in my program taught me how to dress in more feminine professional clothes and style my long hair—to present myself as though I was one of them, and had always been.

I could tell you a lot of things about graduate school, the triumphant and the terrible. But those stories would only serve to distract you from the real issue, like they did me. Because I've written those paragraphs and deleted them and written them again, only to say that in grad school I tried to become *my own kind of girl*, as Dad had once suggested. But mostly the girl was a costume I wore, a role I played. She wasn't all true. She couldn't be.

That is, in grad school I tried to stop thinking about gender, but the nature of my performance meant I thought about gender more than ever before. I tried to convince myself that my childhood didn't shape the person I was, even as the desert of my youth haunted my dreams.

Years went by. The echoed voices of my Tucson friends grew fainter until, one day, I realized I couldn't remember what they sounded like. But the boy I was continued to linger in the background of phone calls with my parents and in the low rumbling of passing trains, his presence ensuring I couldn't forget where I'd come from, or how much farther I still needed to go. Somehow, I had become the person he couldn't imagine. I wondered what the boy would think, whether he would be proud of my accomplishments or disappointed that I'd strayed so far from the people and places he cared about most. Whether he would understand why I left the desert. I wanted to believe he would. But it bothered me that I couldn't say.

For the first time since leaving Tucson, I missed home. I flew back and visited Mom and Dad in their casita, and walked across the grassy University of Arizona mall, and stopped by to say hello to the teachers at Second Street School. When I returned to my doctoral program, I began to write about growing up in Cactus Country. About the oppressive heat, and the boys I knew, and the anger in our hearts, yes, but also about what it felt like to pry jumping cholla needles free from bare skin, to see the colors of a broad sunset streaking across the desert skyline, to breathe in the smell of creosote, mulchy and wet after the rain. The more I wrote, the more I remembered. The more I remembered, the more I returned to myself.

The boy I was does not know there are other children like him. He only knows his own body, his own desert. How to keep pace with the boys in the pack and how to blend into the brush under gnarled ironwood trees. The boy only knows how to survive. That's all I've ever known how to do. So when I started writing the stories of my childhood, I still wasn't sure how to make narrative sense of them, or what significance they held for me now, so many years and miles removed from the park. But I had faith in the boy's perspective. I let him lead the way, and in time, writing brought back the questions I had about who I was, and why. About what it meant for a gender to exist somewhere within and between male and female, for a body to feel both right and wrong at the same time. About how many others grew up looking for these answers, and where they ended up.

Fifteen years had passed since I'd first scoured the message boards under the covers in the Airstream, staying up late to search for any trace of a story like mine. Now when I went online, I could find all kinds of articles and books and blogs written by trans people. In them, I read some of the stories I'd been missing: kids who grew up feeling different, without the words to explain how or why. Kids who saw themselves in a gender they hadn't been born into, who both did and didn't understand what that meant. We had all come of age with this secret knowledge about ourselves, many of us without any sign of others who felt the way we did. The boy I was didn't have the language to describe himself as one of these kids. But he knew to look for them, all the same.

For months, I wrote by day and gathered evidence by night, comparing my childhood experiences to those of trans writers, cataloging the common themes. The humiliation of being forced to use the wrong public restroom, and the joy in simple affirmations like wearing the right clothes or getting the right haircut. The gut-wrenching body horror of an unwanted puberty, and the giddy rush of finding another person like you, even if only on a screen. These experiences, it seemed, were so entrenched as to be rites of passage during the time I and many trans people had grown up. I began to realize that I had not been a tomboy, as adults had often encouraged me to think, but a real boy whose appearance I had actively cultivated, who I'd modeled my behavior on and dreamed about becoming. The boy who I still saw—had always seen—when I looked in the mirror.

That the boy and I are transgender, that this was the answer we'd been searching for, seems obvious now, even simple. But, then again, the most important revelations often are.

The missing pieces came together more quickly now that I knew what to look for. Online, I made fast friends with other trans folks and began to search for a second word, one that would help me make sense of my mixed-up, turned-around, in-between gender story. A name to encapsulate the type of trans journey I'd been on for more than thirty years. My new friends asked if I considered myself genderfluid, a person whose gender identity changes over time. I'd only heard this term to describe more or less nonbinary folks whose gender expression might alternate between more femme and masc outward appearances on a daily or weekly basis. But for many genderfluid people, the changes are much slower, with transitions occurring over months or years, like mine have.

Genderfluid felt exactly right. I began to introduce myself this way, to start using they/them pronouns again, to finally express the thoughts and feelings I hadn't known how to talk about during my boyhood. Offline, I set about finding queer friendships like the ones I'd had with Angel back when he still lived in Cactus Country, and Gavin before I left the 9th Street house. My university's LGBT Center introduced me to OUTgrads, a campus group created by and for queer graduate students. At first, I was nervous to join them, worrying I might not be queer enough or in the right ways. My story was long and complicated. My gender wasn't evident on my face. I'd only been out for a few months. But I wanted a chance to meet other people like me, to get reacquainted with the community I'd been missing.

To my relief, the OUTgrads readily welcomed me into the group. I attended meetings and went on picnics with other trans students, more friends I could relate to about struggles and successes in academia and commiserate with about navigating binary bathrooms and institutional transphobia. When I was with the OUTgrads, I enjoyed the same sense of warmth I'd once felt horsing around with the Cactus Country boys in the desert. My new friends reintroduced me to queer culture through their favorite memes and music. We swapped queer books and video games, and made plans to celebrate Pride together as a group. I had found, as Mom once assured me I would, my people.

But my favorite part of OUTgrads was listening to the wonderful stories my friends sometimes told about experiencing gender euphoria, building loving families, and managing successful careers. About growing older and beginning to enjoy the pleasures of a long, well-lived life. I may never know how to talk about my childhood in a way everyone understands, or how to perfectly describe what it feels like to live in a gender that's always on the move. But when I hear stories like these, I can begin to imagine a future for myself. One where I lay the ghosts of the past to rest within the pages of a book. Where the only question I ask is what new kinds of joy might await me, now that I know where to find it.

The year I finished writing this story, I gave birth to a baby, a child whose face looks remarkably like mine once did, and who may or may not someday grow into the kind of boy I used to be.

One late, tired night while I rocked my sleeping infant, I searched on my phone for Cactus Country, not sure what I would find. The park is still out there, just as I remembered, an island in the desert off Interstate 10. The surrounding area has been developed now, with big-box stores and fast-food chains encroaching into what was not long ago miles of remote, pristine desert. The land between the park and the railroad tracks where I once roamed in boyhood so far remains untouched. But in the time since I left Tucson, Cactus Country has become a "55 and up" senior community. The playground where I spent so many long, hot days with the boys has been razed to make room for more campsites. Our favorite palo verde tree is gone. Kids are no longer welcome to stay in the park. I cannot bring my own children to see the place I grew up, a thing I had not known, until that moment, I might want to do.

But maybe it's better that I can't go back.

Because someday, when my children are old enough, I want to tell them about the Cactus Country I remember. About the place where brilliant cactus flowers bloomed awake in beams of morning light and pale ashes rained from the sky, shimmering under the desert sun like snowflakes. The place where lost javelina with quivering snouts searched for their families by moonlight, and ragtag bands of children found signposts under the railroad tracks written just for them. Where broken boys with sunburned faces could be beautiful, kings worthy of inheriting the desert they called their home. A place where a Cactus Country boy would always be a Cactus Country boy.

In the end, we are left with what the body knows. Its memory runs deep, rooting us to our past no matter how far away or long ago. Whether or not I ever return to Cactus Country, the ghost of the boy I was is still running somewhere out in the desert. When I close my eyes I can feel the hot sand stinging the soles of his bare feet, the rough edges of rocks held in his closed fists, the stiff strands of hair stuck to his sweaty brow. The boy was born in this desert, shaped in its image, and he never left it, even as some parts of him—his memories, his secrets, his story—live on in the person I have become.

At the beginning, the boy was searching for the words he needed, the words he wasn't sure he would ever find. Now I have written them here for you. This is how our story ends, the boy's and mine, but it isn't really the end. There are so many stories, so many lives like ours, that have yet to be told. I give our story to you, and listen for yours.

ACKNOWLEDGMENTS

THANK YOU TO the brilliant Abby Muller, who was never afraid to ask the hard questions, the ones that always led me to the right answers, with incredible nuance, grace, and candor. I will always be grateful for your keen editorial vision and careful attention to detail; *Cactus Country* wouldn't hit the way it does without you.

Thank you to all the outstanding, thoughtful folks on the Abrams team who helped shepherd this book into the world, especially: Eli Mock, Annalea Manalili, Sarah Masterson Hally, Andrew Gibeley, and Christian Westermann. I continue to feel so lucky for my story to have landed in such caring, capable hands. Big thanks, too, to Kelly Winton for a gorgeous cover that feels so true to the desert as I knew it.

Thank you to my inimitable agent, Maggie Cooper, fellow tea drinker and lover of sweet treats, for having my back and for always making the time. I am so grateful for your faith in the strength of my story, and for all your warmth, optimism, and humor on its long journey to becoming this book. *Cactus Country* will forever feel like ours.

Thank you to the literary magazines in which excerpts from this book have previously appeared, and to the generous editors who worked with me, namely Jill Talbot at *American Literary Review*; Eryn Loeb at *Guernica*; Marisa Siegel, Lyz Lenz, and Julie Greicius at *The Rumpus*; and Nancy Holochwost at *The Sun*. Thank you also to the First Pages Prize and the Sandra Carpenter Prize for Creative Nonfiction for selecting *Cactus Country* as the 2021 Readers' Pick. And thank you to the Barbara E. Allushuski Graduate Fellowship as well as Ohio University's WGSS department for your enthusiastic support of me and this project.

Thank you to my online buds for the amazing community and friendships I've leaned on since the early days of the pandemic, when much of this book was written: agogg, baldr, dau, emuz, nitenite, rose, snow, spooky, vanilla, vector, vel, vi, zackmon, and the whole Twilight Onion crew. Each of you carries a small fragment of my heart <3.

Thank you to the many dozens of Cactus Country boys I grew up with, including those not depicted in this book. Twenty years on, your friendships still loom large over my heart in the very best way. Thank you for always playing hard, for loving me like a brother, for teaching me how to be me. You are beautiful and so much more than enough.

Thank you to all the teachers who believed in me long before I believed in myself. Mrs. Goldwasser, thanks for keeping my secret; I loved your class best of all. Thank you to my middle and high school English teachers, whose love of prose resonated deeply with me: Mr. Wauer, Mr. Hill, Stewart Croft, Chad Blair, and Sarah Bromer. And thank you to Erica Saunders, who always saw the best in me, especially when I was at my worst.

Thank you to Jenny Douglas for your faith and trust in me, and to every co-teacher and child I've had the pleasure of working with at Second Street School. The lessons each of you taught me about the importance of kindness, patience, and community continue to be central to my classroom pedagogy and, more recently, to my parenting style. So much love to you, always.

Thank you to the writers Krys Malcolm Belc and Katherine "Kati" Standefer, each of whom read parts of this book and offered feedback at critical stages of its development. I could not have written several of *Cactus Country*'s more emotionally fraught chapters without Kati's incredible trauma-writing doula services, which I recommend without reservation (katherinestandefer.com).

Thank you to my fellow writers who read sections of this memoir in workshops and between classes, or whose friendship otherwise got me through grad school—truly, too many folks to list here—and to the OUTgrads for always making me feel welcome. Thank you to my Creekside sisters for the camaraderie and the residency: Erica Trabold,

Kara McMullen, Kristina Tate, and Laura Laing. And a special thank-you to my best and dearest friend, Sarah Haak, for all your fierce love, excellent advice, and steadfast encouragement of me in everything I do; I hope to always return the favor.

Thank you to all of my wonderful writing professors and mentors at the University of Arizona, Oregon State University, and Ohio University, especially Daisy Pitkin, Fenton Johnson, Alison Hawthorne Deming, Christopher Cokinos, Elena Passarello, Karen Holmberg, Justin St. Germain, George Estreich, Marjorie Sandor, Bianca Spriggs, Mara Holt, Eric LeMay, and Dinty W. Moore. This book contains a little of the best writing advice from each of you.

Thank you to Ander Monson, who deserves his own line, for dropping everything to read my essay that day after workshop. Thank you for your mentorship when I needed it most, for your continued support, both near and far, and for being a friendly face in the writing world. I owe so much of who I have become—as a teacher, a writer, and a person—to your generosity of spirit, and I carry that ethos with me in everything I do. Thank you a hundred times, a thousand times. It will never be enough.

Thank you, Mom and Dad, for allowing me to write the intimate details of our lives in these pages and for honoring my perspective; I know it wasn't always easy for you. Thank you for trusting me to follow my own path and for raising me to live life on my own terms, in pursuit of those big dreams, just like you always have. I love you both more than words can say. Everything I write will always be, in some small way, for you.

Finally, thank you, Jason, for being the first to encourage me to write about Cactus Country. For your genuine interest in the stories I told about my boyhood, and for patiently listening to so many drafts read aloud as I tried to make it perfect. For everything that is good in my life, thank you. I owe this book, and so much else, to you.